Unmaking War
Remaking Men

Other books by Kathleen Barry

Female Sexual Slavery (1979), (1983)

Susan B. Anthony: A Biography of a Singular Feminist (1988)

Prostitution of Sexuality: The Global Exploitation of Women (1995)

Vietnam's Women in Transition (editor), (1996)

How Empathy Can Reshape Our Politics,
Our Soldiers and Ourselves

Unmaking War
Remaking Men

Kathleen Barry

PHOENIX RISING PRESS
OF SANTA ROSA

Phoenix Rising Press of Santa Rosa
www.unmakingwar.net

Second printing 2011

Book Design and production by Joel Friedlander
www.TheBookDesigner.com

Permissions:

Muntazer al-Zaidi, "Why I Threw My Shoe," Comment, Guardian News, September 17, 2009. Copyright Guardian News & Media Ltd., 2009. Used with permission of the publisher.

Brian Turner, excerpt from "What Every Soldier Should Know" from *Here, Bullet* (Alice James Books, 2005; Bloodaxe Books, 2007). Copyright © 2005 by Brian Turner. Reprinted with the permission of Alice James Books, www.alicejamesbooks.org, and with permission of Bloodaxe Books.

Robert Hare Ph.D.. Note from "A Psychopath in Prison," *Without Conscience: The Disturbing World of The Psychopaths Among Us.* (New York: Guilford Press, 1993), p. 21. Used with permission of the publisher.

Mona Fayad, "To Be a Shiite Now," used with permission of the author.

Evelyne Accad, "Lebanon, Summer, 2006," used with permission of the author.

Cover images licensed under a Creative Commons Attribution 3.0 License, original work © Copyright by originators, http://www.flickr.com/photos/. Complete license is available at http://creativecommons.org/licenses/by/3.0/

Publisher's Cataloging-in-Publication
(Provided by Quality Books, Inc.)

    Barry, Kathleen.
        Unmaking war, remaking men : how empathy can reshape
    our politics, our soldiers and ourselves / Kathleen
    Barry.
        p. cm.
        Includes index.
        LCCN 2010931173
        ISBN-13: 978-0-9827967-0-2 (pbk.)
        ISBN-10: 0-9827967-0-6 (pbk.)
        ISBN-13: 978-0-9827967-1-9 (eBook)
        ISBN-10: 0-9827967-1-4 (eBook)

        1. Masculinity. 2. War. 3. Empathy. 4. Military
    education. 5. Military training camps.   I. Title.

    BF692.5.B37 2010   155.3'32
                    QBI10-600162

First Edition

For my brother, *Danny Barry*

The chief reason warfare is still with us is neither a secret death wish of the human species, nor an irrepressible instinct of aggression, nor, finally and more plausibly, the serious economic and social dangers inherent in disarmament, but the simple fact that no substitute for this final arbiter in international affairs has yet appeared on the political scene.

Hannah Arendt, *On Violence*, 1969

Contents

Acknowledgements

While I take responsibility for all of the interpretations and analysis in *Unmaking War, Remaking Men*, feminist networking, a cornerstone of my life, came together in sometimes amazing ways for this book. Over long dinners with Evelyne Accad and travel to her homeland, Lebanon, a short paper I had written mushroomed into this book. She brought her sensitivity to her people to her comments on every chapter. I am grateful to Paul Vielle for his thoughtful reading and comments. I enormously appreciate Nadera Shaloub-Kevorkian for opening her home and her rich world of contacts to me in Jerusalem and the Occupied Palestinian Territories, providing me with vital understanding for this book. I was fortunate to reconnect with Renate Klein and Susan Hawthorne who keep feminist writing alive through Spinifex Press in Australia. They read chapters as I completed them with the kind of enthusiasm every author dreams of having in her corner and with rigorous, critical questioning that both challenged me and strengthened this book. Thank you to Cynthia Enloe for her generosity in reading the completed manuscript which was only outdone by her valuable comments, insights and resources on militarism. As I began this book, I benefitted from comments, questions and suggestions from Ann Neel and Lynette Hoelter as well as ongoing support from Elaine Leeder.

Specific chapters were significantly enhanced by the reading of those who generously gave of their expertise. I am thankful to Ibrahim Hussari for commenting on chapters with his astute insights into the Arab world, especially that of Palestinians and to Ruchama Marton in Israel for directing me to critical resources in my writing about the Jewish experience of wars. I am grateful to Ronald Castro Fernández in Costa Rica who was untiring in the documentation he researched and provided me on the condition of women in his country. Thank you to psychologist Roger Kotilla and social worker David Barry who provided me with critique and support of my use of psychological concepts they drew from their work with prisoners. I am most particularly grateful to have been given William Cross's and Steve Hassna's firsthand experience of combat and to have been drawn into understanding its toll on soldiers.

I have found that family is of one's making. My extended family came together for me with support that brought me through writing this book. For that I am grateful to Denise Pouillon who is a light in my life, Sandra Barkdull and Richard Cleveland for their faith in me and this book, Dan Barry for helping me over rough spots, and Carl Blake who kept me on course with this book when I tried to take on more than it could handle, and the friendships of Barbara Gray, Barbara Larson, and Nancy Gallop. Through it all, being able to turn to Christine Naber has provided me with reassurance and strength when they were lagging.

Thank you Joel Friedlander, this book's designer; you made turning my manuscript into a book a work of art. I am grateful to Sharon Goldinger for her meticulous and faithful copyediting. She not only put on the essential finishing touches but helped me clarify and expand my writing when it was too terse. Caren Parnes was the outstanding proofreader for this book. And thank you Jean Weisinger, photographer extraordinaire, for capturing my image and making me laugh.

The Value of Human Life

The ocean was particularly rough that day. A rescue helicopter hovered at the far end of the beach where the attention of the random array of people was focused on the base of the cliff. Four rescuers were carrying a black, zipped body bag up to the road. The victim's family was being led away by the state highway patrol.

A collective grief hung over the beach that was absent of its usual playfulness. The beach goers had just seen a father dive into the water, rescue his drowning son by hurling him over the fierce pull of the waves to safety only to be caught himself by the next, stronger wave. In one swoop, the wave sucked him up and crashed him to the ocean floor before sending him out to sea where the rescuers in the helicopter found him.

It was over. But the people at the beach that day could not go back to their activities as if nothing had happened. One woman, her cheeks puffy and red, told me the details through her sobs, tears mounting with each sentence. Her husband and children sat behind her in mute sadness. No, she did not know the man who drowned nor his family. Soon she and others began to pack up their things. This was not a beach day.

A life, untimely taken, had been snapped in an unsuspecting moment. As the family was led away, one could feel the overwhelming sadness among the strangers on the beach—a shared grief even in their separateness from each other. One could imagine the family, what it must have been like for them to prepare for a picnic at the beach, not knowing that their lives would be devastated in a few short hours—not knowing that their loss that day of a husband, a father, would ravage their hearts. How could life go on normally for them? Or for us?

What did it mean to those people who watched the boy fighting for his life, saw his father rescue him, then saw that man die? They were strangers whose lives were altered, whose tears and sadness were immediate. Shaken, I was drawn into their implicit unity, a force that seemed to hold this random array of people together. What produced this palpable shared grief that seemed to unite people who did not know each other, did not speak with each other?

Shared human consciousness. In moments like these, we rediscover the spirit that fires our humanity. We find that beneath all of the ideology, politics, myths, and beliefs that parcel us into different groups, beyond our separate loyalties to our cultures, religions, ethnicities, or races we humans deeply value our own and each others' lives. Unless one's humanity has been distorted or perverted, the most normal reaction when strangers witness another's loss of life is to feel the grief for a life just lost—even the life of a stranger.

After the body had been removed, others began to arrive, setting out their blankets or chairs, throwing Frisbees and walking their dogs along the shore. For them, no evidence remained of the tragedy from earlier that morning. Life had returned to normal. But I was unable to take in the stunning views and magical light that usually bring me peace and delight at the ocean. As I walked along the shore trying to absorb what had just happened, a young woman, dangling keys on a ring from her finger, was asking passersby, "Did anybody lose their keys?" I asked where she found them. "They just washed up on the shore." I shuddered to the core of my being, it seemed, thinking of the keys slipping from the pocket of the thirty-two-year-old father as the water took his life. The friend I was with gave me a knowing shrug that spoke volumes and said simply, "Let's go," as if there was no more that could or should be said in the face of such loss.

When we human beings see life threatened or slipping away, especially in an untimely fashion, we are united by a force of consciousness in which neither race nor gender, ethnicity nor nationality matter. We act instantaneously. Either we try to save the life at risk, or, like those standing on the beach, strangers to the victim, we strain as if we are willing the person's victory over the odds. Our lifesaving responses are as collective as they are spontaneous, whether we are silently urging life's victory against those odds or running to get help or actually attempting a rescue. We accept unquestioningly that our reaction is normal to the extent that if anyone should persist in his or her playfulness in the face of such human tragedy, we become suspicious and question her or his sense of decency.

We react, not only from personal ethics, not only from our brain's response to another's distress, but first and foremost from that consciousness that we all share because we are human. This shared human consciousness is not something special that is invoked in the face of tragedy. It is so basic to being human that we usually do not even notice how it filters through our daily lives into all of our interactions. Interaction—which is how we socially engage with each other—is where our shared consciousness is made. Shared consciousness required humans to develop language to communicate with each other, and to interact with their own selves, making us human because we *are* social beings.

At crucial moments such as the drowning at the beach, it may seem as if we are driven by instinct to the unfolding tragedy. But, on closer look, we find that intention plays a stronger role. The people on the beach, not only the victim's family, were making conscious decisions to be there. They chose not to go on with their playfulness, not to turn away, not to disregard the drowning boy. Instead, they stood there watching and crying. And because they did not turn away, the tragedy unfolding before them poured into their own lives. They allowed it in along with the grief that swept over and enveloped all of them, and that made their reactions immediate and spontaneous but also conscious and intentional.

With only a hint of what it was like at the beach, most people recognize that they have experienced this collective grief; they know it in their hearts. Their feelings are not confined only to those of their own family or clan, ethnicity or race, gender or sexual orientation, or nationality. Those differences do not disengage us from that deep life force within us that propels us to save and protect human beings whose lives are at risk. Each time I tell the story of the drowning that day on the beach near Bodega Bay, people spontaneously connect to it with similar stories of events from their own experiences that elicited reactions like the one I described. When I speak of the value of human life to a friend or in a lecture, I am greeted with heads nodding yes, telling me, "I know what you mean." Most of us know implicitly that when faced with situations such as that drowning, our consciousness makes us aware of ourselves as actively engaged, sometimes helping, other times gripping on to all the force of hope we can muster even when we are only bystanders.

And then, as if all of this means nothing at all, there is war.

While the United States was entering the most bloody year of its war against Iraq,* in one summer month of 2006, Israel dropped 4.6 million made-in-the-USA cluster bombs that in their unpredictability were meant to kill randomly across southern Lebanon.[1] Against a country that is three-quarters of the size of the state of Connecticut, the Israeli Air Force launched more than 7,000 air attacks on Lebanon between July 12 and August 13, while the Israeli Navy conducted an additional 2,500 bombardments.[2] The invaders do not bother to distinguish between civilians and soldiers. One in three of the 1,180 Lebanese civilians killed were children. The Israeli civilian death toll was 43. Nearby, the U.S. forces were waging war in Iraq, where the civilian death toll had already passed 650,000 and would climb to over 1.3 million by 2010 and where nearly 3,000 American soldiers had already been killed.

Those wars against Iraq and Lebanon, initiated by the most heavily militarized states in the world, were both planned in advance. Both were launched against states that posed no imminent threat of inva-

---

* In this book, I reject as a fiction the language that suggests that the U.S. war against Iraq was a coalition of states' military forces and likewise, that "Nato led forces" drive the war in Afghanistan. Both invasions and all forces are under U.S. military command. At the time of the invasion of Iraq, U.S. troops numbered 250,000 of the total 297,000, 45,000 of which were from Great Britain. Where "coalition" suggests a united effort and common purpose, the threats made by the United States to countries that did not participate with it in its war, hardly indicate global assent to the U.S. war.

sion to their attackers. Neither war was a preemptive war as the invading state leaders then claimed because neither Lebanon nor Iraq had planned an attack to preempt before they were invaded. They were war crimes—the "willful killing, torture or inhuman treatment, including... willfully causing great suffering or serious injury to body or health, unlawful deportation or transfer or unlawful confinement of a protected person, ... taking hostages and extensive destruction and appropriation of property, not justified by military necessity and carried out unlawfully and wantonly" according to Article 147 of the Fourth Geneva Convention.

Both wars, as all wars do, shattered the shared human consciousness that draws people together to save human life, a consciousness that was so evident when that man drowned at the beach. They beg the question: why do wars persist in the face of our human urge to save and protect human life? To answer that question, this book looks beyond the prisms of nationalism or even ethnic identity to envelop all of humanity. It goes into combat where "death blossoms," as some soldiers say, and replaces the paradigm of war with the palpable awareness of our shared human consciousness. It upends the "soldier's sacrifice," a euphemism that those at home—politicians and families—employ to elevate soldiers' deaths as valiant, as if killing and war were noble, as if more soldiers should fight and die to vindicate the ones already dead.

As an American I live with a deep shame over the death and destruction the United States has inflicted on people around the world. But it is not enough to expose my country's crimes. This book frames them in a new paradigm, one that charts a course to unmaking war and remaking men. This new paradigm is already emerging in our consciousness and through our actions. It has been awakened by men who refuse to fight in combat, enlivened by feminists such as the Afghan women who courageously reject not only the U.S. occupation but their oppression by Afghan "fundamentalist warlords and misogynist terrorists"[3] as well. This new framework of understanding is a human rights paradigm because it places the dignity of human beings and their rights above all other considerations. It is a feminist paradigm because it confronts the power of masculinity as it is socialized and constructed for war as well as female complicity in that power. And yet because shared human consciousness transcends nationalities (nationalism), races, ethnicities, classes and gender, this feminist human rights paradigm is global, encompassing all human beings.

To answer that question—"why do wars persist in the face of our human urge to save and protect human life?"—this book focuses directly on the masculinity of war, from soldiers in combat to the leaders in the White House and around the world, from how masculinity is made to how militaries turn men into remorseless killers, and it looks at how, in that same masculinity of war, resistance forces fight the occupiers and defend vulnerable peoples.

The making of soldiers for combat is the dehumanization of men, and recognizing that is the first step toward unmaking war. I first began to think about dehumanization of men for and in combat during Israel's 2006 summer war against Lebanon when something struck me as oddly wrong about the reports of civilian casualties as "the loss of innocent life." I know, of course, that the term "innocent lives" refers to civilians and especially means women and children. But something jarred my consciousness when I heard the term "innocent lives," which is rarely used to report the civilian causalities in Iraq and Afghanistan when it is Americans doing the killing. To divert Americans from thinking about their soldiers killing innocent people, the media and military rely on cold, calculating language such as "collateral damage."

Embedded in our language of war is our social agreement about human life. That term "innocent lives" nagged me until I finally asked myself, "If we agree that it is wrong to kill civilians in war, then there must be others who *can* be killed. Our language, even that which we use to expose killing civilians, condones killing. That is, we, as societies, states, countries, peoples, conspire to agree that it is alright to kill some people, those whose lives are not innocent. Who are these people?"

Men in combat.

In the paradigm of war, it is acceptable, if regrettable, inevitable, and unavoidable that men will be killed in combat—on every side. Everyone knows that. Indeed, no wars could be fought without that conviction. After all, the 120 Israeli soldiers and 250 Hizbullah fighters were killed in that Lebanon war. By 2010 over 4,300 American troops had been killed in Iraq and 1,000 in Afghanistan.

When U.S. soldiers' death toll hit 4,000, Americans had, apparently, had enough and began to demand withdrawal of the United States from Iraq. It was as if the first 3,999 deaths were acceptable because they were inevitable and because they were mostly men. It was as if we have some kind of magic but unstated limit to the number of soldiers killed in combat we would condone. It is there in that acceptance of the inevitability of death in war that we destroy the value we hold for human life in our collective consciousness. And we are all diminished by that act.

What about women in combat? According to the U.S. military, there is no such thing. Yes, increasing numbers of women are serving in combat zones in Iraq and Afghanistan, but as medics, technicians, truck drivers, at checkpoints, and some in combat. They are not supposed to be sent to fight in combat even though many have been caught in firefights or had to respond to being mortared. As of this writing in 2010, that is still the U.S. military's position. Political scientist Cynthia Enloe points to the military's "inner sanctum of masculinity" that has included "the submarine corps, armored divisions, fighter plane squadrons, paratroopers, irregular elite forces such as the U.S. Army Special Forces, and the infantry regiments."[4]

What are they to us, those men who are sent off to kill, who come home without limbs or their sanity—or return home in coffins? Beyond the grandiose claims of patriotism, nationalism, religious beliefs, and ethnic identities, what are they to their country, to their people, really?

They are *expendable*!

Expendable lives. To the United States. To Lebanon. To Palestine. To Britain. To Israel. To Australia. To Iraq. To Afghanistan. To Russia. To Georgia. To the Sudan. To China. To Zimbabwe. . . . In every war of aggression, for every war of liberation. In every defending military and militia. In every country, of every people.

How in the madness of war do so many human beings throughout the world—who share an unconditional love of life, who are connected to each other through the life force that urges us away from death to spontaneously want to save another's life and to protect one's own—come to accept war as inevitable? How do we sustain as valid a belief in the distinction between "innocent," civilian, or noncombatants' lives and the lives of those in combat? Who are we to determine who can and who cannot be killed as if the power of the state supersedes the value of human life, of every human life? How do we hold in our hearts, against our shared human consciousness, the conviction that men will be killed in combat and that it must be that way?

Every society makes men's readiness to fight in combat a matter of their manhood. Upon that illusion a ready body of soldiers is made for state leaders—presidents, prime ministers, ayatollahs, and dictators alike—to call up to fight and be killed in their wars. That is why militias and resistance forces of the countries that are invaded and occupied can rely on their own steady supply of human beings whose lives can be sacrificed in fighting the aggressors.

Men's expendability is inscribed in international law. When I began this work, I had not expected to discover that all those men in combat, on every side, when they are "engaged in hostilities," are even forsaken by international humanitarian law. While laws do not say that yes, one class of human beings, men who are soldiers in combat, can be killed, Article 3.1 of the 1949 United Nations Geneva Convention indirectly, yet nevertheless decisively, holds that only those *"persons taking no active part in the hostilities, . . . shall in all circumstances be treated humanely*, without any adverse distinction founded on race, colour, religion or faith, sex, birth or wealth, or any other similar criteria" (emphasis mine).[5]

So, according to international law, persons taking "active part in hostilities" do not have to be treated humanely? True. Soldiers' human rights to protection against torture are restored, at least legally, only when they stop fighting or when they have been taken captive by their enemy. That is why we are so outraged to discover that the United States, in violation of the Geneva Conventions, has tortured prisoners of war. Powerful human rights organizations such as Amnesty International and Human Rights Watch keep our attention focused on the inhumanity of killing civilians and torturing prisoners. But soldiers who are still in combat know that they are killable as long as they are fighting. It's the law. They are our *expendable lives*.

Think of what would happen if the Geneva Conventions did not suspend the human rights of soldiers while they are in combat. If soldiers in combat could not be legally killed, legally there could be no war. In the Universal Declaration of Human Rights, human beings, through their nation-states, have agreed that the right of human beings to live is unconditional and unequivocal, that human rights cannot be abrogated or abolished, nor can these rights be segmented into categories for some and not for others. Human rights are inalienable and inherent to being human. They cannot be revoked.

By excluding those engaged in hostilities from protection of their right to live, *the Geneva Conventions actually violate the Universal Declaration of Human Rights of 1948*, which guarantees that "everyone has the right to life, liberty and security of person" (Article 3). "All human beings are born free and equal in dignity and rights" (Article 1), and hence, "everyone is entitled to all the rights and freedoms set forth in this Declaration, without distinction of any kind, such as race, colour, sex, language, religion, political or other opinion, national or social origin, property, birth or other status" (Article 2).[6]

In revoking the human rights of soldiers in combat, the Geneva Conventions segment them into two classes: civilians (presumed to be women and children) with human rights, soldiers in combat (men) without them. That renders human rights conditional according to the class of persons one belongs to (those who are and those who are not engaged in hostilities), violating the principle that those rights are inalienable to all human beings.

Ultimately, the Geneva Conventions compromise everyone's human rights. Instead of prohibiting war, they accept it as inevitable and then regulate it. The reason is to limit the loss of human life in the civilian population and to protect prisoners of war only when they are no longer "engaged in hostilities." But, in fact, the loss of civilian life has risen from 10 percent of all casualties in World War II to 97.77 percent in Iraq and 78 percent in Lebanon in one month of 2006. Such is the fallacy of regulating war. Bereft of their human rights, soldiers in combat have only their own military-trained brute force to protect their lives. That is how male aggression and violence become inscribed in international law.

It does not have to be that way. In this book, I introduce new choices we can make about how we socialize boys, how the military trains soldiers for combat, how we choose our leaders, new means of resistance to occupation, and how we are governed in a globalized world.

By the conclusion of this book, it will be evident that world peace will elude us until we demilitarize states, eliminating their militaries and leaving states to police within their borders, and we establish a global peacemaking military to address violations across borders as well as crimes against humanity within them. But even demilitarization will not be enough. War will not be unmade without remaking masculinity. That is an imperative, if we are to have peace. But we must first ask new questions of men if we are to learn how they were made expendable.

Men, we need to know how you internalize, while growing up to be a man who may join a militia, or a military or paramilitary, that you may be killed by the time you are 20 or 31 or 19, or as young as 12 and 14 for boy soldiers who are drafted into Third World wars? When as a child you saw in movies and in the news that in combat it is always *men* who are fighting, *men* who are maimed in war, *men* who are killed, how did you come to accept this? While you were playing with other children were you beginning to understand that in a few years you might come home from a war without limbs or your sanity? Or not come home at all? What happens to that awareness in you as you are developing a sense of self? That is, how does your own expendability affect the formation of your life? You've not been asked these questions before.

The answer to them is stunningly, frighteningly simple: masculinity.

Masculinity requires that men's lives be expendable. Violent masculinity is modeled, socialized and taught to boys until it becomes an unconscious reaction to being expendable. To ensure that young people, both boys and girls, do not miss that point, the military brings the violence of war into their lives with video games. At the Army Experience Center in Philadelphia, the U.S. military spent $13 million to build a video arcade that is filled with games so that teenagers can enjoy simulated combat attacks in mock-up army vehicles. Although the army is legally prohibited from recruiting children and teens under the age of seventeen, teens of thirteen are allowed into this center where all games are free and army recruiters circulate talking to them. Peter Lehu, with the organization The World Can't Wait, describes the atmosphere and the large touch-screen monitors where teens are introduced to career opportunities in the army. "One particular screen shines a brightly-colored graph that shows dubiously that a life in the military will lead to a six-digit salary, more than any teen could hope for as a civilian."[7]

The center is all about virtual experience. The gaming stations recreate regions of Iraq complete with Arabs to shoot down or "blow away" as some teenagers express their excitement. Research is conclusive and clear: "violent video games are significantly associated with: increased aggressive behavior, thoughts, and affect; increased physiological arousal; and decreased prosocial (helping) behavior."[8] Peter Lehu, observing the effects of the teenagers virtual experience, found, "If watching kids in chairs shoot enemies with a video game controller supplied by the Army is disconcerting, then watching them hunched over giant machine guns shooting out of helicopter windows at nameless Arab simulations is horrifying."[9] Recruiters are waiting for them when they leave to promote the military way of life.

The Army Experience Centers that are being developed around the country are only a more slick version of video arcades around the world. After meeting with a project director on men's violence in Bethlehem in the Occupied Palestinian Territories, I searched out an Internet café. Inside, I found several young Palestinian men sitting around a huge screen each with a control device in his hands, playing Kill Baghdad. This kind of scene is played out all around the globe because those games are available worldwide.

Those young men in Bethlehem and the teenagers in the Army Experience Center in Philadelphia must disconnect themselves from the likelihood that the killing they are seeing on the screen could actually happen to them one day. If they did not distance themselves, the knowledge of their own expendability would be unbearable. As sentient beings, we simply cannot go forward in our lives with a death sentence dangling in front of us.

Miraculously for them, in a virtual world created at the U.S. Army Center they learn to want to kill Arabs but nothing happens to them. They are immortal and superior to those who tried to kill them "virtually." Further, I suggest that in the real world, playing these games has subdued their higher levels of consciousness, making it impossible for them to fully understand that they may become the "expendables" of war. The more that boys enjoy the virtual reality of war, the less real the consequences of war are to them. They see themselves both as men who can go out and kill and as teenagers who are impervious to being killed. They are merely virtually expendable.

As the expendability of male lives slips further away from these young men's consciousness, playing at killing Arabs in the U.S. Army Center brings racism together with the experience of being shot at and having bombs explode around them. Labeling people of other races and ethnicities as enemies, killing them because they are different than you, is the racism that is implicitly internalized with *core masculinity*. After shooting down Arabs, they turn to sip their soda drinks. That racism mixes with the reality of their own *expendable lives* and goes somewhere else.*

Some would argue that women, children, and families are also the expendables of war. In this book, *expendable lives* refers to the class of human beings who are identified by their male gender, are socialized and then trained to know themselves—years before a gun is pointed at them or their truck triggers a roadside bomb—as those who can be sacrificed in war. Male expendability is a corollary to the sexual objectification of girls and women who are socialized to know themselves as sexual objects, a powerful and destructive process that is fed by what I have called elsewhere the prostitution of sexuality.[10]

Our societies impose powerful negative sanctions on men who refuse violent masculinity. Boys who are not aggressive, who cower when attacked by other boys, and who will not fight, are bullied and taunted for being wimps or wusses. Those men who are caring, soft and tender risk ridicule for being effeminate, that is, like a woman. That misogyny and its contempt for all that is female is a foundation of male aggression that forms into what I call *core masculinity*. It is core because it precedes all other ways of being a man and because it traverses all classes, cultures, states, ethnicities, and races.

Core masculinity contains both men's expendability and their contempt for women. It requires women's complicity in accepting men's protection, which justifies the aggression and violence expected of them. It is universal not because it is in male biology but because states and movements require men's lives for combat. But its near universality testifies to its power not to its inevitability. Nothing is

---

* June 2010: unrelenting pressure from a coalition of antiwar groups was successful in closing the Philadelphia center.

"natural" about this type of fighting or this type of masculinity in any culture. It is made by society to serve the warring needs of macho state leaders as well as the needs of resistance or liberation forces. If the masculinity of war were natural, male aggression would just happen on its own. Society would not have to mount the powerful social pressure of *core masculinity* it imposes on boys and expects from men.

The first step in unmaking war is resisting military recruitment and the controlling, painful sanctions that keep a militaristic masculinity in place. Being tough, aggressive, and unfeeling are roles and behaviors that are not only expected of boys but that are normalized in sports. It is likely that only a few boys and men will enjoy fighting, roughhousing, punching, and kicking and not internalize that violence and allow it to shape their identities. More likely, violent sports like boxing and football that involve hitting, tackling, shoving, and pushing set the stage for violence and for war. The traumatic brain injuries that often come with these sports exacerbate aggression. They also reinforce male expendability.

As recent studies of masculinity have shown, many types of masculinities exist and the diverse experiences of being a man differ by culture, class, sexual orientation, and life interests. But *core masculinity* is imposed on boys by society through its expectations and requirements of manhood. The protector role, the role of the aggressor becomes so ingrained from repeated reinforcement from birth that it precedes all the diversity of masculinities as academics and men's movements write about them,[11] and as author John Stoltenberg has shown in his classic book, *Refusing to Be a Man*.[12]

I have spent a lifetime working against men's violence against women. Some readers may wonder why male expendability should matter to me. Why am I turning to men now, when women and children are most harmed by men in war and in their homes? To begin with, *core masculinity* does not arise in a vacuum. Women are culpable in perpetuating male expendability. Male expendability requires women's acceptance of men as their protectors, hence it requires they have soldiers and/or husbands to protect them. Protect them from what, though? The violence conjured by *core masculinity*! That chauvinist circular thinking, requires the protection of women from the violence that comes with rendering men expendable. And finally for many women in danger that protection is imperative.

Buried underneath this presumption of protection is another burning feminist question: can women ever expect full equality in a state or society where men, who deny that equality to women, are rendered expendable? As long as some human beings, men, are taught that they are superior to other human beings, women, and that they are supposed to sacrifice their lives to protect those who they have been taught are inferior to them, women's full equality is impossible. The presumption that war is inevitable is likewise a mandate for gender inequality and male superiority because as long as men are sent to war, in exchange for the expendability of their lives, they will be granted and taught superiority over women. False superiority is what men receive for their expendability. And it feeds upon the learned aggression that they will call upon in combat, the aggression that later will make many of those same men hate themselves.

But most of all, I turn now to the expendability of men's lives because while adhering to the Universal Declaration of Human Rights, I cannot parcel out the value of human life, defending it for some, ignoring its devaluation in others. And I know that when human rights are safeguarded for some at the expense of others, we are set up for deeper, more long-term violence from those who have been deprived of their rights. We cannot contain male violence against women as long as men's lives are rendered expendable.

Making Men Expendable

Considering the masculinist devaluation of men, should anyone be shocked that, having been made expendable, so many men dare not get too close to others? In everyday life, most American men would have us believe that they are not good with all that feeling stuff. At first I was entertained by the current vogue of male self-deprecation in American comedy where men bring us to side-splitting laughter with their portrayal of themselves as people who recoil when, in intimacy, a woman says, "Let's talk," or who will agree to anything their wives ask if it means they'll get sex. They let us see them as vulnerable, possibly, for a moment, even as inferior. They are the men who are "from Mars" and behave like they should be sent there. Aw shucks! They just can't help it! And isn't there something kind of cute about admitting it?

It is not that men are from Mars; it is that their masculinity is shaped from having to suppress their humanity as the result of being made expendable. This devaluation of their lives and their own fear make disconnection safer than compassion, violence more realistic than connection. And it makes cowardice the norm.

Emotional disconnection of men is socialized in boys to the extent that it becomes their standard for manhood. Of course vast differences in how boys internalize these social expectations range from the total rejection of them to the extremes of macho behavior and bullying. But I have observed another aspect of that expectation of men. In relation to combat, I suspect (and men's gender roles bear out my suspicion) that the emotional disconnection from others that permeates masculinity is men's nearly universal survival response to their having been rendered expendable. For how could there not be deep fear of being killed in war, of having to kill others in war?

Men, knowing that you may die very young, neither by accident nor from illness but in war, how do you grow up? How do you become who you are? I want to know what happens to you as you learn to conform to the death wish of masculinity. As you watch the photos and IDs of men killed in combat rolling down your television screens on the evening news, how do you internalize the awareness that you could die in a few years in combat somewhere? A friend of mine remembered with a sarcastic laugh, "Yeah you learn that you are just cannon fodder."

"They just don't think of it," more than one mother has said to me about their sons and the reality that they could be killed or kill others in war. If we dig beneath surface reactions, we find that it is not that boys and men do not know that they may be expected to make that patriotic "sacrifice" when they are young. Rather, with the optimism of being young, many assume that they are immune to the possibility of death in their youth. And that allows them to accept and actively pursue the warrior role as a measure of their manhood.

Fear is the only sane response to being rendered expendable, the legitimate human emotion one feels when one's life is at risk. But *core masculinity* teaches that fear is unmanly; if it is felt, it must be stuffed away. It cannot be shown. *Core masculinity* papers over fear with violence, a way to prove manhood. The aggression expected by *core masculinity* most often yields cowards. That is the violence I see when young men scream "cunts" from their cars at eighty-year-old women who are standing on street corners holding Peace Now signs as they mourn the deaths from war with the organization, Women in Black. That is the violence driving soldiers who kill women and children in the country they have invaded or rape the women serving in the military with them. Cowards attack and harm people who cannot defend themselves. And cowards are the other men who cover for them.

The dominating behavior that results from *core masculinity* is cowardice. We usually think of cowards as those who are not strong and tough when it is required of them and do not have the courage to face difficulties or pain without fear. But a coward who is wedded to *core masculinity*, "harms or attacks people who are weaker or unable to defend themselves."[1] Crudely, the military makes that heroic; the society treats it as bravery.

In *The Things They Carried*, writer Tim O'Brien tells the story of a young man who had protested against the Vietnam War and then received his draft notice at the age of twenty. Until that moment, "I felt no personal danger; I felt no sense of an impending crisis in my life. Stupidly, with a kind of smug removal that I can't begin to fathom, I assumed that the problems of killing and dying did not fall within my special province."[2] When he realizes that all that makes up war has actually entered his life, his expendability becomes conscious. He speaks of "the rage in my stomach. Later it burned down to a smoldering self-pity then to numbness."[3] Filled with terror, he walks off his job and heads for a remote region of Minnesota. "I did not want to die. Not ever. But certainly not then, not there, not in a wrong war."[4] He is physically sick, emotionally racked, and has hit a breaking point.

He knows that he should head for Canada and refuse the war. But something else pulls on him. "Intellect had come up against emotion. What it came down to, stupidly, was a sense of shame. Hot, stupid shame. I did not want my people to think badly of me."[5] Would he be unmanly to his family and friends and even strangers if he did not go to war? Despite those fears, he is ready to dive from a fishing boat and swim a mere twenty yards to Canada to escape serving in combat. But he can't. He cries.

He is a coward, not because he cries but because he does not swim those twenty yards and therefore does not exclude himself from fighting and killing. "What embarrasses me much more, and always will," he confesses, "is the paralysis that took my heart."[6] That is how irrational masculinity is in its expectation that men accept the expendability of their lives.

This story exemplifies the countless other young men who are expected to respond not to their own deep values but from the often brutal standards of masculinity. "Right then, with the shore so close,

I understood that I would not do what I should do. I would not swim away from my hometown and my country and my life. I would not be brave."[7] He makes a decision—choosing the demands of masculinity over his humanity. It is a decision that would lead him to take others' lives, and it would haunt him for years to come.

Later he reflects, "It had nothing to do with morality. Embarrassment, that's all it was. And right then I submitted. I would go to the war—I would kill and maybe die—because I was embarrassed not to."[8] The military counts on the cowardice that is deeply ingrained in *core masculinity*. In this rare, deeply honest glimpse into the moral dilemma that young men face when expected to fight in war, we see the power of masculinity that boys learn from childhood, that feeds wars with *expendable lives*. And because men, like all human beings, are always acting subjects of their lives, they have to find ways to live with their decisions. Some justify them with patriotism, others flaunt them in hyper-masculinity, or, reversing those decisions, some are now refusing cowardice and deserting the military, unwilling to fight and kill in war.

Most men, after all, value human life even in the face of the irrationality of war that makes them violate their own humanity. That is why I ask: Men, is being expendable and knowing that you may have to fight and die in war too much for you to know consciously? After all, being expendable is contrary to your life force. It goes against your own growth and development. If you were imagining your own mortality, fully aware of being expendable, you would not be able to go on with your daily life. There would be little point in planning a future, developing projects, making plans. Why bother if your life is without value and likely to be sacrificed in a war? That is what the guys on the front discovered in retrospect in the classic *All Quiet on the Western Front:*

Albert expresses it: "The war has ruined us for everything."

> He is right. We are not youth any longer. We don't want to take the world by storm. We are fleeing. We fly from ourselves. From our life. We were eighteen and had begun to love life and the world; and we had to shoot it to pieces. The first bomb, the first explosion, burst in our hearts. We are cut off from activity, from striving, from progress. We believe in such things no longer. We believe in war.[9]

Young men are not allowed to know that aspect of their expendability before they enlist in the military. The devaluation of their lives
is shown to them as heroic, manly sacrifice. But there are levels of
knowing and perceptions that we cannot afford to know consciously
will go somewhere else in our being for storage. The unconscious protects us from knowing the unbearable by absorbing that which is too
much for us to live with in conscious reality.[10]

When as a girl I watched romantic movies, I was internalizing
the expectation that one day I would be swept off my feet by some
handsome man who would love me and take care of me, give me pas-
sionate kisses, and I would make babies. Those movies were complete
with the expectation that I would live through my husband. They were
boilerplate lessons in male identification from which I would have to
wrest myself later if I was to have my own identity and shape my own
life. What are boys watching and internalizing when they see all those
soldiers being mowed down in that war movie? Do they see their
own limbs flying into the air, their warm blood chilling in the air as it
spills out of them? Likely not. Rather, *core masculinity* fortifies them
with that distancing that allows them to separate and disengage from
those messages to the point where killing becomes entertainment. In
distancing and disengagement, the unconscious takes over and becomes the holding place for men's expendability.

Unconsciouses are not all alike. Incredibly varied types of person-
alities form in the unconscious process of burying expendability. Yet
patterns can be found. The trick of the unconscious is that it is not
discriminating. It is irrational. It lies. It is fraught with contradictions.
For example, we corrupt our shared human consciousness while we
hold the contradictory beliefs that we value human life above everything else at the same time that we accept the inevitability of men killing and being killed in combat. Men's deaths in combat are consciously
intended. Military leaders plan for them, and men themselves are expected to put their lives at risk. In contrast, we are meant to believe
that civilian or innocent lives taken in war are mistakes, unintended
consequences of combat.

Mothers and wives and lovers who accept—even applaud—their
men going off to combat live with the contradiction of the human life
force that focuses on saving and protecting human beings and their

own knowledge that there is a high likelihood that their spouse, partner, son or daughter will likely kill other human beings and that they may not come back alive. Politicians regularly elevate that acceptance with the heroic language of the "soldier's sacrifice," as if one's son killing or being killed in war should make any parent proud. We are asked over and over again to violate our shared human consciousness rather than act from the human life force that makes killing or putting oneself in the line of fire intolerable.

For you young men about to become soldiers, facing your own expendability invokes your unconscious. Without much effort on your part, your unconscious protects you from that which is antihuman and saves you from that which is consciously unbearable to know by tucking it away so that you do not see it and cannot easily find it. You live as though your expendable life is compatible with your life force, which has inherent in it the urge to protect and save human life. You learn to believe that your life force is for protecting at the expense of yourself. You have internalized this inhuman reality that is lost to your consciousness. Your anger and aggression are sealed, disconnected from feeling for others as well as yourself.

Core masculinity seals anger and aggression away in the unconscious where it becomes the source of the rage that the military will tap to prepare you for combat. It is the same expendability that feeds into the expectation that you exist to protect others, women and children especially, which often turns to violence against women. Here is the unconscious source of men's emotional disconnect and suppression of their own feelings.

Since I began writing this book, one of the most common misgivings people have expressed about my thesis that expendability is built into masculinity is, "What about women? They are serving in the wars in Iraq and Afghanistan." Yes, as we have already seen, women in the military are inching their way toward combat. In fact, as of 2007, 20 percent of the service units in Iraq included women; seventy-one U.S. servicewomen had been killed in Iraq.[11] Because women are serving in combat zones, the common belief is that they are assigned to fight in combat. To correct that, the military narrowed its definition of combat thereby enabling it to put women in combat zones but not assign them to actual fighting, yet use them unofficially in combat if needed.[12]

Most of the time, being in a combat zone is different than being in combat. Women are taking serious risks and increasingly becoming the objects of hostile fire in Iraq and Afghanistan. While these wars have taken a proportionally larger toll on servicewomen than in any prior U.S. conflict, women are not even sent for combat training before they deploy. Yet some find themselves caught in the crossfire of combat. In 2005, Sergeant Leigh Ann Hester was in a military police convoy that was ambushed. She "maneuvered her team through the kill zone into a flanking position where she assaulted a trench line with grenades and M203 rounds. . . She then cleared two trenches with her squad leader."[13] She was the first woman since World War II to receive the Silver Star for valor in combat.

Women's more influential role in relation to combat is found back home in the support many give to making men expendable for war. From women's expectation of male protection to parents' socialization of sons into *core masculinity,* neither male expendability for war nor female vulnerability to male violence arises independently of each other. We women who were not socialized from childhood into the expectation that we would fight in war and you men whose expendability and violence invokes our vulnerability are intertwined in that dance of death that is war.

Growing up with two younger brothers, it never once occurred to me that I would have to join the military, go to war, register for the draft (although later I joined the protest against it), or refuse to serve my country. At the age of twenty, I did not wonder whether I would come home from the war without some limbs or if I would come home at all. I did not have to face the possibility of being thought of as a coward if I did not put my sanity and my life at risk for my country's wars. I was more concerned with how to delay or avoid getting married and resist being turned into some man's housekeeper, the prevailing working-class goal for girls of my age back then. My young, developing sense of self did not imagine sacrificing my life for my country, nor was that expected. I have never had to think of myself as someone who would bomb or attack neighborhoods, villages or military installations. Those scenarios had nothing to do with being a girl or becoming a woman.

Only now, much later in my life, do I wonder about that working-class trade-off my brother Danny was making when he enlisted in the army. Already he had learned at home that while he might be beaten, he could not hit girls, especially his sister. In that same home, my two brothers learned that the masculinity expected of them was exempt from the inferiority assumed to be inherent in all women. It was their reward for being expendable. And in the way that females are implicated in male expendability, that same home is where and how I learned to be a woman. To escape our abusive home, Danny enlisted in the army at seventeen. He was set up for that sign outside the army recruiting office: "Uncle Sam Needs You!" Imagine being needed, he remembered thinking at the time.

In stories of American men fighting with their lives on the line in Iraq, deceptions at the recruiting office that include promises the military never intends to keep, along with the working-class need for money for college or to pay off family debts figure prominently in men's decisions to enlist.[14] A naïve sixteen-year-old boy signed up to be called at seventeen, he says, "mostly because I thought it would be a good way to make a little money during high school, and because I was assured that nothing would ever happen, our country wouldn't go to war."[15] The year was 2001.

Military recruitment relies on boys knowing their expendability. Since the draft ended in the United States, the military has developed other ways of tracking teens and trapping them in the service. Under the No Child Left Behind Act of 2001, high schools must give military recruiters the names and contact details of all of their juniors and seniors. Students are usually not informed that they may opt out and refuse to have their names given to the military. Antiwar writer David Goodman has discovered that the number of students who opt out has increased significantly. Undeterred, the military has fought back, aiming its ads at their parents. Only 5 percent of those parents would recommend the military to their children, yet the ads try to draw them in: "Your son wants to join the military. The question isn't whether he's prepared enough, but whether you are."[16]

By 2004, one-fifth of all military recruiters in the United States were under investigation for lying, coercing, and making false promises such as promising that boys would not be sent to Iraq if they enlisted. Aimee Allison and David Solnit have shown how the Department of Defense explicitly exempts the military from consequences for lying to get new recruits by stating that recruiters may change the terms of enlistment documents without notice. The bonuses they offer are more like loans.[17] In 2010 the U.S. military was enticing new recruits with, "There are many benefits to joining the Armed Forces, but few directly affect your pay as much as enlistment bonuses. In fact, if you enlist in the military you may be eligible for up to $40,000 in cash bonuses." Then come the disqualifiers—the ones they name—"bonus will depend on the service branch, education level, civilian experience, specific job specialty...and length of contract," and the ones they don't name.[18] Actually, "65 percent receive no money for college, and only 15 percent ever receive a college degree," according to Allison and Solnit.[19] With eight-year enlistments that are often extended, combat is not a place for job training. "There aren't many jobs for M240 machine-gunners stateside."[20] But it does shape young men through their twenties, the most formative years of becoming an adult. How else, other than lying and making false promises, can the U.S. military attract men when the job description includes a much higher than usual probability of being killed?

Both women and men accept that the likelihood of dying or being disabled in combat is part of being a man, writ large into masculinity by the state and by cultural and social values. I became acutely aware of the extent to which we not only live in masculinist society but also to the extent to which it lives in us one evening in Paris.[21]

I had slipped away from my writing to see a new, much acclaimed film, *Indigènes*. (*Days of Glory* is the title in English.) The film portrayed indigenous Algerians, Moroccans, and black Africans from the French colonies in Africa who were recruited and used by the French to fight the Nazi occupation in France only to suffer humiliation at the hands of the French with whom they had enlisted. In the racism that is inherent in war, it soon became evident to me that those indigenous North Africans were used in that war in much the same way African Americans were used by the U.S. military in World War II—human beings, because they were Arab or black Africans were sent to take the first line of fire from the enemy.

The film began with North African men tearing themselves apart from tearful families, their expendability engaged on behalf of their colonizers, the French. Like most of the audience, I became caught up in the men's subjectivity, their feelings, their reactions to racist slights and offenses by French soldiers, their loss of buddies and brothers, their longing for their families, their eagerness to return home, and their uncompromising fight against the Nazis.

As the first men in the line of fire, their numbers quickly dwindled. Finally, of those few left, a small band of the *indigènes* were surrounded by Nazis in a remote village. I found myself so drawn into the battle that I was writhing in my cinema seat, relieved when they picked off one Nazi after another. At some moment, my own physical discomfort from the contorted position into which I had wrestled myself during the battle drew my attention from the film to my body. I let my focus rest on myself for a moment, observing my reactions to the violence in the film. I was shocked to see that I had been urging the killing that was on the screen before me. I was becoming disengaged from my own humanity.

This was not the same urge that I experienced that day on the beach near Bodega Bay. This urge was for death. The Nazis, not to mention the looming, monstrous horror of the Holocaust, offered no other possibility. That was not a trick of the director or the script. It is the paradigm of war—kill or be killed—and I was writhing in it, if only in my imagination.

Sure it was a film, sure they were Nazis, but only then did I realize that I, who reject the death penalty and oppose all wars, was urging the killing of some. I was relieved each time they, the *indigènes*, killed a Nazi soldier. I could only have that reaction to urge killing by disengaging from my own life force and from connection to all others. In that act of severing our connection to others, they become killable.

In my defense, the film was meant to evoke those reactions in me. Its good-guys-versus-bad-guys scenario is typical of most World War II films, the masculine paradigm of war in which the enemy, the bad guys (in this case Nazi soldiers), are without humanity. Viewers saw Nazis in a way that soldiers are trained to see their enemies on the battlefield, be they Vietnamese "gooks" or Afghan and Iraqi "rag-heads"—objects without humanity.

During the film, just as soldiers in combat, we come to know nothing of the enemy's families, nothing of their subjectivity, their likes and dislikes. We did not see them eating meals together or pining for loved ones or having flashbacks to memories of childhood. Objectification turned to depravity, we saw them only as killing machines. And in fact, that may be what they had been reduced to by the Third Reich. That is how states engage men in combat to carry out their crimes against humanity.

In the film, success was when Nazis were killed. The depravity that began with the ruthless, depraved extermination of Jews turned with seamless continuity to the annihilation of the Nazi soldiers. But the breakthrough message of the film, and it was a real breakthrough that brought about French recognition of the *indigène* fighters for the first time since World War II, was the extent of French military racism. That was where my attention was supposed to be focused—becoming conscious of this form of racism and applauding the heroism of men from the former French colonies who had not before been recognized as heroes. And well they should be, as they finally are now because of the film. But gender drives the issue deeper.

It was not until I was walking back to my studio after the movie that I realized that never once did I put myself in the place of those doing the killing—neither the French nor the *indigènes*, and certainly not the Nazis. I never imagined myself being one of those who was trying to kill the other. I just wanted the *indigènes* to live, and someone, not me but the *men*, the indigene soldiers to kill the Nazis. I relied on men to do the killing.

Although it was only in a movie, assuming the role of the protected gender is where my disconnection from my own humanity began. It was as if I was saying, "Men—I want you to get them—those Nazis, those enemies. Certainly I cannot do it. I am not trained. I am not aggressive. I am not violent. You must do it." That is the bargain isn't it? Women will produce, rear, and nurture men's children, and men will protect us. That is how war connects women and men. The very meaning of masculinity is embedded in the expectation of women's vulnerability that is men's excuse to fight—to protect us. You men and we women have both internalized, indeed, embodied our masculinist society in which male power makes the world more violent and then offers women protection from it by killing, which provokes more violence against us.

I am walking through the minute details of my experiences in this film as they show how easily anyone can slip into that gendered death trap. I watched myself, and I realized that instead of fully engaging in the force of life that is my connection to all human beings and refusing the entire kill-or-be-killed war paradigm, I was assuming that someone else would do the killing: men. Only then did I ask myself how different my reaction to the film might have been than that of many of the men in the theater. After all, I thought only of someone else killing the Nazis. But could these men feel that way? Had some of those men sitting in the theater seen themselves in the place of soldiers fighting against the Nazis? Had some of them actually fought in the French Resistance? Or would some of them be fighting in the next war? Or was this film part of their socialization into, and preparation for, being called upon to kill? Have any of those men around me killed for their countries? We are not supposed to ask these questions. We are expected to leave unspoken the crimes of war that rest silently on men's hearts. "Not any longer," I thought.

Another, more rational and heartfelt, more human and hopeful way must be found. Fortunately, the work of remaking masculinity is already underway, undertaken by men including, maybe especially, those deserters who refused to kill for their countries. But first, we must know how men are made into remorseless killers for war and why they are expected by their militaries and militias to behave in ways that, if they were in civilian society, would be considered criminal and would be punished.

Remorseless Killers:
Military Training

Most new military recruits are not seasoned macho men or super-masculine women when they join the military. Although some, as we saw after the September 11, 2001, attack on the United States, just want to "kickass," revenge being their excuse, most are naïve seventeen or eighteen or nineteen-year-olds who enlisted either because they could not find a job or their unemployment benefits ran out or because they thought they could earn enough money for college by joining the military. Two weeks before the 2003 invasion of Iraq, one soldier who joined the U.S. Army to get money for college remembers seeing the sign at the recruiting station that told him of the $40,000 he could earn if he enlisted. He said to himself "That could be mine. I'll be a man. I'll earn the money myself." A recruiter told him that he would not be deployed. None of it was true. "I was 19. I knew nothing of the world. I believed everything everyone told me."[1]

One marine veteran who enlisted at seventeen to get money for college admitted that "I didn't understand the world, politics, foreign policy. I was oblivious." He found the conditioning in boot camp training to be "ruthless and merciless." He learned the repetitive U.S. Marine chant "Kill! Kill! Kill! Kill without mercy!" It was as if it chilled him to the bone to speak of discovering that in order to be a Marine, "violence had to be motivated." When he was sent into combat, that conditioning to violence drove his actions. "It didn't occur to me that it was wrong. I didn't think about it." He didn't until he got home and the deconditioning began.[2]

New military recruits learn that they are "government issue," "GIs," property of the United States just like the uniforms issued to them. Steve Hassna, a former U.S. Army drill sergeant who put young men through basic training, explained that it is all about "how strac (strategic, tactical and ready for action in combat or strategic, tough, and ready around the clock) you are, how sharp you look. You have a button line that comes right down your shirt, and that button line should line up with the button on your fly, your belt buckle centered. You have a foot locker. The foot locker has a display. Every single display is exactly the same in the barracks. If I come into the barracks and find one single display out of sorts, then every single footlocker goes out onto the middle of the floor. Till you get it right. You will get it right over and over and over again because I'm in charge and you're not."[3]

The marines are known for being tougher on new recruits than the army. Long after returning home as a veteran, one marine colonel with the U.S. Marines anti-terrorism unit was still unable to shake off the fear that began his first day in boot camp when some marines strapped him to his bed with duct tape, beat him severely, and forced a bottle of liquor into this throat.[4] This hazing, called "beat downs," where marines beat up on each other just for the hell of it, is not only their way of having fun, but for them, it becomes synonymous with being a marine. Trying to prove they are manly men, they do not even see the cowardice inherent in their behavior.

Consider what is happening in basic training: New recruits, isolated on a base, are separated from their families and friends. They are not allowed to use their first names—their own or anyone else's. Anything that formerly defined them, including their clothes, is taken from them to "strip them of their old civilian identities before building new Marines." This is just one of the calculated strategies to disorient them.[5] From the beginning, they are subjected to extended periods of sleep deprivation, the most basic tactic of torture. They must meet new and often impossibly extreme standards and are humiliated at the slightest infraction or the possibility of the slightest infraction.

The purpose of military training is to wipe out the recruits' identities, to disconnect them from how they knew themselves before joining the military, and to diminish their sense of their own agency until their wills are subordinated to military command. The recruits' identities are standardized as they are stripped of the notion that they can make their own decisions or even have their own intentions.[6] And they are rewarded for this loss of self. In their degradation, soldiers learn that they are superior to civilians who are not as neatly organized as they are in the military and who do not have the power of life and death over others. They are told that they are "professional," a status elevated beyond what many young working class and poor recruits could have hoped for in civilian life.

Under any other analogous conditions such as induction into a sect, prisoner of war brainwashing, or fraternity hazing, the treatment that recruits are subjected to in military training would, by the standards of our societies, be considered inhuman, cruel, and most often criminal. Brainwashing involves:

- Intensive, forcible indoctrination, usually political or religious, aimed at destroying a person's basic convictions and attitudes and replacing them with an alternative set of fixed beliefs

- The application of a concentrated means of persuasion, such as an advertising campaign or repeated suggestion, in order to develop a specific belief or motivation[7]

In the military, having stripped down recruits' sense of self and disengaged them from our shared human consciousness, their human agency is replaced with a singular loyalty to the others in their unit. This loyalty is exclusionary. It does not extend to those outside of the military. Then they are ready to commit themselves to follow the U.S. Army values which include loyalty, duty, respect, selfless service, honor, integrity, and personal courage.[8]

Selfless service is to "put the welfare of the Nation, the Army, and your subordinates before your own."[9] But "selfless" means absence of your own self. Brainwashing is complete. As a soldier of the U.S. military you do not bear true faith and allegiance to your own self as a healthy ego requires. These military values look very much like the loss of self that psychologists find characterizes women who lose their identities to the men they love. They describe the selflessness of women who value their lovers or husbands by devaluing themselves and in the process lose their own identities. Selflessness is how women's subordination to men is secured in their psyche, and it is how men are subordinated to the military.

In basic training "you have to get everybody to understand that this is a complete team effort. When you come into the barracks for inspection, you get down and you should be able to see one set of foot lockers, one set of beds, one set of books," according to Steve Hassna. If anything is out of line—one shoe, one bed—the drill sergeant dumps everything onto the floor. Hassna told his men to "check your buddy, check your bunk mate, you are working together. You have to be able to do your thing and cover your friend."[10] You learn not to let others down. The cost of doing so is too high.

You are separated from your friends, family, and all you have known. You can count on no one else, it's you and the others in your barracks. Commanding officers scream orders and belittle the recruits in front of their units, reminding them that they are "expendable," "worthless." These scenes, always taking place in front of their buddies, are public displays of moral indignation that sociologist Harold Garfinkle refers to as "degradation ceremonies."[11]

If you are in the military, your total identity has been reduced to something lower than most of you have ever known and that degradation makes you reliant on and bound to the others around you. That is how you become a unit, one in your degradation. You fear being belittled, ridiculed, humiliated if you do not hold up your part. But you are even more concerned about letting down others in your unit. In effect, your empathy and connection to shared human consciousness are being reconfigured to serve military needs—to make remorseless killers.

Normally, outside of the military, most of us want our friends, those we choose to bring close into our lives, to come alive in positive, caring environments that will elevate and not degrade us. But when your identity is reduced and degraded, the loyalty of friendship is made from humiliation and out of fear. These men already share being expendable and have survived practices that have dehumanized them. These experiences tie them to each other even more tightly because they rip each individual apart from the larger shared human consciousness.

In boot camp or basic training degradation is meant to build up resilience in recruits and to create a force that will overcome the basic human resistance to killing their own kind. Psychologists now call brainwashing "mind control" or "thought reform," which I tend to think of as the effect watching television for too long will have on me. This military training is not at all benign. Nor should anyone feel comfortable with its heinous practices.

Psychologist William Cross remembers the first day of training at West Point when he was told, "These are your classmates. You are going to be with them for the rest of your life. You don't dump on your classmates."[12] That sounds good—you get lifetime buddies, and you are forever loyal to each other. But it has a sinister underside to it. These loyal friendships are crafted in the degrading and punishing treatment of new recruits. Bonding forms during brainwashing and through the stripping away of each new soldier's sense of self. If you were the one who was out of line and caused the sergeant to dump everyone's bunk or foot locker, you see it is your fault that everyone has to clean up the barracks all over again. Friendships form in the context of fear and intimidation.

When your closest friends are those who have gone through the same humiliation and degradation, you become convinced that because you are in the military you are so different from nonmilitary people that no one on the outside will understand you. Your differences from those on the outside, like the unity forged in any mind-control sect, seals your bond with each other. That is how the military assures itself that you men will remain in combat even when combat as it is today violates everything you know, value, and trust. As a soldier you must be there to protect your buddy even when doing so contradicts common sense. At that point, you are prepared to kill other human beings.

Even then, the resistance of human beings to killing their own is so powerful, as Lieutenant Colonel Dave Grossman who studied the effects of killing in war notes, "that it is often sufficient to overcome the cumulative influences of the instinct for self-protection, the coercive forces of leadership, the expectancy of peers, and the obligation to preserve the lives of comrades."[13] For example, SLA Marshall, a former soldier turned military historian, found in a study of U.S. soldiers in combat that only 25 percent of them fired their guns in combat during World War II.[14] Our human life force, oriented to protecting and saving lives, powerfully resists killing. As Grossman also found, even with their training, soldiers in combat resist killing, especially up close.

Since SLA Marshall's research, the military turned its attention to increasing its soldiers fire and kill rates. In training soldiers to kill, to get men to override their humanity, the military employs reflexive conditioning with repetitive shooting in which they bypass their thinking and their own moral code. It is the same method that Pavlov used to train that dog.

The ultimate goal of combat training is to prepare soldiers to kill without remorse, to act without a conscience. Think about it—having no feelings about taking the life of another human being! The goal, remorseless killing, requires redesigning the soldiers' humanity. In target practice, a man's image is placed on the target, which as Major Peter Kilner, a West Point instructor, points out enables "soldiers to overcome their aversion to killing by conditioning them to act spontaneously to conditions that are combat-like yet morally benign."[15]

Still, the military found that firing at an image of a human face was not enough to overcome soldiers' resistance to killing human beings. So it intensified its training by teaching them instead to fire at locations—a house, a car, something (not someone) moving in order to get men to override their humanity. They are instructed to fire without thinking and spray large areas with fire. While they are mowing down human life, they see only trees or buildings or cars.

One new recruit who was training in the Marine Corps could not make that leap and override his conscience. When he went out with his unit to the shooting range and looked at the target 500 yards ahead of him, he realized "All you could see was a little blur." That is when it struck him that the target "could be a woman and a little girl." His empathy engaged, and at that moment he knew that he could not go to war. He began the long torturous process of filing for conscientious objector status, which made him the object of ridicule, abuse, and beatings from other soldiers. But he did not relent until he was discharged.[16]

To prevent empathetic reactions like that of this conscientious objector, Marine Corps training glorifies killing. One former soldier from Iraq Veterans Against the War remembers the demands of his National Guard training; "I callously screamed out brutal chants about slaughtering kids in schoolyards and laughing about the way napalm would stick to their skin. We must've screamed, 'Kill!' hundreds and hundreds of times to get into our heads that this was our purpose as soldiers."[17]

Journalist Thomas Ricks quotes a Marine Corp drill sergeant, "'An M-16 can blow someone's head off at 500 meters,' he teaches. 'That's a beautiful thing, isn't it?'"[18] And the marines make his sense of beauty their own with resounding "Yes, sirs." One soldier pointed out that "it becomes muscle memory," and adds "you don't think about it. You just do it."[19] Not surprisingly as the Haitians found out after their 2010 earthquake, the marines on a rescue mission cannot even hand out emergency food and water supplies to the earthquake victims without screaming at them and pointing guns in their faces.[20] Wherever they are, everyone who is not one of them is their enemy.

Shifting out of the paradigm of war, connecting to our life force that was so evident that day on the beach near Bodega Bay, we might ask, "What kind of training should soldiers be given before going into combat?" Most efforts to rethink military training focus on postconflict and peace-building militaries. But we need to rethink military training for conflict that escalates into combat. A feminist and human rights paradigm asks different questions: "What if soldiers were taught to value all human life? What if they were expected to act from consciousness of their interconnection with others? What if they killed only as the last resort, when under attack and purely in self-defense?"

In the paradigm of war, valuing human life is considered too dangerous for the soldiers. But is it? We see firefighters entering into extremely dangerous conditions, risking their lives. They rely on their training and each other. The fire is their enemy. But their focus and intent is not only to put out fires; it is first and foremost to save lives.

We would be badly served if they put the fire above the human lives at risk inside. Their determination to protect and rescue people whose lives are at risk does not make them weaker or more vulnerable. Indeed, it drives them. In taking risks to save lives, they do not displace themselves from their own humanity nor is their training focused on destroying their identities. We all need them to be fully present when they enter that burning building to bring out those trapped inside. But we do not see evidence that teaching skills for negotiating in a situation to prevent it from turning into a firefight are valued tools in U.S. military training.

If a roadside bomb just blew up your buddy's vehicle, if you are being mortared and attacked, you don't necessarily see your attacker. But for most infantry soldiers, combat is usually close in, face-to-face, and physical. What if you were to see human beings at the end of your gun? First you would likely think of tactics other than killing, such as negotiating or trying to take prisoners. You would know from your training, as the firefighter knows, that you are prepared to do what is necessary to save your own life and that gives you the opportunity to avoid forsaking the lives of others. If you were trained to kill only as a last resort, your state would not be able to commit war crimes because remorseless killing is required when a state has no reasonable basis for invasion and combat.

Instead of training to kill only as a last resort, the military wipes out soldiers' resistance to killing. In a *Frontline* interview one army private talked about how that training lowered soldiers' resistance to shooting, saying "it was so much like basic training, they were just targets out there, and I don't know if it was the training that we had ingrained in us, but it seemed to me it was just like a moving target range, and you could just hit the target and watch it fall, and hit the target and watch it fall, and it wasn't real."[21]

"Watch it fall." "It wasn't real." In combat, that "it" will be the woman driving her children to school or the Iraqi sniper trying to kill you. That use of the word "it" is a measure of the social distance soldiers achieve from those they kill, in order to kill. That "it" is spraying large areas with gunfire. That "it" is the objectification that is necessary to override a human's resistance to killing.

Training soldiers to shoot randomly is the making of bullies, the fulfillment of cowardice. The figure, the 25 percent of soldiers who fired in combat during World War II, only rose when soldiers were able to fire at locations rather than people. By the Korean War (1950-1953), the military had succeeded in increasing the number of soldiers who fired on the enemy in combat to 55 percent.[22] But the military knew that it could do even better, shift its focus, change the language until soldiers understand that they are not ordered to go out and kill human beings, but instead they are "clearing" an area or a house. Once soldiers were trained to clear an area, the U.S. firing rate in the war against Vietnam rose to 90 percent and left 3 million Vietnamese dead.[23] Civilians accounted for 70 percent of that war's casualties.

By the time soldiers' eight-week training and combat training are completed, men's expendability is fully activated. Those destined for combat will be sent for further training. After eight weeks, marines train another week with more target practice. Observing training at Parris Island, Ricks noted that "the rifleman is also anonymous: not a famous individual, not even mattering as an individual, but as a member of a group."[24] For the marines, it is the group that matters.[25] The loss of self deepens.

Group loyalty drives soldiers into anonymity, disengaging them from shared human consciousness, making one's self unknown even to oneself. Until then, the knowledge of their expendability has been incompatible with human consciousness which normally is forward looking and thinking about the future. With this training their expendability is activated and comes into consciousness as soldiers going into combat know they may not come out. They go anyway. They are expendable and that "sacrifice" of their lives, limbs, or sanity is what their state or militia expects of them, as do the people back home. That sacrifice may seem to them as if it is the nature of their masculinity, so deeply ingrained in them that it feels essential to being a man.

Deserters will tell a different story. And most of those who do not desert, because they defied their own human integrity, will pay for that "choice" with post traumatic stress disorder (PTSD) and a lifetime of painful memories.

Fear of reprisals keeps soldiers looking out for each other. You give your buddies your support and loyalty. Your survival depends on them. More importantly to you, their survival depends on you, which is why you do not notice that your friendships are being built upon dehumanization. Still, if you could think about it, most of you would know that you would not make friendships that are based on supporting each other in killing. But no alternative relationships or support are available either in training or in combat where on a daily basis your unit is all you have. The military has carefully calculated every step in this process of male bonding, manipulating it so that soldiers will violate their own life force—so that they will kill.

You are a unit and, male or female, you are indoctrinated into the masculinity of war. When you stand up and take ridicule and hazing, the masculinity of war is affirmed in you. This is part of how you learn to survive life-threatening, ego-destroying experiences. Soldiers in combat in Iraq and Afghanistan report that this is the training that gives them the confidence to face the situations they are in as invaders and occupiers who are always unwelcome by people concerned with their own self-determination. But those soldiers in combat are men, and they are battle-ready.

No one says to them that they have been trained to do that which is criminal in civil society. Nor do they get to think about the validity of invading a country that poses no threat to their own. Brainwashing is complete and military authority is brutal. The U.S. military is a law unto itself.

Peace will remain an illusion as long as the U.S. military trains its own soldiers as well as Iraqi and Afghan soldiers in remorseless killing and as long as military leadership rises from the ranks of remorseless killers. Unmaking war necessitates not only sweeping changes in military training, it requires another kind of military. But I get ahead of my story. How we go about unmaking war depends on knowing more about how it is made.

First Kill:
The Soldier's Loss of Soul

The first thing many GIs are told when they are new to a combat zone is to forget everything they've learned. The actual language is "that's all chicken shit." They won't be shining their shoes or making their beds so that a quarter bounces off of them. Most of the time on maneuvers in combat, soldiers don't even have a bed. On maneuvers in Vietnam, every time soldiers changed location, they likely had to dig out their "bed" for the night, which, if it was not deep enough, could become their grave before morning. And above all, soldiers in a combat zone do not salute any officer because that move could identify the officer as a target. It matters not at all whether a soldier's shirt is buttoned in alignment with his fly zipper (or whether it is buttoned at all). That is the same shirt that he wore yesterday, that he slept in last night in the field, and that shirt will be on his back until he returns to his barracks.

Then why did soldiers have to suffer humiliation to learn all of that precision? That was so that the military could reshape their basic human needs to connect with others and produce in them the desire to belong to a team effort to kill. Research on the brain has found that when people make judgments on their own that go against the group, their brain scans show areas associated with emotional salience (the right amygdala and right caudate nucleus regions) are highlighted. According to psychologist Philip Zimbardo, "this means that resistance creates an emotional burden for those who maintain their independence—autonomy comes at a psychological cost."[1] The military relies on the high cost of that emotional burden for going against the group. It is what keeps soldiers fighting.

In a study of World War II Reserve Police Battalion 101 in Poland, Christopher Browning found that "the Battalion had orders to kill Jews but each individual did not do so. Yet 80 to 90% of the men proceeded to kill, though almost all of them—at least initially—were horrified and disgusted by what they were doing." Why did they keep on killing? "To break ranks and step out, to adopt overtly nonconformist behavior, was just beyond most of the men. It was easier for them to shoot." Those who refused to shoot knew they were leaving the burden with their buddies. Those who "did not shoot risked isolation, rejection and ostracism" in a very tight-knit unit. Further, if they did not shoot, it was as if they were morally reproaching those who did. Not shooting meant that they were not living up to their masculinity.[2]

Military male bonding can be so powerful that it can even make you act in ways that you never would have considered, not because it took bravery to do it, but because it required that you suspend your common sense. Psychologist William Cross points out that you get a "cold focus on your own responsibility to uphold your end of things, and if you fail, you are not just failing yourself, you are failing your buddies. When I first jumped out of the airplane, I was the first one out. Somebody later asked why I jumped and the first thing that came to my mind is that I jumped because I'd be ridiculed if I didn't."[3] Tim O'Brien captured this embarrassment in *The Things They Carried*. It made a young man go into the military, go to war, and kill.

How else can we explain 150,000 American soldiers entering combat and walking from the border of Kuwait into the Iraqi desert on March 20, 2003, having just been told that one in three of them will die in the invasion? Most accounts of this war jump to the next point—that Iraq had no Weapons of Mass Destruction (WMDs) and so one in three soldiers were not killed as planned and predicted. But I want to linger over that announcement to the troops and ask why these men who were walking into a perfect staging area for Saddam Hussein's weapons of mass destruction did not mutiny?

Those soldiers had heard the same intelligence that their commander in chief presented to Congress and the American public. "Right now, Iraq is expanding and improving facilities that were used for the production of biological weapons," President George W. Bush told the United Nations in an address on September 12, 2002. A month later he escalated his charges against Iraq to include chemical weapons: "Iraq has stockpiled biological and chemical weapons, and is rebuilding the facilities used to make more of those weapons."[4]

On October 5, 2002, Bush told us what Iraq would do with those weapons. "We have sources that tell us that Saddam Hussein recently authorized Iraqi field commanders to use chemical weapons—the very weapons the dictator tells us he does not have."[5] A few days later on October 7 in Cincinnati, he escalated his rhetoric to the ultimate terror: "The evidence indicates that Iraq is reconstituting its nuclear weapons program."[6] Those statements were all lies from the president of the United States and being used to justify invading another country. Worse, neither Americans nor Iraqis had any protection from the warring consequences of the president's lies as both the U.S. Congress and military accepted them as facts.

Sergeant John Bruhns was in that invasion of Iraq. He remembers that as they spanned out across the southern Iraqi desert where there were no villages or cities, he and his buddies were talking about how they made perfect targets for Saddam Hussein's WMDs. They wondered why their commander in chief would put them in that position.[7] But they pressed on. That is when many combat soldiers say to themselves, "well, this might be my time to die," or "maybe my number has come up," and they go forward into combat. They were not mutinous, those 150,000 soldiers fanning out in the empty Iraqi desert, even though, as far as they knew, they were invading a country with WMDs to use against Americans—them.

Why did they not refuse to go forward? Ah! That would be unmanly, cowardly. In other words, the military has turned manhood into a suicide pact. The men's manhood and military training propelled them into what seemed sure to be their death march. But they could not let their buddies down. Each of you knew that the guy next to you is thinking the same thing about how he cannot let you down. So you march in unison toward a likely death. You have been trained so well that you override your own life force and even your sense of self-preservation. You even diminished your genuine connection with others—for if you were marching in tune with your shared human consciousness, your duty to your buddy would have been to convince him to desert too. In fact, you would try to convince others to desert. That is how you actually save and protect human life. And it could lead to unmaking the war that you were sent there to make. But in the military that is unmanly.

Only if you soldiers step outside of military-think will you be able to see that if people cannot act to save their own lives, then they cannot really be expected to protect the lives of others. For a soldier to try to save his own life would mean refusing to be rendered expendable. But the military relies on its training of you that required you to believe that your own life is without value, thereby making a sham of the belief that you are in combat to protect others.

Sergeant Steve Hassna vividly remembers his first days in the combat zone in Vietnam. When you arrive, "you are brand new. You are so green you're like Day-glo. You don't know what to do—you are overwhelmed with everything going on around you." Steve looked around to see the soldiers in his platoon straggling back in from several days of fighting. "These guys are coming back armed to the teeth! They've been out on operations, in combat, looking for the bad guys." He was army, they were army, but he was not yet one of them.[8]

Steve stepped forward to meet his commanding officer, who looked him over and said, "If you are here after about a month, if you are still alive, we'll talk," and walked away. Steve went out with his platoon on maneuvers. "Nobody's talking to me. I stumbled over every single twig, stump or rock in my way." The other guys are thinking "you are a newbie, stay away. Go over there. You're going to do something stupid and get me killed." And yet, they are supposed to be there for their buddies.

How long does this go on? How many times do you go out on maneuvers in combat with these guys and no one talks to you, no one wants you around them? You don't know. And you do not even get a chance to think of how contrary this is to your training to be loyal to your buddy. Nobody has told you what it will take to be considered one of them, part of their group in a war so far away from home in a place where you are likely to die. And you are eighteen, maybe nineteen years old.

Then you find out. You kill. You try not to notice what is happening inside you. The other guys are there, and you are introduced to a new kind of camaraderie: "If you take somebody out—now you've joined the club"—the "8½ pound pressure pull—the pressure it takes to pull the trigger."

Until the military forbade them, Internet blogs and short YouTube clips taken by U.S. soldiers during firefights in the Iraq war provided ample evidence of the elation that takes place when you take someone out. The soldiers sound like guys in video arcades but with a bit more desperation in their voices. Marines in a tank on an empty street of an Iraqi village see something that's outside the range of the camera recording the event. "Shoot that motherfucker!" comes a screaming order. Then, "get down!" On the screen you see three teenage Iraqi males in tee shirts and jeans running down the street. They have no weapons. Maybe they threw rocks at the tank. Maybe they had weapons and dropped them. As viewers, we don't know. And we don't know if the soldiers in the tank know. Then another command from inside the tank, "Use the 16!" In the intensity of the moment, the young soldier does not stop to ask himself why his commander did not order him to take the two unarmed boys as prisoners.

More sounds of gunfire on the video clip. One of the young men running down the street falls into a heap on the pavement. "I got him, sir." Adrenalin is running high inside the tank. An order is shouted to the driver, "Slow the fuck down." The soldier who shot the teenage boy on the street, insists on getting through to his commander. "We got the motherfucker, sir," with the pride in his voice of a boy announcing his success to his parent.[9]

Dave Grossman found from his interviews with combat veterans that after killing an enemy soldier at close range, the shooter often experiences "a brief feeling of elation upon succeeding in killing the enemy." Later, that kind of bravado usually disappears and is replaced with self-disgust when "the soldier is faced with the undeniable evidence of what he has done, and the guilt stage is often so strong as to result in physical revulsion and vomiting."[10] One soldier told him that after shooting an enemy soldier who was attacking his comrades, "I can remember whispering foolishly, 'I'm sorry' and then just throwing up ... I threw up all over myself. It was a betrayal of what I'd been taught since a child."[11] An Iraq veteran remembered the first time he arrived in a combat zone with the U.S. Army, and a small child rolled something under their truck. His commanding officer told him to shoot the kid. "I lost faith in why I was there." From that day on, "I was only there to defend the person next to me."[12]

Men, is that how your military training makes you sidestep the value of human life? Are the hypermasculinity of military training and loyalty to your buddy enough to make you suspend your own life force? Will you wear that indifference or even satisfaction we see in the movies when some macho man kills the other guy? Or is what we see on your face the smugness of patriotic pride?

Apparently not. Soldiers, we can see that often in combat when you face one another, look into each other's eyes, and then kill him or her, you are sickened by your own act. From many combat soldiers accounts it is evident that some of you cry, others vomit, some of you wet your pants—involuntary reflexes against violating your own humanity in taking the life of another. Repeated cases of soldiers being unable to fire on their enemies abound. Fortunately the military has abandoned the practice of shooting on the spot those young men who freeze when they are supposed to fire.

Soldiers have many different stories of their first kill. What is common to most of them is that at that moment everything in their lives and beings changes. Almost every soldier says that. But before you think about what you have done or analyze your reactions, feel your feelings, at the instant that you know deep inside of you that you have broken the bonds of your own humanity, the guys all around you show you that you are one of the group. Grunts, pats on the back let you into their camaraderie, the club of men who have killed in war. They can let you in because you can no longer look at them as different. You've proven yourself and your manhood. You are a true soldier. Not because your footlocker is perfect. You do not even have one. But all of that training, marching in unison, has brought this human being to this moment when being part of the group is more important than anything else—than oneself, than human life.

When a marine automatic machine gunner had what he called his "first confirmed kill" in Iraq in April 2006, "my company commander personally congratulated me."[13] His victim was an innocent man who posed no direct threat to him or his unit. Part of his shame when he returned home was that he killed the man in front of the man's friend and father. Those congratulations and pats on the back that go out to every man for his "first kill" are meant to repress his shame, to overlay it with the assurance that he has met the standards of manhood that the military and his country have set for him.

Then you soldiers who were not remorseless killers before enlisting discover something else. You, all of you who have fired your guns, who have passed the 8½ pound pressure test, know that you are different from all of the rest. Some of you know it immediately. Others will see it later in nightmares and traumatic flashbacks when you get back home. But you do not speak of why. You have changed. There is a rupture in your being. You have that sick feeling that you can never go back to who you were before that first kill. The continuity of your lives, which the rest of us take for granted, is ripped out of you.

The first time soldiers kill another human being, their reactions reveal not only the repugnancy that humans have for taking each others' lives, but the damage killing does to their own humanity as well. This is more than psychological harm. It is loss of soul. Shared human consciousness still insists itself on you even when you violate it, even when you degrade yourself.

In spite of all of that destruction of the soldier's humanity, the U.S. military is still puzzled over why so many soldiers commit suicide! "The most frustrating thing is trying to find a cause," General Peter W. Chiarelli, the army's vice chief of staff, told the Senate Armed Services Committee.[14] The 158 army suicides in the first half of 2009 were such a dramatic increase over the total of 128 suicides for 2008 (which itself at 20.2 per 100,000 soldiers was higher than the national suicide rate), the military commissioned a research project to find out why the incidence of suicide was rising. But they seemed to miss the obvious connection between turning soldiers into remorseless killers and soldiers killing themselves.

In 2009, the National Institute of Mental Health launched a new research study in collaboration with the army which was based on the assumption that post traumatic stress disorder, family issues, alcohol abuse, and neurobiological factors might each play a role in soldiers' suicides.[15] Stress? Of course stress is related to suicides inside and outside of the military. But in no other place but war and conflict zones are human beings required to kill other human beings without feeling and then treated as heroes and manly men for doing so. Those soldiers were set up as potential suicide victims when they began their military training. Many blot out the reality of being a killer with alcohol and drugs even though they are prohibited as well as pornography. After the U.S. tripled the number of soldiers deployed to Afghanistan, the Pentagon reported that the number of soldiers seeking treatment for opiate addiction in its Substance Abuse Program rose from 89 in 2004 to 529 in 2009. In the last year, with President Obama's surge in troops, the number dramatically increased to 50 percent.[16]

Nor was I particularly surprised when U.S. Army Major Nidal Malik Hasan, a military psychiatrist about to deploy to Iraq, walked into the Soldier Readiness Center on one of the largest military bases, Fort Hood in Texas, and opened fire killing thirteen and wounding thirty before he was brought down by a woman civilian police officer who was one of the wounded. In fact, his own U.S. military training and the hours upon hours that he listened to men in psychiatric sessions talk of committing unspeakable acts and the utter military devaluation of human life left me wondering why this kind of massacre does not happen more frequently.

While the complex web of factors that form around an act like that is unique to that particular killer, each is drawn from an environment that has ruptured the fabric that holds our human life force in place. But politicians and the media seized upon his name and his religious beliefs, diverting Americans' attention away from how the military makes killers and toward anti-Islamic, anti-Arab racism by making Hasan out to be a Palestinian terrorist. We cannot forget that when the Oklahoma City bomber Timothy McVeigh and the buddy who assisted him took 165 American lives in April, 1995 they used the training and ideology of the enemy they learned in the military.

As Steve Hassna's story of Vietnam and the first time he killed unraveled, he spoke not of killing but of "taking someone out." That was the first time I was aware of the power of not speaking that word "kill." But by the time of the U.S. war against Iraq however, "kill" had become a rallying call of soldiers and marines. I knew that Steve was going to continue talking about how it felt to make it into the group. I interrupted his narrative. Before shifting to the others, the "club," I wanted to know about him, I wanted him to tell me about how he felt the first time he killed another human being.

Staying in the present tense of the firefight that he was talking about, using his own words for killing, I asked him "When you take someone out, what happens to *you*?" To keep our attention close to this experience, I continue in the present tense. He tears up. But his reference point is still the other guys—his buddies. "Essentially you join a club" A long pause. I think, he is wondering if I get it. I see behind his words that he is questioning whether I can possibly comprehend how important it is to be part of that club at that moment. But then he continued, "that you can never leave." Quiet—tears, just a few. Then I can barely hear him say "You become part of a fraternity," before another really long pause.

My unanswered question still hangs heavily over us. Finally, in almost a whisper, "I think the closest I can get to it. . . You inadvertently have a hole . . ." long pause and he looks away, then to the floor. ". . . in your soul." Huge tears that had welled up in his eyes drop directly to the floor. I try to hold mine back. Absolute stillness hangs between us in the midst of the café's clanging cups.

Over the years, Steve has had to answer this question that I asked about what happened to him the first time he took someone out, and it is clear to me that this is as much as he can say about it. I do not press him for more. He knows that something of his humanity was ripped apart at that moment, and there is no going back to the guy he was before that. All of his socialization to be a man and his training in the military have served this moment. He is not dead, but, in becoming a killer (the word that is not said), something of his humanity died. And the hell of it is that he knows it and must live with it for the rest of his life.

Then we, the people and politicians who send soldiers to the destruction of their soul and spirit, lock that loss in their hearts. To make up for not welcoming Vietnam veterans home as heroes, today people spontaneously applaud soldiers in airports and politicians repeatedly thank them. President Obama, visiting U.S. soldiers in Iraq in April 2009 told them "You have performed brilliantly on every mission that has been given to you." Speaker of the House Nancy Pelosi returned from one trip to Iraq to tell the press that "our soldiers are perfect."

"Loss of soul" repeatedly comes up when soldiers tell us what happens to them when they kill. When Staff Sergeant David Bellavia describes how in self-defense he plunged the blade of his knife into an Iraqi who had been firing on him and his men in Fallujah, he realized, "I was soulless. My innocence was gone. I could never have it back again."[17]

Camilio Mejia became a conscientious objector when he saw that "I could be killed in more than one way. It wasn't just the physical death; it was also the many deaths of the soul every time you kill a human being...We die, little by little, each time someone gets killed, until there is no soul left, and the body becomes but a corpse, breathing and warm but void of humanity."[18] That is why, as we shall see, diagnosing the trauma of combat as post traumatic stress disorder only skims the surface of describing the harm to soldiers from being in combat.

Professor William Cross, a combat veteran and a psychologist who counsels Iraq veterans, put it this way: "Each of us has a different experience [of killing] that has been emblazoned on us. A lot of people are unwilling to talk about their experiences because they have a sense that their experience is not glamorous or worthy. It's been my experience that the trauma [of killing] is something that touches something in people, that awakens their spirit and can potentially destroy it. [In that act] there is a sense of betrayal by your parents, your church, your government, God." That loss is the unspoken that is embedded in and covered up by platitudes about the 'soldier's sacrifice.'

Forward observers are soldiers attached to infantry units to bring in artillery support. They brought in support for the unit flown in by helicopter that Cross led on a combat mission. "The forward observers are well thought of because they are able to protect people in the unit."

But Cross saw that something had happened to the forward observers out there in field operations. Hanging around during off-duty hours, they would talk about "how many rounds it would take to take out a village." Cross, noting the macho in their talk, was sickened, "There is something very overpowering about that." When he went in after the forward observers with the helicopters, "You see the devastation of that. And it wipes you out."

Most soldiers do not engage in Bill Cross's kind of soul-searching while they are in combat. The effects of brainwashing and the loss of self that is imposed on them during military training shut down their reflection and diminish their consciousness. The war paradigm provides all of the answers they need at the moment until weeks or months or sometimes years after they get home, when their psyches disentangle from brainwashing and conditioning. But there in combat, as one sergeant said of how he felt about killing, "If you are in this environment, its fine. It's a hoot to be honest with you ... No civilian job can compare to the infantry. You are trained to kill people. I have no hesitation about it. It's what I do. It's my job."[19]

On the other hand, one military police officer had the job of guarding those the United States took as prisoners in Iraq. But he said, "I was not able to make that jump to turn those men into sub-humans. The act of treating them as sub-humans creates atrocities. I just felt my vital spirit bleed out of me."[20] He turned in his weapon to his commanding officer, and he too embarked on the grueling experience of becoming a conscientious objector in a military unit where defection was treated as being lower than life itself.

How do we understand the various meanings men give to their experiences of killing in combat?

Answering that question is as vital to unmaking war as it is to remaking men for we cannot even begin a quest for lasting peace until we know what has to be undone in men. Nor can we expect men to break out of the dehumanization that military training and combat does to them until we are all drawn back together in shared human consciousness. To get there, I turn to how human beings interact with each other.

Human interaction is the glue of all human connections—for better and for worse. At the core of every interaction we have with each other, we interpret the meaning of the other's words, gestures, behaviors, and actions not only with objective knowledge we have about the situation we are in, but personally, subjectively in our felt experiences.

Suppose you, for example, just told me "that you got a hole in your soul" the first time you took someone out in Vietnam. As I have never taken anyone out, I cannot use my own experience to interpret the meaning that experience has for you. But I refuse to say to myself that I cannot understand. For if I do, I disengage from my own life force that is fed by our shared human consciousness. I will not use either my disdain for war nor my lack of war experience to distance myself from you. Even when I write about how you got that hole, as I did in the preceding pages, in order to come close to your subjectivity, I stay in the present moment and speak of "you," instead of the more distanced "he" or "him." Being present with you allows me to have no excuses to not know.

I too am human; I have experienced violation of my soul, not in killing but in another way. There! I have found it—a beginning point for me to understand the violation of your soul, the hole in your soul. I have found a place in me from which I can enter into your personal subjectivity. Other ways can be used to empathize with you and connect to your suffering. This one is mine.

Trying to understand your experience in combat, I have to bring everything I know to bear on it if I am to interpret the meaning that hole in your soul has for you. If I do not, to me you will become just another veteran who has seen horrors that I believe I can never understand, or more likely, that I just don't want to know. If I do not interpret the meaning your experience had for you, or if I grab on to some ready-made explanation like "well, that's men for you," I push you back, and I become to you just another someone who has entered your life but neither can nor will try to understand what war did to you.

I bring to our encounter an objective knowledge that comes from basic assumptions I am making about you. For example, I am thinking of you as someone who very likely was not reared to kill, who enlisted to serve his country thinking he was doing something good. That, I understand, is what you mean when you say "I was a true believer."

Implicitly, I get it. I listen, I ask more questions. You are interpreting, discerning the meaning of the questions I ask. You may be wondering if I get it, or you may just assume I don't. That is how genuine interaction works—each of us trying to interpret the meaning of the other, shifting between assigning meanings already established by society and those we glean directly from each other, touching each other's pain, joy, frustration, satisfaction. That is how our subjectivity brings us in close to each other.

If I do not try to get at the meaning your experience has for you, I am left with stereotypes: sure you killed in war, after all, men are macho, or killing in war is heroic so you must feel strong and heroic or your macho made you do it. And when I fix pre-established explanations to your words and actions, I reduce you to an object again, pushing your humanity beyond reach. That is objectification.

Then I wonder, are you objectifying me into the no-one-can-understand numbness of your own loss of empathy? Or are you engaged with me here as part of your soulful mission to help people understand why wars should not be fought? Don't both of these forces in you work together, contradictions that you can shift in and out of to find the balance between survival and change?

All of our interactions involve those basic elements—interpreting the meaning of the words or gestures of another and then responding with our own words and gestures based on the interpretation we made, and then receiving the other's interpretation of our response. We interact in this way whether ordering a cup of coffee or trying to interpret the meaning of a veteran's experience of killing. The basic elements are the same.

In our interactions, if we are present, that is to say not distanced or dissociated, we are subjects to ourselves—feeling what we feel, bringing those feelings and our senses into the interpretations we are making. If we extend that feeling and sensing, that felt experience to another, not only do we act from our own subjectivity but we enter theirs. Interaction deepens as our subjectivities connect until we can put ourselves in the place of another and interpret what a situation means to that person.

By carefully attending to words being said, feelings and gestures and expressions that come with the words, not flinching, being there fully, subject to subject, we restore each other to our shared human consciousness and affirm the value of human life. We are melting away objectification. That is the interaction that humanizes us, sparks our souls. It is something we do whenever we seek to genuinely interpret the meaning of the experience of the other. That is the interaction that will diminish the numbness of soldiers in combat as well as anyone attuned to systematic harm. In this kind of interpreting the meaning of the other, we have found our empathy, the route to our souls. It is the nature of being human.

Each time I try to enter into a soldier's experience of combat and killing—when I see a youthful eager face like that of Steve Hassna's in his photo taken just before he enlisted and then look at the tough, remote don't-mess-with-me stance of photos of him in Vietnam, as I listen to him and other veterans talk about how killing forever changed their lives—I feel a terrible heaviness on my chest, sometimes palpitations. For we cannot go to where they were without being affected ourselves. But if we do not go there, we cannot find ways to undo war. If we open ourselves to our own human empathy, we find there the force that is equal to the task of unmaking the wars that wreak destruction of the human spirit.

To know what combat means for soldiers, their experiences must be spoken. When Iraq Veterans Against the War held Winter Soldier hearings in Washington, D.C. in the spring of 2008, courageous and vulnerable soldiers spoke the unspeakable, told us what they did, the dirty secrets of war. They not only were reclaiming their own humanity, but giving us their subjective experiences, that point of human connection from which we can interpret the meaning their experiences had for them. When we do, when we feel their pain, then we know and understand. Only then can we act wisely.

One's soul and the goodness of the human spirit implicitly sets boundaries that limit how far humans go into harming others. Those boundaries are reinforced by values and ethics that are meant to contain violence against others. Even *core masculinity* that promotes and socializes aggression is constrained by humanity's repulsion for killing other human beings. Those are the checks and balances, the controls on human behavior that are defied outrightly in war, especially since major military powers now ignore even the restrictions of international humanitarian law against killing civilians that are laid out in the Geneva Conventions.

Further, we need to consider the implications of this most often unspoken reality of combat and killing. Is there really room for women in that fraternity of death made up of the grunts that men become even to themselves? Is that why the military has refused to officially assign women to ground combat or frontline fighting and does not even train them for it? Perhaps women's exclusion aims not to protect them but to not disrupt the male bonding that is built upon expendability and cowardice and then sealed with remorselessness.

Despite all of the military efforts to suppress shared human consciousness in combat soldiers, it continually reasserts itself, revealing how difficult it is to snuff out our life force. Now, more and more men are choosing to refuse their own expendability, and women are choosing not to expect it of them. That is the beginning of writing a new social script that will in fact redefine masculinity.

This new masculinity, already a work in progress, will be easier to achieve than the effort it takes to make killers because it will work with rather than against our human life force. It is based on empathy from our connections with each other. But that personal challenge invokes another enormous change—remaking the military. From that new norm we will require a different kind of military training—one that focuses on protecting and saving human life, one for which killing is the very last resort. First, we will look at just how far the military functions outside the law, human ethics, and just plain decency.

Preventive Killing

Whether it is Iraq or Afghanistan, George W. Bush's or Barack Obama's wars, or anyone else's war in the world, as a soldier in combat you are there to kill the enemy. But you are not sure who the enemies are because when you invaded, they did not go out and get uniforms to identify themselves as resistance fighters as the Geneva Conventions requires of them. Your military command tells you that your enemies are fighting an "unconventional war" as if they are not playing fair in the killing game of war, as if you are.

As combat soldiers, your problem with the Iraqi and Afghan or any insurgency your military provokes is that you don't know how to distinguish between an ordinary citizen and an insurgent. When you have to make the call of whether to kill that man coming across the field carrying something, or those two women driving too close to your Humvee, or those teenagers who you suspect may be armed, you face the uncertainty that Iraq veteran Brian Turner did in this excerpt of his poem "What Every Soldier Should Know":

> There are bombs under the overpasses,
> in trashpiles, in bricks, in cars.
>
> There are shopping carts with clothes soaked
> in foogas, a sticky gel of homemade napalm.

Parachute bombs and artillery shells
Sewn into the carcasses of dead farm animals.

Graffiti sprayed onto the overpasses:
I will kell you, American.

Men wearing vests rigged with explosives
walk up, raise their arms and say *Inshallah.*

They are men who earn eighty dollars
to attack you, five thousand to kill.

Small children who will play with you,
old men with their talk, women who offer chai—

and any one of them
may dance over your body tomorrow.[1]

That is the soldier's terror—he does not know who his enemy is. If in doubt, soldiers, already hyped to "Kill! Kill! Kill!" are ordered to kill, "just in case." That is preventive killing. Then they kill, just in case but without orders. Then they kill just because they can. All are murders.

After the release of the film *Fahrenheit 911*, in March of 2004, one soldier in Baghdad wrote to its director Michael Moore about his battalion's approach to killing. "It's hard listening to my platoon sergeant saying, 'If you decide you want to kill a civilian that looks threatening, shoot him. I'd rather fill out paperwork than get one of my soldiers killed by some raghead.' We are taught that if someone even looks threatening we should do something before they do something to us. I wasn't brought up in fear like that, and it's going to take some getting used to."[2]

Implicit in the soldier's phrase "getting used to..." is the struggle of soldiers to overcome their own humanity, to break away from shared human consciousness—that interconnection among humans that protects lives—and get used to killing another human being! To guide his decision-making, each American soldier carries a plastic card, the U.S. Military's "Rules of Engagement," that tells him who he can shoot and under what circumstances. "Engagement" is a euphemism for attack, firing on, killing if "there is a reasonable certainty that a proposed target is a legitimate military target." But as a soldier, how do you determine that? You do not have to make that decision on your own if you are ordered to shoot by your commanding officer. But you did decide to follow his orders. On your own, faced with someone who does not look like an American, how do you get to a "reasonable certainty" to kill her or him? How does it differ from being just what any individual decides to do in the moment when preventive killing is a condoned strategy of war? What if you are scared or not sure or just don't give a damn?

The Rules are as vague as their title is misleading. Veterans returning from Iraq testify to how in combat zones the Rules are changed over time—at first by their commanding officers and later by the soldiers themselves who just ignore the Rules. In the initial 2003 invasion of Iraq, one marine reported that according to the Rules their units were ordered to shoot anyone in Iraqi uniform. By the time his unit made it to Baghdad, he "could shoot anyone that came closer to me than I would feel comfortable, if that person did not immediately move when I ordered them to move after I told them to move, keeping in mind," he added, "I don't speak Arabic."[3]

Once, as one marine reported, going out with his unit on assignment to blow up a bridge, when they were ambushed, they turned to shoot "at anything and everything [read "everyone"] without bothering to identify targets."[4] (Brackets added.) Dehumanizing words and racist slurs such as "ragheads" or "haj" reduce Iraqis into objects of ridicule and contempt, making it easier to kill them.

One marine who had three deployments in Iraq pointed out that over time no one paid attention to the Rules at all. They shot at Iraqis—civilians and resistance fighters alike—without any constraint. When soldiers were on the road it was not uncommon to take pot shots from their Humvees at any cars around them traveling on the same road, even those pulled over on the side of the road. They aimed either at the car's radiator or windshield, maybe killing the driver and passengers or just destroying the car. But they never bothered to stop to "conduct a battle assessment."[5]

Many soldiers were laden with "drop weapons."[6] When they kill anyone who was armed or when they uncover a cache of Iraqi insurgent rifles, they confiscate the arms and carry them with them. Then when they kill "innocents," as they call the civilians they shoot down, they drop the confiscated weapons next to bodies leaving no basis for questions, no investigation, just another dead insurgent, should anybody wander by and ask.

Returning from Iraq, one U.S. Marine reported that according to his command's interpretation of the Rules of Engagement, if they encountered a person with a weapon, they had to call the command post. But after seeing some of their buddies blown up by improvised explosive devices (IEDs) or killed by insurgents in firefights, soldiers seething with anger, said "we didn't bother to call the command post."[7] They just shot.

Then the command post's interpretations of the Rules changed. One marine reported that "if a town or city that we were approaching was a known threat, if the unit in the area before us took a high number of casualties, we were allowed to shoot whatever we wanted." Noting that everything [read "everyone"] they saw, they engaged [read "shot"] it [read "him or her—man, woman, child"], he described one woman coming by with a bag. "We lit her up" with a grenade and "when the dust settled, we realized that the bag was full of groceries."[8] (Brackets added.)

Another marine recalls receiving a command: a taxi had been used to set off a roadside bomb, and the Rules changed once again—they were to shoot any orange and white taxi, the typical color of Iraqi taxicabs. Later, new orders came down: "If they carried a heavy bag and shovel, take them out."[9] Think about it, someone, a military officer sitting in a command post, decided that it is reasonable to kill any human being who is Iraqi and is carrying a heavy bag and shovel. Then consider that it was common in Iraq to see men and women carrying bags and shovels as people were trying to rebuild their homes and shops and schools and clinics as fast as the military bombings and mortars demolished them.

When you are there on the ground and see everyday people reconstructing bombed-out villages, how could you not conclude that most of them are just ordinary civilians? That, however, is the normal human interaction from which soldiers are expected to be disengaged and it leaves them incapable of interpreting what they are seeing and then deciding on a reasonable course of action. Military training combined with *core masculinity* to destroy soldiers' ability to put themselves in the place of another makes valid interpretation of the meaning of others' behaviors impossible. When that happens to you, you impose meaning from your preconceived ideas or the rote learning that came through brainwashing. They are the enemy. Any of them. Things. Objects.

If anything natural can be attributed to human nature, interaction is it. Interaction is what makes humans social, connecting us to each other. Language is our means of interpreting our interactions and without language, one cannot fully function as a human being. We find its foundation built into the very nature of how we interact with each other. I am not speaking of the quality of any given interaction but rather the fundamental act of interpreting the meaning of the other's words, gestures, and acts even as one's own meaning is interpreted in return.

When a soldier returns from Iraq, rips off his dog tags, and tells us, "I am not a monster anymore," I have to interpret what that means. My interpretation begins by needing to know what made him think of himself as a monster while he was in Iraq. Looking squarely at the situations he and others with him were in, understanding what was required of them by their commanders, asking how and why they followed orders that would make them feel like monsters when they get home, finding out why they were there in the first place, I am able to reconstruct the context of the situation he and his fellow soldiers were in. Only when I know his situation can I genuinely interpret the meaning of that one phrase, "I am not a monster anymore" as that soldier meant it.

Empathy, as we have seen, requires taking a further step. In the case of that soldier, I try to put myself in his shoes until I get to the point that I can say with a high degree of certainty, "I know what you mean." That knowing stems from interpretations we make from our interconnections, from our experience of oneness. Genuine interaction does not impose pre-fixed meanings on our interpretations of each others' words and gestures. We come in close, through empathy.

Cultural relativism asserts that we are so different from each other—separated by gender, race, life experiences, culture—that we could not possibly know, not to mention feel, what another is experiencing. It is an opaque wall that blocks some from knowing the experiences of others' and it is so dense between men and women that it is assumed that I, a woman who has never been close to combat, could not empathize with a man who has killed. But that, quite frankly, is not true for me, for any woman, for anyone. As humans, we are endowed with not only the ability but the need to interact. We could not make meaning without it.

The consequences of *core masculinity* and military training closing down soldiers' abilities, needs and desires to interpret the meaning of others' experiences are dire. U.S. soldiers, from their helicopter on October 23, 2007, in the early morning near Djila, did not see Iraqi men in a ditch alongside the road. They saw "emplacers," which is military speak for people who put bombs or IEDs in place, the most common means of attacking U.S. forces in Iraq. No other explanation for the appearance of men in a ditch occurred to them because they did not see human beings. They saw only objects who, to them, were potential killers.

They not only refused to interpret the behavior of the men they saw, they interpreted everything that was happening around them to be about themselves, the American soldiers. The military and its invading soldiers believe in their own superiority, which makes them supremely arrogant and self-centered. To those U.S. soldiers in the helicopter, the Iraqis on the ground were emplacers out to kill them. Unlike words we commonly use for people in the fields like "farmers" or "peasants," that imply that they are human beings and suggest a particular way of living, "emplacers" is a cold, distanced, disengaged term meant to keep soldiers' humanity distanced from the "objects" they are targeting that become known to them as insurgents.[10]

The *Counter Insurgency Field Manual* instructs soldiers to understand "insurgents" not as men fighting in a resistance to U.S. occupation but as "propaganda units."[11] That instruction appeals to the assurance given to soldiers that they are "professional," that is, they are businesslike in that their behaviors conform to standards of a properly qualified person. Presumably telling soldiers they are professionals helps convince them that killing is a responsible act.

Actually, those supposed "emplacers" were men; human beings were in that ditch. More specifically, they were farmers working in their field in this rural area of Iraq where men rise early, 4:30 in the morning, to irrigate their fields before the blistering heat of the day sucks any water out of the ground. Able to see only emplacers, the soldiers in the helicopter "fired and killed two of them. A third ran back to his nearby house presumably to take cover. But if the soldiers saw him only as another emplacer and not a farmer, then they would see him taking cover not in his home but in a "safe haven," the term they use to indicate the place where criminals hide. The U.S. soldiers' report read, "During the engagement, insurgents used a nearby house as a safe haven to re-engage coalition aircraft." The helicopter "engaged" (read "'fired upon") the house. That is how, if the incident were reported at all, we would hear about it back in America on the six o'clock news and in news reports around the world.

On the ground, Abdul al-rahman Lyadeh, a relative of some of the victims saw the second air-strike from the helicopter that killed fourteen people and destroyed their home. Journalist Dahr Jamail, who exposed the incident learned from another witness "that four separate houses were hit by the helicopter. A local Iraqi policeman, Captain Abdullal al-Isawi, put the death toll at 16—seven men, six women, and three children with another 14 wounded."[12] Then as the final death knell to empathy, those deaths were reported to their generals as collateral damage as if the human beings killed were storage sheds or plows.

Could that massacre of peasant farmers have been averted? Not likely. Maybe it would have helped if the soldiers knew something about farmers in desert climates and used that knowledge to interpret the meaning of the men working in the ditch. Made blind by their training and their masculine, American arrogance, with their absence of empathy, that is, their remorselessness, they turned themselves into murderers.

In April 2010 Wikileaks released a video taken from an Apache helicopter of U.S. soldiers gunning down fourteen Iraqi civilians including two Reuters reporters in a Baghdad suburb in July 2007. To the horror of most newscasters who reported the video, the soldiers were joking about their kill, which Wikileaks referred to as "collateral murder." The U.S. military, under pressure to investigate the incident, concluded that the actions of the soldiers were in accordance with the law of armed conflict and its own "Rules of Engagement."[13]

Saturated with stories like this one from the wars in both Iraq and Afghanistan while writing this book, I saw on the video an ordinary day with soldiers doing what they ordinarily do in combat where in addition to killing they are taking mortar fire most of the time. But I was heartened by an apology to the Iraqi people that appeared shortly afterwards from two Americans. In An Open Letter of Reconciliation and Responsibility to the Iraqi People: From Current and Former Members of the U.S. Military, Ethan McCord and Josh Stieber, they admitted: "From our own experiences, and the experiences of other veterans we have talked to, we know that the acts depicted in this video are everyday occurrences of this war."[14]

These air strikes are the same war tactics that U.S. troops took into Pakistan and into the escalated war in Afghanistan once Barack Obama became president. Random killing, being easier from the air, led to the U.S. military dropping 1,853 bombs in Afghanistan in the first half of 2008. The total for 2007 was 3,572.[15] While the United States had dropped nearly 10,800 cluster bombs in Iraq, British allies used almost 2,200 according to reporter Paul Wiseman.[16] In one U.S. bombing of rural Afghanistan villages in August 2008, according to Kai Eide, the UN's special representative in Afghanistan, the United Nations Assistance Mission in Afghanistan gathered eyewitness testimony to the killing of ninety civilians, sixty of whom were children.[17]

Preventive killing. Random killing. How do you even count the Iraqi or Afghan or Pakistani dead? The United States does not bother. The Internet database Iraq Body Count regularly publishes updated death tolls. But to confirm an Iraqi death due to war, it requires two sources. This is much like the old laws on rape that, absurdly, required eyewitnesses. By mid-2008 Iraq Body Count documented between 86,312 and 94,174 Iraqi civilian deaths from the U.S. war since 2003. But those documented deaths are only the tip of the iceberg.

In a 2007 survey, fewer than half of the U.S. Marines in combat thought that Iraqis should be treated with respect, and only 55 percent of all soldiers and 40 percent of marines would report another soldier who had killed or injured Iraqi civilians, according to a Penta-

gon report.[18] Preventive killing of Iraqis in Fallujah, Haditha, or revenge killings by the U.S. military contractors like Blackwater will continue to go uncounted unless an exposé is pursued such as the 2008
indictment of Blackwater soldiers for the murder of seventeen Iraqis
the year before, (against whom charges were dropped on a technical-
ity in U.S. courts in 2009).[19] Under occupation by the U.S., criticism
from the Iraqi government was rare. All the while, casket makers in
Iraq could not keep up with the demand in the early years of the U.S.
war there.

To address the problem of uncounted Iraqi dead, researchers
from the Johns Hopkins School of Public Health in conjunction with
an Iraqi research team interviewed a representative sample of Iraqi
households to find out how many had relatives who had died from
violence in the war. Household reports were then objectively verified.
Because the sample was representative, their results from this study
can be generalized to the entire Iraqi population. The Johns Hopkins
study found that by 2006, 655,000 Iraqis had been killed in the war.

In 2007, the generally accepted and frequently quoted body
count (which is regularly updated) was thirteen times smaller than
the number that came from the household survey research conducted
two years earlier. The U.S. invasion and occupation of Iraq had provoked and unleashed warring factions within Iraq to take vengeance,
not only against Americans and their allies but against each others'
communities, until that figure of Iraqis killed because of the U.S. war
reached well over 1.3 million by 2009.[20]

The Iraqi death rate from the 2006 Johns Hopkins study was confirmed by other studies. Research from the Opinion Research Business of London in conjunction with the Iraqi Independent Institute
for Administration and Civil Society Studies conducted a survey of
Iraqi households between March 2007 and August 2007 and estimated that 1,033,000 Iraqis had been killed.[21]

Nevertheless, despite the random, preventive killing by U.S. soldiers and the unrelenting bombing, in 2009 the Iraqi government,
still under U.S. occupation, released death tolls for the period 2004 to
2008. Seriously undercounted, the 85,694 is the minimum Iraqi death
toll reported by the Iraq Ministry of Human Rights for that period
even though Iraq had no functioning government at the time and few

records were available. Other flaws in the report come from excluding all of the deaths as a result of the invasion up to the end of the first year of the U.S. war. Insurgents deaths were also excluded from those figures. It found that 1,279 children and 2,334 women were killed during that period.[22]

Returning to the value of human life that was uncovered in the collective grief of the people on the beach that day near Bodega Bay, we cannot avoid seeing that Iraqi, Afghan and Pakistani lives are simply of less value to the U.S. military forces than American life. When I conduct a search in the computer or at the library for "value of human life," I am referred to the so-called right to life campaigns, which sacrifice women's dignity, their right to control their own bodies, and even their own lives, to sustain pregnancies at any cost. Or I am directed to life insurance company actuarial tables for the dollar amounts they ascribe to the value of a human life.

A U.S. government program set the value of Iraqi and Afghan life at the same amount it paid for property damage—an average of $1,212 per person up to a maximum of $2,500 per dead Iraqi or Afghan.[23] Compare that to the payment of $100,000 in 2002 to each U.S. family, "for those whose death is as a result of hostile actions and occurred in a designated combat operation or combat zone or while training for combat or performing hazardous duty."[24] In 2006, that payment for an American life lost in combat was raised to $400,000 through Servicemembers Group Life Insurance.[25] Does that lesser monetary value of Iraqi life reflect an ease in killing Iraqis or is it just the difference in the cost of living in the United States and Iraq? Or is it a measure of racism in war?

The military relies on racism to shape soldiers' views of their enemy. American patriotism reduces non-Americans to lesser human beings and enemies, painting Arabs, Iraqis, Afghans, insurgents, Sunnis, Shiites and others with broad strokes that label them terrorists. Michael Carey, an Iraq War veteran and Harvard law student, provides us with an example of how the U.S. military unofficially sanctions racism against U.S. enemies in his article, "Anti-Arab Racism in the Military." In his view, racism is natural or instinctual and innate, "not necessarily an unnatural perversion that obstructs an innate human tendency to love everyone." And it is functional; "it is one product of an instinctual need humans have to limit the group of people to who we show sympathy."[26] Carey argues that cohesion in the military comes from an instinctual capacity to limit our caring to those close to us. That is why soldiers have less sympathy for those people who are not in their military.

While Carey invokes sociobiology as a kind of intellectual justification for his thesis, he is merely mirroring what every GI knows: in war, support for your buddy and unit is as far as sympathy for others *is allowed* to go. As that loyalty is the result of a training based on brainwashing or mind control, claiming that it is instinctual or innate is simply false. If our ability to sympathize with others were biologically confined to those who are like us, with whom we share similar features, nationality, or family, it would not have to be further diminished through the often inhuman rigors of training. The allegiance that insulates them from the world in which they go to war would be automatic. As Carey himself points out, "The military will want to encourage soldiers to identify with their unit and dehumanize their enemy," which is not so different from the insularity of families riddled with abuse where the nasty secrets of beating and sexual assault are guarded by treating those outside of the family as potential threats, even enemies. But in war, according to Carey again turning to sociobiology, the exclusion of others from your human family is not racism, it is human nature.[27]

We have to make a decision here. If it is true that it is in our nature to sympathize and care only for those who are close to us, then shared human consciousness is a sham. Interconnection is an illusion. More likely, through paternalism of the family we learn that men are our protectors and therefore, we must confine our caring, sympathy, empathy, and keep it within our family. That is, we must sell out our shared human consciousness, trade it in for paternal protection under which closeness and connection stays within the family. The rest of the world be damned. To hell with strangers.

The mindset of the occupier of a nation-state is not unlike that of an abuser who controls a home, for whom the "other" is merely an object upon whom the abuser imposes her or his meaning. The reason for the hatred is not that he does not understand his victim's Arabic tongue, it is not because she is a woman who is from Venus as opposed to being from Mars as the popular defense of *core masculinity* goes, but because human interaction has been reduced to objectification. Either the soldier has refused to interact when faced with the enemy or has been so effectively brainwashed that he has lost his ability to very simply ask himself, "How would I feel about these guys pointing guns at me if because of them I have no water, the garbage piles up around my house, I have no hospital to take my sick child to, because of them—those Americans?"

However, contrary to the patriotism that expects us to accept war, remain loyal to our soldiers, objectify the enemy, and support killing and murder, our humanity does not require of us that we distinguish between empathy for soldiers and for their victims. Indeed, our shared human consciousness requires us to empathize with both, which is what brought me to try to understand men in combat and from there to discover how they came to accept their *expendable lives*. Empathy, however is not enough. In the politics of empathy, our government, the military, and soldiers must be held responsible for the crimes they commit in war, including those that the military does not consider criminal.

Does the $298,000 rise in payment to the family of a U.S. soldier killed in combat reflect an increase in the value of what his life was actually worth? Of course it doesn't. It is payment for his expendability which is called "sacrifice" over his flag-draped coffin. It is hush money, a payment to reassure families of fallen soldiers that their loved ones' lives were worth it.

In civil society, we construct criminal codes to prevent killing. But the United States allows its military to function outside of the law, beyond the reach of human ethics. We make laws to prohibit anyone from taking another's life, invoking our moral code that no one challenges as valid even though some violate it. We protect our shared human consciousness because we know that it protects human life. In civil society, we make murder the most serious and heinous of all crimes and one for which we reserve the most severe punishment. But when the United States invades another country and its soldiers kill other human beings with impunity, generally those who murder Iraqis and Afghans are not held accountable.

This moral code is why the French government initially charged the journalists with not giving aid at the scene of an accident when they chased Princess Diana's car into a deadly crash in a tunnel in Paris. We demand of our doctors that they prolong life, that they work at finding newer and better ways to keep us out of pain, to restore our health, to keep us active. We make it criminal for a doctor to intentionally harm or destroy a human being's life. We demand the strongest justice for the victim. When Americans awakened to the disregard the health insurance industry has for human life and people's well-being, they found that insurance companies not only deny needed care, even life-saving interventions, but they also degrade all of human life and make the diminished value of human life normative. When Americans found repugnant that the value insurance companies hold for human life is the profit they can make from our illnesses and injuries, their outrage led them to demand an overhaul of health care in the United States.

Many of us struggle against the state when it takes as its right the power to end a human life by imposing a death penalty. We construct local, national, and global institutions to reduce infant and maternal mortality, to eliminate hunger. We do all of this to protect and enhance human life. We make rituals, laws and institutions that support and enhance human life, and in doing so we are conscious of ourselves acting together and being responsible to each other. From our life force, we make our love of life legal and institutional.

Except in combat. We exempt our military from upholding the life-saving standards that drive our society and sustain our own humanity just as we exempt our soldiers from the protection of human rights. We will have to come to terms with allowing our military to function outside of the norms, values and laws of our society and our state if we are to unmake war.

Grunts: From Soldier To Sociopath

In combat, once you set out on the mission of a killer, being tough prevails over having a mind and a soul. "You become like a bull. A grunt." And you don't give a damn. Marine veteran Tyler Boudreau explains that grunts "see the world as threat and response, attacks and counter-attacks, offense and defense, allies and enemies, winning and losing."[1] When all the shades of grey are ruled out, your behavior goes to the extreme, and you may act out sometimes in bizarre ways. But being a grunt is more than that.

Boudreau tells us that joy is the most dominant emotion of battle for many soldiers. He remembers how he and his buddies reveled in the battle they had just fought. "Did you see the rockets? Did you see 'em fly? Did you hear the bullets smacking our sides? Did you feel the heat and thunder? Did you smell the burn? Did you know what the edge looked like before now? Did you ever know we'd be hanging over it so far?"

Why the soldiers' reaction? "Joy to have finally answered the question of myself: Will I stand up and fight, or will I curl up and die? Joy to have found myself still standing when it was all over."[2] That joy is actually not joy at all but hysterical excitement from relief of fear combined with the need to hide the cowardice it takes to kill and destroy.

"In the course of ten minutes in a firefight," Steve Hassna told me, "I experienced and saw almost every emotion you can think of. Hysterical laughing to uncontrollable sobbing to screaming, people yelling for help, people taking command." That hysteria follows directly from remorse having been driven out of you.

Grunts become more than indifferent to the lives they have taken. They are pompous about it. Moving out on maneuvers with "the club," Hassna and his buddies, the "hardcore people" in the fields of Vietnam, reassured themselves with bravado:

> Yeah, though I walk through the valley of the shadow of death
> I will fear no evil, for I am the meanest son-of-a-bitch in the valley.

That tough talk comes not from being the meanest-son-of-a-bitch in the valley, but because your humanity has been reduced to that of a grunt. You don't think of the depravity involved in some of the tactics you learn in the field. For example, you may have been issued a "bait-and-kill" packet. Direct from the U.S. Department of Defense of the Bush administration, "bait and kill" was a tactic where soldiers strew fake weapons and bombing materials on the ground and then hid nearby to wait for an Iraqi to pick them up. That was the soldiers' signal to blast the life out of them, for if they picked them up, they must be insurgents out to kill American troops. The U.S. soldiers were not to stop and wonder or even question if the person they saw coming into their lure was a child picking up stuff to play with or a parent picking up debris that might be dangerous to children or a neighbor who wants to clear litter from her or his yard. You bait, then you kill because you are a grunt.

The soldiers' hysterical excitement from having fired, killed, and come out alive papers over their emotional emptiness. They sink into the depravity of combat. It gives them the impression that they have feelings. But in fact, they become cynical with that I-don't-give-a-damn attitude Steve Hassna described. For Hassna and his buddies in Vietnam "don't mean nothing, don't mean a thing" became a mantra.

Being a seasoned soldier, you don't think of what you have done, don't feel what you are doing, you don't care, you just do it. By reverting to "don't give a damn," or "don't mean a thing" you can kill when you have to as if without remorse. I say "as if" because we truly do not know where the remorse has gone in those soldiers. It was in most of them before they went into combat.

Steve Hassna told me that in combat "you cannot afford to be emotionally involved in what is happening," and I finished his sentence with "it would be too dangerous." But I had more to learn about the power war has to destroy the human spirit. He corrected me, "or you'll become even more insane." Soldiers are not trying to stay less insane because it feels better but because if they let go and feel, "then you become dangerous to everyone around you. You cannot afford emotional distress."[3]

But in combat you *are* emotional distress. You live in a constant state of hypervigilance, never knowing when or where the next attack will come. You are ready to attack. One Iraq veteran testified that "you can only take so much when people take pot shots at you. It wears you down. I stopped caring and became apathetic."[4] That numbness again. For most of you, that is not who you are. Your body and mind do not know what to do with you, so you go numb. Feeling stops. Growing up, your psyche coped with being expendable by pushing it to your unconscious where you could not see or feel that devaluation of your life. Even with the brainwashing of basic training, most of you were not ready for your "first kill" in soldier jargon. Then you killed—there were congratulations and slaps on the back. Your loss of soul followed, and numbness, another layer of protection, took over. Now you really are inured to killing. The death tolls mount on your soul, but you do not feel it. You are numb.

The military counts on you soldiers going numb so that you can kill without a second thought. There is something deeply cold-hearted about pushing human beings into conditions that take them beyond the limits of human endurance, keeping them there, and pushing them further to kill. Normally we associate that kind of inhumanity with sadists.

In fact, psychologists find that numbness is the most common characteristic they see in war veterans. That numbness is actually a form of depersonalization that takes over when your perception or experience of yourself is so changed that you feel detached from your own mind and body. The groundwork for being numb was set into motion with your socialization into *core masculinity* where you learned to distance yourselves from others, from your own feelings. "But," as Steve Hassna explains, "numbness out there while you are in combat, you don't even know it. It's a way of saving what little sanity you have left."

As a soldier in combat, that numbness is how you experience depersonalization—it is as if you are an outside observer of yourself, but you assume that the outside is inside you. Your expendability is complete. And you were not killed. You just lost your soul and ruptured your psyche, but you are still in combat. You dare not notice. Depersonalization pushes unbearable reality into the unconscious.

In combat, the present is chaos and demands hypervigilance. Fear, panic, anxiety, and violation explode. There is no escape. But there is a lot of down time—just driving trucks, sitting, and waiting. That is when living in the present can be intolerable. You do not want time to think about what you have been doing out there in the killing fields. If your mind turns to another time, another place when you are not in the chaos of battle, you wonder what you'll do when you get back home or imagine your life with those you left behind. This is more than just natural loneliness; it is living in the future because the present is unbearable.

Or you desert. James Burmeister enlisted in the army in 2005 because a recruiter convinced him that he could serve on a "humanitarian mission" in Iraq. "In many cases our platoon was required to engage in exercises that were designed to attract fire from insurgents." Burmeister could not obey those orders. "Army gunners would then return fire with 7.62 millimeter rounds that would 'literally tear the limbs and appendages off the intended targets' or .50 caliber explosive rounds that when used against 'human targets' would cause them to 'literally explode or evaporate.'"[5] He was instructed to place fake cameras on poles and label them U.S. property. He and his team were then supposed to shoot anyone who tried to take the equipment. "These citizens were almost always unarmed. In some cases, the Iraqi victims looked to me like they were children, perhaps teenagers."[6]

When Burmeister found that he was sent to bait and kill Iraqis, he made a decision to desert the military, a decision for human life—his own as well as the lives of Iraqis. He asked his commander to let him become a conscientious objector, but his request was ignored. At the end of his next leave to Germany, Burmeister did not return to Iraq. Instead, he deserted and he went AWOL (absent without leave). He exposed the secret military bait-and-kill tactic. The *Washington Post* investigated and revealed the full story. He was arrested and pled guilty to going AWOL, but that was not punishment enough for the U.S. military. Although he had exposed a war crime, instead of being hailed as a hero, in July 2008 he was punished with a court-martial and sentenced to six months in prison.

In deserting, Burmeister reminds us that a choice is always there to make. Rather than disengaging from shared human consciousness and following the military's expectation that he act from human depravity, he joined the courageous movement of soldiers who refuse to murder human beings on behalf of their country. Courage to Resist estimated that by 2009, 39,900 or 1.9 percent of the total enlisted members had deserted from the U.S. military. This number is over twice the rate of desertion prior to 2001 when the rate was .78%.[7] The number of deserters from the U.S. war in Iraq is twice the number of soldiers who have been injured or died in combat.[8] This trend, as we shall see in a later chapter, is the beginning of remaking masculinity and redefining the military.

As a sociologist, I search for social constructs that can explain the inhuman, cold-hearted behaviors and practices that drive soldiers in combat to psychic breaks and loss of soul. To establish a standard for assessing the behaviors of soldiers in combat that turns them into grunts, I turn to how those behaviors are treated when they occur in civilian life. For example, soldiers in Iraq have reported that when they were alerted that a village would be bombed, off-duty soldiers would gather for a party on nearby house tops with their beer to watch and cheer. Back home a beer party to celebrate the destruction of a village with bombs, knowing that villagers are dying under them, is behavior that is so far outside of accepted social norms and moral conduct of civil society, it is unthinkable. Not only would they not applaud the destruction of towns back home, but such celebrations would be repugnant to their own human consciences.

Enjoying harm to other human beings is the behavior we find in sociopaths. Most psychologists have abandoned the term "sociopath" and prefer instead "antisocial personality disorder." Here, I am retrieving from the psychologists' waste bin the term "sociopath" with all of the associations of depravity that go with it. But instead of focusing on the diagnoses of individuals as psychologists do, I am concerned here with understanding *collective* behavior that we normally associate with criminality.

In civil society, sociopaths lie, hurt others, and some kill. Usually their behaviors are criminal—but what makes their actions sociopathic is that they intentionally do harm to others without cause and without remorse. They have no feelings of guilt, no second thoughts for their criminal acts. More likely we will see them puffed up with bravado. Rapists, murderers, and many white collar criminals, who bilk people out of their pensions or their savings, who play ponzi schemes and bring down the economy just because they can, are sociopaths. Consider the criteria used for diagnosing antisocial personality disorder, (ASPD). A person must display at least *three* of the following characteristics:

- Failure to conform to social norms including respect for law

- Deceitfulness, lying, and conning

- Irritability—aggressiveness and repeated physical fights or assaults

- Reckless disregard for the safety of self or others

- Consistent irresponsibility such as failure to keep a job

- Lack of remorse—an indifference to or rationalization for having hurt, mistreated, or stolen from others

If we turn those behaviors (except for consistent irresponsibility) into social conditions and look again at the military's expectations of soldiers in combat, we find that soldiers are required to conform their behaviors to the amorality that characterizes severe mental disorders. Further, as soldiers in combat still tend to be men, and those diagnosed with ASPD (including sociopaths) are much more likely to be men, we see a strong correlation between gender and combat behaviors and sociopaths. The aggression and power of *core masculinity* combined with the men's *expendable lives* make it not surprising then that 3 percent of men but only 1 percent of women meet the criteria for ASPD in the general population. The prevalence of sociopathic behavior in combat makes it seriously under-diagnosed.

I am not making psychological diagnoses of soldiers here. I am using psychologists' criteria to establish a social condition that is generated by the military. The newest generation of Winter Soldiers, veterans from the Iraq War, who are trying to heal themselves as well as us, the nation that has sent them to destroy and kill, reported the common practice in Iraq of having a buddy take your photo with your "latest kill," standing next to the dead body with a big smile as animal hunters do.[9] Some soldiers refused to have their photos taken with an Iraqi corpse. But their refusal was not out of consciousness that what they were doing was immoral or even amoral. Instead they admitted that if the dead Iraqi was not their kill, they should not take credit for it.[10]

Where empathy might have been, callousness and sometimes glibness reigns. That is the sign of a sociopath, which, when it has infected a collective as large as that of combat soldiers and the military, is a social condition I refer to as the *sociopathic condition of war*. Wars of aggression—wars that are made for reasons other than imminent threat of war by another state—are themselves large-scale sociopathic conditions with the militaries generating sociopathic conditions. The military has reduced itself to a sociopathogenic institution.

Sociopathic behavior was foreign to most soldiers before entering the military. Rather, it has been induced in them through training. In combat, it is ordered. Sociopathic behavior among soldiers, I suggest, results not from some proclivity to amorality but from the depersonalization that brings about numbness to feelings when one is committing acts of depravity in war that are driven by military conditioning and brainwashing.

In the Winter Soldier hearings, one marine testified that the Rules of Engagement "put soldiers in situations where their morals are at odds with their survival instinct."[11] The work of the military is to normalize amorality for soldiers in combat, the same amorality found in sociopaths. Major Peter Kilner, a West Point professor, acknowledges, "We train them how to kill, but we never explain why it's okay when they do what we train them so well to do, so they can be at peace with their consciences for the rest of their lives."[12] He is trying to find ways to help ease soldiers' consciences that are disturbed, as they should be, by killing.

When "average" soldiers are mixed with criminals as well people entering the military who are already sociopaths, it is difficult to tell the genuine sociopath from a normal person who is required to enact the behaviors of a sociopath. Placing normal human beings in sociopathic conditions, especially those persons whose humanity is already compromised by having been made expendable, sets the stage for mental breakdowns. This, as I see it, is where post traumatic stress disorder begins for most soldiers.

Once sociopathic behavior is activated in soldiers, it takes on a life of its own. In a study that replicated prison conditions, psychologist Philip Zimbardo found that when good men, for his study was only of men, are put into bad situations, they behave in pathological ways that are alien to them. Zimbardo recruited male volunteers for his Stanford prison experiment and placed them in a mock prison, half of the volunteers taking roles as guards, the other half as prisoners. Within a week, the men's behavior had so degenerated, the guards treatment of prisoners so dehumanized the men, that the experiment had to be called to an abrupt stop. Zimbardo's study reaffirms a vital fact of life: human nature itself is not evil but situations that some people create such as prisons and war are.[13]

As if it were not bad enough that the military requires sociopathic behavior from men in combat, the U.S. military is now compensating for those it loses to death, injury, and desertion by increasingly replenishing its ranks with criminals, actual sociopaths from civil society. Until the military became stretched thin, being convicted of crimes disqualified convicts from serving in the police forces in their cities or joining the ranks of soldiers in combat. Despite the fact that the military is required to screen recruits for criminal records, alcoholism, and drug abuse, "since the beginning of the Iraq war, waivers for Army recruits with felony arrest or conviction records more than tripled, from 459 in 2003 to 1,620 in 2007," a study for the *Sacramento Bee* newspaper found. While this study did not follow a classic research protocol, its review of the military files of 250 military personnel revealed that 120 had criminal records that included felonies, serious drug, alcohol and mental health problems.[14] These recruits bolster the sociopathic conditions of war for the rest of the soldiers.

Put women into the military and deploy them to war zones and we find that their risk is not as much from the enemy as it is from serving alongside those soldiers who have been reduced to sociopaths. Thirty percent of American women veterans report having been raped while in the military making it more likely that women will be raped by a fellow soldier than they will be killed by the enemy.[15] Soldiers' free-flowing access to pornography and their frequent uninhibited sexual harassment of women has turned into an epidemic of sexual violence against female GIs in the military.

In recent years, rape in war has finally been recognized as a crime by the Security Council of the United Nations. The 2008 Resolution 1820 "demands the immediate and complete cessation by all parties to armed conflict of all acts of sexual violence against civilians with immediate effect" and urges that "all parties to armed conflict immediately take appropriate measures to protect civilians, including women and girls, from all forms of sexual violence."[16] What about raping women soldiers? There is an echo of the Geneva Conventions here—just as soldiers in combat are excluded from human rights protections, so women soldiers are excluded from Resolution 1820.

What about women serving in Iraq and Afghanistan like U.S. Army Private LaVena Johnson who was raped and murdered on her base in Iraq on July 19, 2005? Upon her death, the U.S. Army notified nineteen-year-old LaVena's parents that their daughter had "died of self-inflicted, noncombat injuries," but added that she did not commit suicide. Then the army reversed itself saying, "A decision apparently was made by higher officials that the investigators must stop the investigation into a homicide and to classify her death a suicide."[17]

LaVena's mother had spoken to her on the phone a few days before, as she did almost weekly while her daughter was in Iraq. She remembered that her daughter was happy and feeling good. Then she was dead. LaVena's suicide did not make sense to the Johnson family. The bullet to the head of this right-handed, nineteen-year-old woman entered the left side. Suicide? Yes, the military said, it was the exit wound from an M-16. Dr. Johnson, a veteran himself, was familiar with this type of gun and could not imagine how his five-foot-one-inch daughter could handle a three-foot-four-inch rifle to kill herself, especially from that angle. Besides, her mother had detected no sign of distress in her daughter. She was happy and excited that she would be coming home for Christmas. LaVena's father demanded an explanation from the army.

LaVena's father, a physician, was suspicious when he saw his daughter's body in the funeral home. The Johnsons challenged the military's ruling on their daughter's death and began their own investigation. When LaVena's body was brought home for burial, Dr. Johnson examined her and found that she "had been struck in the face with a blunt instrument, perhaps a weapon stock. Her nose was broken and her teeth knocked backwards." She had been dragged and her body bore scratches and teeth imprints. The rapist had tried to burn her.

After two years, with no cooperation from the army, they finally received photographs through the Freedom of Information Act that were taken of their daughter's body when it was found in Iraq. Later when the photographs were released, "the photographs of her genital area revealed massive bruising and lacerations."[18] With the same authority it uses to cover up soldiers' murders of Iraqis, the army closed the case and the House Armed Services Committee concurred with the military's version of LaVena Johnson's death.

When the violence of male domination that we see in wife abuse and rape engages with the sociopathy of war, we are no longer dealing with Zimbardo's "good men in a bad situation" scenario. Soldiers are sunk into the depravity that comes from being a grunt. As feminist writer Susan Griffin pointed out in a germinal article back in the 1970s, in the U.S. rape is an "all-American crime."[19] Given that one in four American women are raped in their lifetime, those sociopaths who rape them match the description of an average male. But the one-in-three ratio of women raped in the U.S. military is significantly higher than that of civilian society.

Rape-murder crimes account for some of the deaths of women serving in Iraq. By the end of 2006 women's death rate reached 2 percent of all U.S. military deaths.[20] Dr. Anne Sadler conducted a 2003 University of Iowa study that was funded by the Department of Army Medical Research of the U.S. Department of Defense. She found that of 556 female veterans of the Vietnam and the Persian Gulf Wars, "79 percent of participants reported experiences of sexual harassment during their military service; 30 percent of the women reported an attempted or completed rape."[21] According to Department of Defense statistics, in 2009 the military received 2,670 charges of sexual assault (up from 2,347 in 2005) involving other members of the armed forces.[22]

Can women really be "buddies" in the military environment of masculinity and expendability, in the world of dirt and grunt and in the meanness of combat? That question does not depend on whether or not women can be mean or act like disgusting grunts. It turns instead on the female presence in what has previously been the exclusive male world of killing, on the military-made-sociopathic fields of fighting.

That is what U.S. Army Specialist Suzanne Swift found when she charged that she was sexually harassed and assaulted by three sergeants while she was stationed in Iraq. She told the *Guardian* newspaper, "when you are over there, you are lower than dirt, you are expendable as a soldier in general, and as a woman, it's worse."[23]

Swift, age twenty-one, refused to go back to Iraq when she was redeployed because she would be again under the command of those who assaulted her, and she was suffering from the sexual assault and post traumatic stress disorder. She was arrested for being AWOL. On December 14, 2007, Swift was convicted by a summary court-martial. She was stripped of her rank and sentenced to thirty days in the brig, a military prison, although she was released a few weeks later for good behavior.

Looking at female GIs from the standpoint of male expendability, one can see that for some men who have lost their moral compass or who never had one to begin with and were attracted to war, the women serving with them are there to be taken. There are other reasons: the women after all have entered what had been a men's-only club, many men consider them inferior because of their gender, or men's unspoken hatred of women for expecting men's protection which is what got soldiers into this place where they know that very likely they may not come out alive, or because as sociopaths they have no feelings.

Men-turned-grunts do not necessarily want to be observed by outsiders who are not grunts, who are not the meanest sons-of-bitches in the valley. But now outsiders are there in the next barrack. You soldiers have internalized that the enemy is anyone who is not like you and is not your buddy in combat with you. Now some of those around you are unlike you. They are women. They cannot be your buddies. But they expect to serve with you men, taking from you your significance, which is your sacrifice, the measure of your expendability. That she has become expendable too, even though she is not officially in combat, makes no difference—she is merely a woman.

Unlike civil society where rapists can be confident they can get away with their crimes, in the military covering up rape is a done deal. Although the soldier whose sperm was found on the sleeping bag of Army Private First Class Tina Priest was charged with rape, her death too was ruled a suicide. Ultimately, the soldier was convicted by the army of failure to obey an order, but Tina Priest's murder went uninvestigated. In calculating the cost of raping and murdering an American woman GI: $714 dock of pay a month for two months, restriction to base for thirty days and extra duty for forty-five days. The cost of murdering your rape victim: $0.00 and no time in the brig. That is the lesson some soldiers take back home with them.

Like the random killing of Iraqi civilians, the military men close ranks to cover up rape-murders by attributing the rape victim's deaths to "non-combat related injuries" or "suicide." It's not that raping fellow soldiers is covered in the Rules of Engagement—officially it's against the law, and that is what puts the edge on it. It's the type of risk that sociopaths pursue.

Many men bring their violence of war home with them. Some brought it from home into war. Fort Carson, Colorado is an army base from which soldiers are sent to combat in Iraq and Afghanistan. In January 2009 it was reported that within three years of coming back from combat in Iraq, nine members of one brigade at Fort Carson had been charged with killing someone. Five of those killings took place in 2008. And that Fourth Brigade has had a significant increase in charges of wife abuse, rape, and sexual assault.[24] In 2007, the Department of Defense received 2,688 reports of sexual assault, of which 60 percent were for rape and 72 percent were service members, but only 181 cases were referred for court-martial.[25]

The rate of rape is higher in the military than in civilian society. Likewise, wives of military men are more endangered in their homes than are wives in civilian society. Wife abuse, which occurs at the rate of 3.1 per 1,000 in the general population of the United States, is more than five times higher in military families—16.5 per 1,000.[26] At Fort Bragg, North Carolina, U.S. Army Sergeant Christina Smith was murdered by her husband Sergeant Richard Smith on September 30, 2008. Christina was one of four military women in North Carolina murdered at that time.[27] Wife abuse and rape can be identified as antisocial personality disorders. When wife abuse is included in the list of mental disorders caused by combat, the number of war veterans suffering from mental illnesses increases to 31 percent according to Karen Seal, a physician and researcher at the San Francisco Veterans Affairs Medical Center.

Sociopathy is the absence of human empathy. In empathy we may discover our courage, for example to save another's life. Strength and courage are *not* incompatible with empathy. It is not necessary to drive empathy out of soldiers' souls to get them to be strong or act bravely. Courage and bravery are writ large in our humanity. But to activate true courage, strength has to be disengaged from the aggression and violence of *core masculinity*. Even strength that is honed by the military can be turned toward saving and protecting human life. Wesley Autrey, a New York construction worker and a Navy veteran used the strength expected of him from *core masculinity*, trained in him by the military, and required for his job in a death-defying, life-saving rescue in the New York subway in 2007.

When a man who was having an epileptic seizure fell into the New York City subway tracks in front of an oncoming train, Wesley Autrey, did not first ask whether or not the person he was about to risk his own life for was of his race or his gender, whether or not he was American. His only concern, beyond that of the man's life, was the safety of his own two daughters who were with him. When the man fell into the subway tracks, in a split second, Autrey spontaneously entrusted his little girls to a stranger, a woman standing nearby. That act stemmed as much from shared human consciousness as what he did next.

Autrey made his next quick judgment. In the face of the oncoming subway train, he jumped down to the tracks, positioned the man who had fallen into the narrow center between the two train tracks, and covered the man's body with his own. The train passed over them with only a few inches to spare. As soon as it stopped, he yelled from under the train to the crowd to tell his daughters he was okay. Spontaneous applause rose from the relieved people on the platform.

That heroism reconnects us to each other in a world given over to war and killing. From Autrey to the unknown woman who held his daughters' hands, to the white man who came out of his seizure to find an African American man on top of him while a subway train passed over them and who instantly complied with Autrey's orders not to move until they were rescued, every second was filled with each person's conscious and intentional action. All of those people on the platform were making choices like those of the strangers on the beach, choices that soldiers are expected to abandon in combat.

Empathy is in the nature of being human, but it is not just an automatic, unthinking impulse. Autrey's decision to jump in the subway was as calculated as it was spontaneous. "Since I do construction work with Local 79, we work in confined spaces a lot. So I looked, and my judgment was pretty right. The train did have enough room for me."[28] The first perception of danger to another when shared human consciousness engages prompts parts of our brains (the motor cortex and the amygdala). Connected to each other, we determine a line of action.[29]

Whether we rush forward to save the stranger, to seek help or just to fervently hope, that line of action comes from the place in us where we make meaning; each meaning is a decision to interpret an experience this way and not another way. When we interpret the meaning of a situation with empathy, we do not do so with disregard for lives at risk. That is where we experience our own human agency, the action we take when we are agents of our own lives. Autrey reminds us of who we really are. In his actions, we feel the life force of our own human agency; we own our actions as distinctly *ours*, each of us interconnected with each other.

If we attribute our agency to religion or god or luck or biological impulses, we cease to know our capacity for empathy. Our own agency slips from our awareness and we diminish our experiences. Our sense of human interconnectedness drops away. We are alone again in the isolated individualism that characterizes Western societies and encourages us to derive satisfaction from spending and getting rather than knowing and understanding each other. Individualism turns us away from empathy with others and diminishes our shared human consciousness, weakening that human urge to save and protect human life.

On the subway platform that day, everyone was deeply reliant on each other, whether they realized it or not, simultaneously acting from within their own selves and for each other—not as isolated individuals, not as disconnected men and women, but as those who know from some place deep in their humanity that they can trust their own actions and each others'. That is human agency fully realized. That full realization of one's own humanity, more than any other reason, is why in the weeks and months that have passed since the "subway hero" saved another man's life, he has been praised and fêted, honored with New York City's highest recognition, the Bronze Medallion, and with scholarships for his daughters. *Time* named him Person of the Year. But Wesley Autrey refused the title of hero. "I don't feel like I did something spectacular; I just saw someone who needed help," Autrey said. "I did what I felt was right." As if that were normal. Because it is.

Autrey became another Everyday Hero (a CNN award he received) who reminds us of what we are capable of when we are fully ourselves, when we act to support and protect another's life over everything else. But in the context of war and combat, he reminds us that being a grunt does not make men or women heroic. With a different kind of military, one that is not under orders to commit crimes of aggression in making war, Autrey's courage would be the kind of strength expected of soldiers.

Psychopathic Leadership
Versus the Politics of Empathy

Imagine being a man with all of the unconscious rage that comes from having been rendered expendable. Combine that with the superiority you have internalized that is granted to you for being a man, the superiority that places you over all those who are not men, those who are considered weak (that is, not macho) men, and over men of classes and races you judge to be inferior to yours. And now imagine that you become the leader of a state or a powerful militia. You not only *have* power, you *are* power.

More than the cowardice that is flaunted by the Israeli military when it bombs cities and villages of Lebanon or Gaza; more than the power of an American soldier to blast an Iraqi, an Afghan, a Pakistani walking down the street only to realize much later that he had just murdered someone and lost his own soul; more than the power of Al Qaeda to blow up airliners or trains to attack United States and other western cities; more than the individual power to forcibly subdue and rape women serving with you in the military, you have the vast power of command over the world's most powerful armed forces.

Heady? Intoxicating? Hard to resist pulling the trigger?

In examining how one U.S. president after another took the military into unnecessary wars, historian Alexander DeConde in his study of *Presidential Machismo* found that presidential power over the military allowed leaders to test and prove their virility. "Consequently few presidents have been able to resist the temptation of using the military machine at their disposal or, when the opportunity arose, of exulting in the role of the warrior."[1]

U.S. presidents are not alone in this cowardice—presidential machismo infects presidents, prime ministers, ayatollahs, and dictators throughout the world by closing down human empathy in the place we need it the most, the highest offices of the land. Leadership positions are feeding grounds for psychopaths, attracting as they do those cunning leaders who are indifferent to human life and absent of remorse. Lying and belligerence mark these leaders' drive into wars on the least pretext or for no reason at all except that they have the power to do it.

The year 2001 was a fateful year for the world. In January, it saw George W. Bush take office as president of the United States, and a month later Israelis elected Ariel Sharon, already known as a war criminal, as Prime Minister and then on September 11, 2001, Osama bin Laden, the self-styled leader of Al Qaeda, attacked the United States. Their commonality was their psychopathology. Their disregard for human life extended even to the lives of their own people. They each intentionally sacrificed soldiers and targeted civilians while covering their psychopathy with the rhetoric of being on a divine mission or fulfilling historic or religious legacies. They each acted as if the people they claimed to lead are superior to any other human beings. They confronted world criticism with their megalomania telling doubters "you are with us or against us." I am drawing together the common pathology of leaders like Bush, Sharon, and Bin Laden in order to derive from the observable reality of their leadership a concept that approximates every leader of their type—the psychopathic leader.[2]

Psychopaths are attractive to those who look to them to be tough and provide them with security but mistake the psychopaths' absence of feeling for strength. Their cold remorselessness is frequently read as strength under fire; their indifference to human suffering can seem like the power to stand firm and their cunning may look like caring.

For most people it is hard to imagine how psychopaths think and act because their behavior is so foreign to most of us. That is the psychopath's advantage, the edge he or she has over everyone else. Psychopaths go to great lengths to represent themselves as normal and caring. Psychologist Martha Stout in her important book, *The Sociopath Next Door*, introduces us to the unfeeling amorality of sociopaths and psychopaths so that we may recognize them. As Stout points out, they are without conscience, feelings of guilt, shame and remorse, to the extent that they have "no limiting sense of concern for the well-being of strangers, friends, or even family members." If you are a psychopath or sociopath your success is in your ability "to conceal from other people that your psychological makeup is radically different from theirs. Since everyone simply assumes that conscience is universal among human beings, hiding the fact that you are conscience-free is nearly effortless." And that leaves you "completely free of internal restraints" to do as you please.[3]

George W. Bush's delayed, abstract, and remote first words to Americans at the moment of the 9/11 attack were "freedom has been attacked," as if he was disconnected from human suffering and death, as if he could not or would not feel the pain of human loss. Peace activist Cindy Sheehan tells of his coldness and disconnection when he greeted hers and the other families whose loved ones were killed in combat. While Sheehan was still reeling from the death of her son Casey in Iraq, Bush referred to him in the distanced language of "the loved one" with as much feeling as he would have had for a lamp shade.

Combine Bush's macho and criminality with his lack of empathy, his disconnection from the suffering of others, his call for people to go shopping just after we saw bodies propelled out of the shattering windows of the World Trade Center's twin towers in New York on 9/11, his (unsuccessful) efforts to reopen Wall Street only five short days after that attack, and you have examples of the dominant characteristics of a psychopath.

In an already terrified post-9/11 America, Bush successfully manipulated Americans' fears and intensified their anxiety. He presented himself to Americans as if he were tough and in control so that they would believe that he could protect them from the dangers he manufactured. The U.S. Congress, apparently beguiled by his lying about threats from Iraq, went along with him authorizing war against Iraq with Joint Resolution 114 in October 2002. The majority of Americans followed once he raised their fears further with haunting alarms of weapons of mass destruction raining down on the USA.

That kind of psychopathy extends the distancing and disengagement found in *core masculinity* to include amoral disregard for the lives of others. Leaders imbued with presidential machismo are indifferent to killing. That is the kind of leadership we saw but may not have recognized after the 9/11 attack on the United States when Bush began preparing for a war against Iraq even while he authorized an attack on Afghanistan to get Bin Laden. In Israel, to intensify fears of Iraqi terrorism and support a U.S. war against Iraq, Ariel Sharon falsely asserted that Yasser Arafat, then the head of the Palestine Liberation Organization, was the Palestinian version of bin Laden and the Palestinian suicide bombers were like blood brothers of the nineteen Arabs (none of them Palestinian) who hijacked the four American airliners, as journalist Robert Fisk reported.[4]

These leaders used distortion and misrepresentation to goad their people into vengeance. Bin Laden escaped the clutches of the U.S. military during its six-week war against the Taliban in Afghanistan from October to December 2001, and Bush showed little interest in pursuing him. Instead Bush turned Americans' attention to Iraq. Even though, at the time, Iraq had nothing to do with Al Qaeda, and, in fact, Saddam Hussein was hostile to bin Laden and even though Iraq had not threatened the United States with war, Bush intensified fear among Americans of another attack. In his fabrication of reality this next attack would bring even worse destruction than 9/11, with weapons of mass destruction raining down on Americans from Iraq. Vice President Dick Cheney, on August 26, 2002 said, "Simply stated, there is no doubt that Saddam Hussein now has weapons of mass destruction." No doubt! That certainty convinced many Americans and most of their Congressional leaders to support war against Iraq.

A few weeks later President George W. Bush began his campaign of escalating rhetoric to raise fear of Iraq's biological weapons. While not mentioning it directly, he linked his campaign of fear to Saddam Hussein's actual use of mustard gas on the Kurds of Iraq in 1987 and 1988. Gas masks appeared in stores and were demonstrated on television. Young people, especially men, were off to recruiting offices and ready to expend their lives to save Americans.

Democrats bought the bait and chimed in. Then Senator Hillary Clinton asserted on February 5, 2003, that Iraq was "continuing to possess and develop a significant chemical and biological weapons capability, actively seeking a nuclear weapons capability, and supporting and harboring terrorist organizations."[5] All were lies. Clinton would later invoke the "if I had known then what I know now" defense, even while her rhetoric remained the same, shifting only from supporting an invasion of Iraq to edging toward war against Iran.

Democratic Senator Joseph Biden, the future U.S. vice president, had already gone further. On September 4, 2002, he asserted that "if we wait for the danger to become clear, it could be too late."[6] But in international law, "there is no self-appointed right to attack another state because of the fear that the state is making plans or developing weapons usable in a hypothetical campaign,"[7] according to international legal scholar Mary Ellen O'Connor. Ever since the Kellogg-Briand Pact of 1928, the United States with other nations have agreed not to take "recourse to war for the solution of international controversies, and renounce it, as a instrument of national policy in their relations with one another." That treaty was abandoned by George W. Bush in his war on terror, as it was ignored by Lyndon Johnson in his war against Vietnam, a country that also posed no threat to the United States.

Biden's warning presaged Bush's disregard for both international and national law, which require that there be an imminent, direct threat of attack for a state to initiate war. But the United States would not be bound by international law or the decisions of the United Nations, and Bush would not even be constrained by U.S. law. With the disregard for human life, a characteristic of psychopaths, he announced to the world that "the war on terror will not be won on the defensive," and that the United States would "impose preemptive, unilateral military force when and where it chooses."[8]

Obviously, Bush intended to ignore the charter of the United Nations. As O'Connor points out, "permitting preemptive self-defense at the sole discretion of a state is fundamentally at odds with the Charter's design. It is an exception that would overthrow the prohibition on the use of force in Article 2(4) and thus the very purposes of the UN."[9]

Speaking to graduating West Point cadets in June 2002, Bush sounded tough. "We must take the battle to the enemy, disrupt his plans and confront the worst threats *before they emerge.*" (Emphasis mine.) He was building up steam to attack Iraq even though that country had neither attacked the United States nor made plans to do so, but because it might. Just in case. He was laying the groundwork to commit war crimes. While claiming the right to wage a preemptive war, which is a right of every state facing *imminent* threat of attack, he was actually preparing to launch a preventive war—to commit a war crime.

He was disregarding defense as the basis of war and in doing so making himself into a war criminal. Preempting an attack before an attack is launched can only be applied in the strictest sense, when a direct threat of imminent attack has been made against one's own country. The United States was not faced with an imminent threat of attack from Iraq. If it were, it would have a legitimate right of self-defense, and international law would allow it to strike an enemy that is preparing to attack if the threat of attack is acute and imminent, according to Article 51 of the UN charter.[10] That right to self-defense includes preempting a planned attack.

The United Nations had appointed an investigating team led by Dr. Hans Blix who after 300 inspections that were unimpeded by Saddam Hussein, found no WMDs or evidence of them in Iraq.[11] Actually, Bush was planning a preventive war, invading another country in case sometime in the future that country might try to attack the United States. As commander in chief of the U.S. armed forces, he was about to make the United States into the very "rogue state" he set out to destroy.

Although he was proposing to commit war crimes, he made his criminal acts sound normal, much like reasonable actions, as if he was clearing the brush on his ranch. And yet, at the same time he sounded so tough that the cadets cheered uproariously. They loved his bravado and cheered him on again when he asserted that "our security will require all Americans to be forward-looking and resolute, to be ready for preemptive action when necessary to defend our liberty and to defend our lives. (Applause.)"[12] I had to wonder; did those enthusiastic cadets have a course in their elite military training at West Point on international law or even U.S. rules of warfare or were their courses riddled with justifications for preventive war?

The cadets who listened to that speech apparently missed something in their training or could not muster their own knowledge and ethics against their president's macho. However the West Point Graduates Against the War take another view. While military personnel must obey lawful orders,[13] their "moral and legal obligation is to the U.S. Constitution and not to those who would issue unlawful orders ..."[14] They cite the Uniform Code of Military Justice (UCMJ), a U.S. law that applies to all military personnel and point out that these cadets and all soldiers take the military oath of enlistment and swear: "I will support and defend the Constitution of the United States against all enemies, foreign and domestic; that I will bear true faith and allegiance to the same; and that I will obey the orders of the President of the United States."[15] But they "have an obligation and duty to only obey Lawful orders and indeed have an obligation to disobey Unlawful orders, including orders by the president that do not comply with UCMJ."[16] They must refuse to obey unlawful orders, orders that are in direct violation of the Constitution and the UCMJ. Legally the U.S. military is constrained by a moral paradigm that protects human beings and requires obedience to national and international law. In other words, the military was constitutionally obligated to refuse to obey the president's orders for a war of aggression against Iraq.

In the context of the post-9/11 America that was still reeling from fear of another attack, Bush's lying and conning had the specific goal of intensifying and escalating those fears, making it easier to put into action his plan to go to war against Iraq. American citizens did not notice the military's failure to stand against orders to commit war crimes. If you are being conned and your fear level is rising at each of your president's utterances, then when he calls for preemptive war, it could sound reasonable—even like protection—which allowed him to assume the role of the paternalistic, protective father the right wing so much favors in their leaders. Paternalism was part of his cover for his psychopathic leadership.

Psychologist Robert Hare, an expert in the study and treatment of psychopathic behavior, characterizes psychopaths as having "a narcissistic and grossly inflated view of their self-worth and importance, a truly astonishing egocentricity and sense of entitlement."[17] They are glib and superficial, pathological liars, cunning and manipulative. These are behaviors often found in criminals.

Bush's demeanor was frighteningly similar to that of criminally corrupt economic leaders and CEOs, from Enron's Kenneth Lay and Jeffrey Skilling to Bernie Madoff. They all controlled their domains with lying and conning, making promises that were only meant to enlarge their own power. Jeffrey Skilling's smirk when he appeared in court and was convicted of fraud and insider trading was not unlike the one George W. Bush wore in most public appearances during his eight years in office. It was the expression of someone who knew that he had just pulled off a big heist and could see how gullible his victims were. Even when there was the potential that Bush, like Skilling or Madoff, could face criminal charges or impeachment as president, it appeared that he could not have cared less.

Although the U.S. war against Iraq was a war of aggression, not of defense, and it violated the UN Charter, Bush had placed himself and the U.S. presidency outside of the law. He violated Nuremberg Principles which is the international law derived from the trials of Nazi war criminals when he committed "crimes against peace." Those crimes included "planning, preparation, initiation or waging of a war of aggression or a war in violation of international treaties, agreements or assurances."[18]

Who would bring him to justice? He knew that the UN Security Council was impotent to act against him if he ignored it. It takes only one vote on the Security Council to derail any proposed action. China, France, Russia the United Kingdom, and the United States are its five permanent members and Bush already had Tony Blair, prime minister of the United Kingdom, on board with him. He knew that alliance made him and the United States immune from potential UN sanctions.

A year into the U.S. war against Iraq, with the death toll of American soldiers and Iraqi civilians skyrocketing, Bush appeared at the March 2004 Radio and Television Correspondents Association dinner, an annual event that is meant to be an evening of humor where even the president pokes fun at himself. Showing a photo of himself looking under a piece of furniture in the Oval Office, he joked, "Those weapons of mass destruction have got to be here somewhere." The next photo showed him looking into the corner of a room. "No, no weapons over there." Then to the journalists' uproarious laughter, another photo of him bent over his desk—"Maybe under here?" he quipped. His psychopathic indifference shocked the heads of state when in July 2008, Bush left his last G-8 meeting as president with "goodbye from the world's biggest polluter!" With a big grin on his face, he then punched the air as if to punctuate the fun of it.[19]

While we have seen how soldiers who were not sociopaths prior to going into combat in Iraq, Afghanistan and Vietnam adopted aberrant and abnormal behavior during combat, we have no such coherent explanation for the criminality of the forty-third president of the United States. For the United States and the world, it matters not whether George W. Bush and Dick Cheney could be clinically diagnosed as psychopaths, although evidence for the latter is especially abundant.[20] My concern here is not with the mental health or lack thereof of those particular individuals. I am not making an argument for either sympathy or treatment for them. (Psychopaths are known to be nonresponsive to most treatments that have been tried.) What matters is that they caused amoral, aberrant behavior that is typical of the most hardened criminals in our prisons to become the standard behavior found in the presidency of the United States.

Witness President Barack Obama's flurry of frightening messages to the American people and the world about Afghanistan's threat to U.S. national security which he followed by a surge of troops and full-scale war there. He then went to that Radio and Television Correspondents dinner in March 2010, and although he does not have the characteristics of a psychopath, he adopted the behaviors of his predecessor. He joked about predator drones, the same drones that were "mistakenly" wiping out village after village, bombing wedding parties, hospitals and schools in mountainous Afghanistan and Pakistan.[21]

Three months into the U.S. war against Iraq, George W. Bush's approval rating soared to 79 percent, which meant that almost four-fifths of Americans supported his war—some from fear their president effectively engendered in them, most with the patriotism that validates their country at war.[22] The United States was at war, and at least 79 percent of Americans apparently did not care about the effects of a U.S. war on Iraqis.

Very few Americans complained about the killing of Iraqi people and the destruction of their country. Those who protested the war were regularly vilified as unpatriotic.[23] If some Americans were revolted by the killing in war, their concern was confined to the increasing number of U.S. soldiers who were losing their lives. Six years later when President Obama ordered an escalation of war in Afghanistan and illegal strikes in Pakistan, even though fewer Americans were in favor of that war, his American support conveyed the same disregard for the Afghan lives being put at risk by U.S. forces.

Patriotism evokes a sense of belonging and in exchange demands our loyalty to our state. Patriotic devotion to one's land and allegiance to one's state as if to one's family yields in a country's people a cohesive identity against the outside world—the other is the enemy. Its model and origin is the patriarchal family—male dominated, violence prone, and closed to the world outside of itself. But it is not an even exchange because patriots are expected to put the interests of their state above even their own lives; the ideology that relies on men's *expendable lives* for war.

Patriotism ruptures our humanity—it segments shared human consciousness, separating us from others who are not of the state or ethnicity or race or religion to which we have given our loyalty. That disconnection from others is sealed with the false belief in the superiority of one's own people above all others, making empathy for those others all but impossible. In wartime, patriotism insures a rigid rupture between us and them. In exchange, we are promised paternal protection from those among us whom we have made expendable for that purpose. Accepting that promise is the first step toward accepting that they can be killed. It is for our safety, as President Obama, following the standards Bush had established in the Oval Office, told us when he escalated the war against Afghanistan.

Requiring that we restrict our empathy to those of our own country, dividing humans into "us versus them" categories, patriotism encourages national arrogance that can become lethal especially when it is backed by the most powerful military in the world. That patriotic arrogance is the source of the American belief, often expressed in

Congress, that Iraqis should have been grateful for the U.S. invasion and occupation of their country. In contrast to every states' patriotism, empathy stretches to the full breadth of humanity. Unless you are amoral, a sociopath, or psychopath who has no feelings and enjoys harming others for the sake of it, you cannot help but want to save and protect any human lives at risk. Empathy propels you into action.

Americans are not always so hardhearted. In those early moments of 9/11, after the Al Qaeda attack on the United States, as if in defiance of death, we witnessed a collective spirit rarely seen in the United States. Many Americans still reeling with pain and horror broke the forces of individualism that separate them from each other and joined in a spirit that came to them from around the world. They ignored the blindfolds of patriotism and acted instead from their connection to life that evokes strangers' compassion for each other that we see time and again when human lives are threatened or taken. Our shared grief became evident—we saw volunteer rescue workers pour into New York City to help search for survivors, strangers step in to cook meals in churches and schools for the workers and survivors and find shelter for those displaced by the destruction. Volunteers were there to console the families waiting for word of their loved ones and even to open safe houses for Arabs who, at that moment, were vulnerable to racist attack. The outpouring of care and goodwill was palpable.

American's caring was tense against a background of macho thirst for revenge. We could hear it on the streets and roadways in the menace of revving engines and screeching brakes. We saw it on their pickup trucks from which they aggressively whipped large American flags behind them signaling a readiness to fight. We saw it in the president's impatience to make war even though the states he chose to target had not attacked the United States.

Despite the threat of American revenge, in those moments when goodwill prevailed over war fever and became a balm for open wounds, there was a sense of possibility in the American people. A few days after the attack, I wrote of "Non-Selective Compassion":

> To say that we are one in spirit, interconnected in being, means right now that we are one with the victims of the Tuesday attack, one with the grieving families. Moreover, if there is a lesson for us as Americans to be learned from this attack, it is that we must be one with

those who are the victims of U.S. bombing and U.S.-sponsored attacks on human life throughout the world . . .

When we are intolerant of terror, we will have to call upon our government to cease and desist—not only its plans for revenge attacks, but its own state-sponsored terror. Only then will we begin to heal, for we can only heal together as one.[24]

Even though the history of wars and the story of masculinity suggest otherwise, for a moment, it seemed possible that the sensitivity of Americans in the face of their own tremendous human loss might stem a tide toward revenge and contain the mounting support for war. If at that moment the United States had had a president who was capable of building upon Americans' shared compassion even while mobilizing a defensive network against future attacks, the entire world would be different today.

Instead, Bush captured and used that moment to escalate American fears until 79 percent of them apparently decided that the lives of Afghans and Iraqis were so insignificant that they could accept them being killed. For the most part, Americans had lost their capacity to identify with the sufferings of others and rejected their own responsibility in their government's terrorism of Iraqis and Afghans. That blind patriotism is not automatic or instinctive. It comes from being torn apart from our interconnections with others. That is where the leadership of the United States took Americans in 2001 and has kept us since then.

Unless they were already sociopaths, psychopaths, or they are driven by *core masculinity* and female dependence on it, Americans actually had to change their behavior to accomplish their complicity in their state's war crimes. Generally, it is not true that Americans are empty of empathy. Those at the beach seeing the man drowned while saving his son did not turn away. American people did not dissociate themselves from the human suffering and massive loss of Asian life when the 9.1 magnitude earthquake in the Indian Ocean in December of 2004 caused the tsunami that took 230,000 lives. The outpouring of raw human grief from around the world was followed by generosity as evidenced by immediately filled donation boxes appearing in grocery stores and more than $7 billion in humanitarian aid from the international community. But then those Asian countries had not attacked the United States. Then again, neither had Iraq or Afghanistan.

The American refusal of empathy for Iraqi losses meant that Bush would be re-elected, a vindication of U.S. strategies, and that Iraqi suffering would be prolonged indefinitely and extended back into Afghanistan and Pakistan. It would take much longer for American empathy to emerge and swell the ranks of the antiwar movements that were under attack for being unpatriotic. That is only part of the cost of American failure of empathy in favor of patriotism.

Empathy, whether it is individual or collective, whether one people, such as Americans, engage in it for another, such as the people being invaded and occupied by the U.S. military, is a political force that has the power to lift the silencing cloak of patriotism. As with all interaction, collective empathy begins by locating oneself in both the subjective, or felt experiences, and the objective realities of those who are occupied by one's country. By entering into the feelings of Iraqis', Afghans', or anyone else's experiences of war, we are able to interpret the meanings that their experience of occupation has for them.

The politics of empathy requires facts—details of the objective situation, in this case, the realities of war—that will inform rather than replace subjective knowing. For Westerners whose states support U.S. wars, that requires searching beyond censored and biased media reports and not merely accepting state leaders' reports on their wars. Fortunately independent media is abundantly available from Amy Goodman's *Democracy Now* to Jon Stewart (despite his disclaimer that the *Daily Show* makes fun of the news), to websites like those of Common Dreams, Truthout, Information Clearinghouse, and Move-On.org.

The realities of the others' situations, the stuff from which we interpret the meanings their experiences have for them, come into sharp focus when we ask of ourselves "what if my country has just gone to the top of the enemy list of the state with the world's most powerful military?" or "How would I feel if I was there in Iraq and just heard the American vice president announce that I will be hit with shock and awe?" Then the inevitable questions arise such as "what can I do to protect my family, my parents, myself?"

Making interpretations from within the other's experience of occupation, you would know that if you were Afghan or Iraqi you are helpless, that bombing is erratic, not surgical as the military claims, that human judgment of those dropping the bombs can be flawed as is the military intelligence that instructs soldiers on where to bomb. That kind of collective empathy reconnects us to the human force for life that makes the killing of others by our state and military intolerable. That awareness is the political consciousness that can propel the force to end war, to remove psychopathic leaders from office and demand diplomatic solutions.

If you are in Iraq, you are looking at your children and worrying that you will not be able to protect them. You turn to your spouse. Neither of you know where you can take your children to be safe. You know that you cannot hide from war; it is a total situation that consumes everything and everyone around you. You know that you and everyone around you are potential targets. You anxiously check on your household supply of candles and matches. You fill empty jugs with water. You do not let your children out of your sight for a second.

Is waiting the worst? Or is it the flashing light that comes with the earth shaking sounds of bombs hitting their targets? When the bombing begins, are you trying to show calm to your terrified children who huddle in your skirts? Each strike is so powerful that it makes your body shudder as your walls and your children tremble. The war has come inside your home, your body, your children. The electricity flickers on and off. Then you are in darkness. Do you realize that it will be years before you will have regular electricity again? As of 2009, only 25 percent of your country will have it back after the destruction of electric power plants in the U.S. invasion.

Days into those wars against Iraq and Afghanistan, basic resources like telephones that most of us take for granted stopped working. The power of the blasts down the road have blown out your windows, and you can see that mortars are landing near your brother and his family's home, but you have no way to find out if they are still alive or if your son has left there and is on his way home or was killed in the streets. When there is a lull in the bombing, many who can, flee. Over the months that stretched into years, those who made it out of Iraq became part of the 4.8 million displaced Iraqis in refugee camps in nearby countries, especially Syria and Jordan, countries whose own resources were stretched and squeezed by the U.S. war. According to Refugees International, by 2009 more than three million Afghan refugees had been registered, 2.1 million in Pakistan and 0.9 million in Iran.[25] That is only part of the burden those countries bear from the U.S. war.

After the invasion of Iraq, to establish American rule there, George W. Bush, who claimed his mission was to bring democracy to Iraq, ironically appointed a "viceroy," the title given to a royal official who rules in place of the monarch. Viceroy Paul Bremmer ruled over the U.S. occupation from the deposed Saddam Hussein's Emerald Palace in the center of Baghdad. One of Bremmer's first acts, against all logic and the best advice available to him, was to disband the Iraqi military—army, air force, and navy, and to close down anything associated with Saddam Hussein's Ba'athist party without regard for the fact that being in the army, working for Ba'athist projects and enterprises was how, if you were an Iraqi under Saddam Hussein, you stayed employed in that dictatorial regime that the United States overthrew. He paid no attention to the fact that for the average Iraqi, working for Ba'athists had little to do with loyalty to Hussein's regime and more to do with income to support their families. Several Americans working in the Emerald City, including Bremmer's predecessor, knew that. But those who opposed Bremmer were fired and sent packing back to the States.[26]

On top of the 40 percent unemployment rate in Iraq before the war began, when the United States disbanded the Iraqi military, thousands more Iraqis lost jobs and family income. Hundreds of thousands of newly unemployed Iraqis flooded the streets. They had just lost their income and ability to support their families and their villages, but worse, many had lost children, brothers, and sisters as their homes were being destroyed by the U.S. military invasion and occupation. Then Bremmer privatized all state-owned factories in Iraq, skyrocketing the unemployment rate, imposing on Iraq the same flawed economy that was about to tumble the economy in the United States.

Meanwhile, the United States, having already destroyed 75 percent of Iraqi power-generating capacity during its invasion of Iraq, saw to it that Bremmer and his American staff luxuriated in the air-conditioned palace with generators flown in from the United States and had a fully equipped hospital that was not open to Iraqis while the Iraqi hospitals had no functioning generators and while the United States was bombing and making more Iraqi causalities every hour. The U.S. invasion ruined the clean water supply in Iraq, and the occupation left garbage mounting in the streets for months that turned into years. In one of the richest oil countries in the world, cars waited in lines miles long for gas—when it was available.[27]

If George Bush's pretensions to grandeur and the American arrogance that provided for itself while leaving Iraqis steeped in squalor were not enough to gall Iraqis, then certainly taking their arms, their military, their jobs, their clean water, their electricity, and their health care away from them would do it. The Bush administration and the U.S. military did everything in their power to humiliate and dispossess Iraqis. That is how they turned the whole country, not just Saddam Hussein's regime, into an enemy of the United States. And that does not even take into account the fact that most Iraqis knew that the United States was there to take their most precious natural resource—oil. That is how you provoke an insurgency or, from an Iraqi perspective, a resistance, against their invader's authority. That is how the United States gave Al Qaeda a new, larger playing field—Iraq—where it had not been before.

The lesson I take from having lived through the impeachment of Richard Nixon is that when the country takes criminality in the highest office seriously, not just as a political ploy to slow down the working of government as the impeachment of Bill Clinton was meant to do, it is possible to restore integrity to the office of the president. Even that lesson was mostly undone with Gerald Ford's pardon of Nixon.

Psychologist Robert Hare, in warning us about psychopaths, asks us, "if another of his kind comes knocking at your door, will you open it?" That is the very question we need to ask ourselves when we are electing our national and state leaders, a question that every voter should ask in considering who they will vote into positions of power. If we are to be wary of psychopaths, to keep them out of our private lives, should we want the kind of behavior they exhibit running our country? How will voters resist being seduced by another like him again?

Hare cautions people about what will happen if they let a psychopath into their lives, a caution that we should consider in determining who we allow to govern our country. A psychopath in prison wrote:

> He will choose you, disarm you with his words, and control you with this presence. He will delight you with his wit and his plans. He will show you a good time, but you will always get the bill. He will smile and deceive you, and he will scare you with his eyes. And when he is through with you, and he will be through with you, he will desert you and take with him your innocence and your pride. You will be left much sadder but not a lot wiser, and for a long time you will wonder what happened and what you did wrong. And if another of his kind comes knocking at your door, will you open it?[28]

The Bush-Cheney political legacy diminished Americans' expectations of their leaders. Having vacated decency, honesty, and adherence to the U.S. Constitution from the executive office, it left President Obama and the Congress to quibble over whether "any laws have been broken," and if so, whether or not any action should be taken, as if breaking the law is a privilege of the U.S. presidency.

As president, as power itself, there were virtually no limits to the crimes Bush could commit. Representative Dennis Kucinich introduced Articles of Impeachment into Congress that included these charges:

- Creating a Secret Propaganda Campaign to Manufacture a False Case for War against Iraq

- Falsely, Systematically and with Criminal Intent Conflating the Attacks of September 11, 2001, with Misrepresenting Iraq as a Security Threat as Part of Fraudulent Justification for a War of Aggression

- Misleading the American People and Members of Congress to Believe Iraq Possessed Weapons of Mass Destruction, to Manufacture a False Case for War

- Misleading the American People and Members of Congress to Believe Iraq Posed an Imminent Threat to the United States

- Illegally Misspending Funds to Secretly Begin a War of Aggression, ...in Violation of the Requirements of H. J. Res114... Absent a Declaration of War...in Violation of the UN Charter[29]

As a national of the United States, George W. Bush is still liable under the U.S. Code for any conduct that is "defined as a grave breach in any of the international conventions signed at Geneva 12 August 1949, or any protocol to such convention to which the United States is a party." Under this U.S. law, "Whoever, whether inside or outside the United States, commits a war crime,...shall be fined under this title or imprisoned for life or any term of years, or both, and if death results to the victim, shall also be subject to the penalty of death."[30] Prosecutor Vincent Bugliosi already has researched and developed the legal case in his book, *The Prosecution of George W. Bush for Murder* (2008) in the deaths of over 4,000 American soldiers.

The decision the Obama administration made not to dwell in the past and pursue criminal charges against Bush and Cheney was a choice to leave in place the psychopathic standards they established for the U.S. presidency. In deciding to escalate the war against Afghanistan in 2009, Obama engaged those standards, employing the same rhetoric and language Bush used to take the United States into committing war crimes in Iraq. The failure of those in the Obama administration and the U.S. Congress to uphold the law concedes to the standards set by psychopathic leaders and makes them the new norms by which we are governed. In the United States, both the Constitution and civil law are suppressed. The military is fully freed to exist outside of the law. These are neither political party nor personality issues; the fundamental ways in which we govern ourselves have been given over to rampant criminality in the highest offices of the land.

Making Enemies—
Humiliating Men

It is two o'clock in the morning and you are sound asleep in bed with your wife next to you and your children in the next room with your mother. Suddenly the crashing sound from the walls around your compound being ripped apart wakes you up in terror. At the same moment, the even closer sound of your front door being kicked down sends shock waves through you and your family. Before you have time to figure out what is happening, you are being dragged from your bed by an American soldier in full combat gear who holds a gun to your face. Your wife shrieks and your children are pouring out of their bedroom and are being shoved by other American soldiers. One of them has your fourteen-year-old son by the neck and has shoved his hands behind his back, fastening them together harshly with plastic cords. Suddenly, the other soldier is doing the same to you. All of that takes place in the first sixty seconds of what the U.S. military calls "house clearing," or "night raids" which is how occupying militaries invade people's homes. They are looking for insurgents or information on them.

Back inside your house, the soldier who grabbed you from your bed throws you to the floor. You are frantic about your children, your wife, your mother, even more worried for your son who you know will be treated as if he too is a suspect. You come to your senses and re-member a neighbor telling you that if American soldiers come into your home, tell them they are "welcome." It is one of the few words in English that you know. You say "welcome" over and over and over. But the soldier shouts at you "Shut-up!" You say "welcome" again. So he shouts, "Shut the fuck up" at you as if he could stop you by screaming more loudly with more profanity. You do not know what he is saying. You think that he does not understand your words in English because of your poor pronunciation. You are squirming on the floor under the point of his gun trying to appease him, trying to see what is happen-ing to your wife and children, and he his getting angrier and more menacing.

In most cases, you have done nothing to bring on this invasion of your home. All the while, you fear that no matter what you say your wife and children will be beaten and raped or killed. You already know of women in your area who have been raped by soldiers—foreign and local. According to Amnesty International, one in five Iraqi women have been beaten and raped "by Islamist armed groups, militias, Iraqi government forces, foreign soldiers within the US-led Multinational Force, and staff of foreign private military security contractors."[1]

Rifling through your possessions, American soldiers are looking for anything that may be suspicious; a flyer or an unauthorized weap-on would do equally well. With the full force of masculine aggression, they scream questions at you, often without interpreters, just as com-manding officers screamed at them during basic training. Not answer-ing their questions or responding in a language they do not under-stand is usually construed as guilt. But of what? Being an insurgent? Possibly becoming an insurgent? Associating with insurgents? Or just being an Arab, an Iraqi or an Afghan?

The soldiers have taken your family outside and separated you and your son from the children and women, who are terrified and crying. Your fourteen-year-old son is trembling next to you. When you try to say something to calm him, you feel the butt end of a rifle in your shoulder. While a few soldiers outside restrain you from reentering your home, you hear the soldiers inside tearing out your walls, ripping your furniture apart, turning over your refrigerator, and dumping all of your food to the ground. Incredulous, you ask yourself why? Breaking dishes and the sound of school books being torn up add to the cacophony.

For a brief second, you think of all the hours you have toiled for that food, to buy those books for your children. Then a bag is slipped over your head. You are powerless. You cannot even see if your wife is okay. You are a man and the U.S. military has just rendered you impotent.[2] That floods you with shame, anger, and fear as you are carried away with your son. You feel ashamed not because you have done anything to put your family in jeopardy, but because you have failed as a man to protect them. Like your invader-occupiers, you too learned *core masculinity* growing up. As a man you are expected to sacrifice your life if necessary to protect your family, to defend your honor and support your people.

Soldiers are trained to clear houses at Camp Pendleton in California before deploying to Iraq or Afghanistan. One marine corporal described the training like this:

> A forceful kick sends the door to the floor and Marines flow into the hallway. Seconds later, the sharp cracking of rifle fire resounds through the building.
>
> "Support up," comes a call from inside the house.
>
> "Marines entering!" More Marines rush into the building, more shots are fired.
>
> "Room clear!" The Marines move on, kicking down another door.

A few more rifle reports mean a few more "enemies" down, dead and deflated. "House clear! Weapons on safe!"[3]

The job is done within a minute, and the marines emerge from the house victorious.

The U.S. military trains Iraqi and Afghan forces to employ these tactics against their own people. An Army Staff Sergeant with the First Special Forces Group based out of Fort Lewis, Washington, trained Iraqi soldiers to clear houses. "We teach them the same three things we learn: speed, surprise and violence of action," he explained.[4] This training of Iraqi soldiers has the effect of insuring that the Iraqi people will suffer from U.S. military tactics long after the United States leaves.

One U.S. soldier reported that he had raided between twenty and thirty Iraqi homes in the eleven months he was in combat. During his tour of duty, a sergeant took part in nearly 1,000 nightly house clearings with ten other soldiers on each mission. According to a recent study of U.S. veterans of the Iraq War, "such raids are a relentless reality for Iraqis under occupation." American forces are ordered to invade neighborhoods where insurgents are thought to operate, "bursting into homes in the hope of surprising fighters or finding weapons," which they usually do not find.[5] Soldiers and marines find the military intelligence that directs them to houses to raid is usually so poor that some soldiers joke when they call in a completed house clearing, "Yeah, I found the Weapons of Mass Destruction in here."[6]

Reporter Dahr Jamail quotes one former sergeant who said, "We would raid people's houses, and 95 percent of the time fail to find the remotest trace that could connect them to any sort of terrorist actions."[7] Many soldiers reported that over 90 percent of the houses they raided yielded nothing incriminating.[8] Many U.S. soldiers believed that it was because the Iraqis were lying to them. They tell us in their cell phone movies and in war stories on You Tube or Military TV that Iraqis, indeed Arabs, are all liars.

One officer of the Marine Alpha Company told the reporter embedded with his unit, "I'm the law as far as I'm concerned . . . I wouldn't want to say they're a nation of liars—but if there is an honest Iraqi out there, I haven't met them yet."[9] Watching some of those soldiers talk about Iraqis, you can see in their eyes that they are sounding off from a conviction that lying is in the nature of being Arab, of being Iraqi, of not being American. Infantilizing those Iraqis or Afghans, the enemy, follows from racism and is wed to patriarchal power. For another marine with Alpha Company, "It's just like dealing with a little kid cause you know they are lying to you." He just wanted to smack them like an aggressive father would his lying child.

Those U.S. soldiers derive their sense of patriarchal authority both from the psychopathy of the president who sent them to war and from the blinding macho of men against women in their private lives.[10] Instead of allowing soldiers in combat to act from their own human empathy, training them to rely on their common sense and to follow human morality to save and protect lives, the military is in step with the psychopathic standards set by the White House. And it systematically draws upon the violence many men unleash at home, in what feminists refer to as "family terrorism" and what I see in house clearings and night raids as blinding macho.[11]

I do not use the term "blinding macho" merely rhetorically. I draw my definition of "blinding macho" from women's experience of abuse in private, domestic familial relations. Blinding macho—one small incident, even an imagined, not-real one, can inflame him. He lashes out in uncontrollable rage—maybe first a slap on the face or a fist to her pregnant belly. He allows himself to go into an uncontrollable rage. Although that rage is often portrayed as something beyond his control, he has done nothing to inhibit it. He lets his violent fury rise to the occasion, so to speak. While his rage may appear uncontrollable, he chooses violence, for he makes no effort to turn away from it. By rising to it, he reveals his blinding macho as the entitlement of his gender—an entitlement based on the belief that because he is stronger, can yell louder, is bigger, and because he is a product of *core masculinity,* he believes that nothing should inhibit him from allowing his rage to take over his being. The bully and cowardice of *core masculinity* has surfaced.

She might protest that she did not do whatever he accuses her of, and he takes the sheer audacity of her protest as defiance of his authority. He hurls furniture, breaks dishes. Or he may calm down this time and retreat. He goes out slamming the door with a menacing "don't let this happen again." She tries to avoid his wrath in the coming days and weeks while he is growing another arsenal of complaints against her. His authority is based on his masculine entitlement to his rage and he knows it provokes fear in her—fear that he expects will produce her compliance, her submission, her subordination. Like the president of the United States who intentionally intensifies his people's fears of an attack and treats any refusal of fear as unpatriotic, at home he sees in her a failure to recognize his authority if she is not fearful, compliant, and submissive. That is how he chooses to interpret the meaning of her words and actions.

Then she slips up again, or she doesn't, but he is sure she has. It really doesn't matter. He throws himself into a rage of hate. He cannot be sure he has fully imposed his authority over her. He has to attack her. The next time is worse—he may hold a knife to her throat, slash her back or cheek, turn on the children. He does this because he can, because there is nothing to stop his violence—it may be fists flinging in the home or bombs dropping on people. It may be provoked by nothing, a small transgression, or a major violation. Neither morality against harming others nor human empathy enter into his thinking. Blinding macho drives his judgment. Deep fear may lurk underneath that blinding macho. Or he may have no feelings at all. Either way, because every act is an interpretation of meaning and in every interpretation all people choose from an array of possible meanings, he chooses to allow his fierce blinding macho to take over his being.

Blinding macho that leads to abuse against women in private follows from *core masculinity*. It is not confined to one class or any culture. It does not know national boundaries, and it is not confined to any race or ethnicity. However, militaries and militias around the globe add to it and give it the authority of combat where it is unleashed on enemies and civilians alike. By then, brainwashing has eliminated most soldiers own decision-making.

Because of decades of feminist work to gain protection for women against domestic violence, an abused woman may go to the police, get a protection order, or file charges that lead to her abuser's arrest. But in the military a man is no longer restrained by humanity's repulsion for killing another human being. In combat, he is put out of bounds of the values and ethics that prohibit violence against others, and is disconnected from the human life force where one is constrained as well as fed by the goodness of one's soul. *That* is the blinding macho soldiers take into house clearings or night raids.

Whether by house clearing or any other abusive and demeaning tactic, soldiers make their male victims weak, vulnerable, and unable to defend themselves. They treat them as abusive men treat their wives and girlfriends. Blinded by their military macho, soldiers render the men they occupy inferior as a matter of course. In studying men and war, Joshua Goldstein found that "normal life becomes feminized and combat masculinized."[12] "Emasculation," the misogynist term for rendering some men inferior to other men as they would render women, means taking another's manhood away. For many men, that is the worst thing that could happen to them for they would then be considered to be like a woman.

Almost every man, Iraqi or Afghan or Pakistani or Iranian, will resist being rendered inferior. *Core masculinity* requires all soldiers to fight against that inferiority, uniformed and resistance fighters alike, to make combat central to manhood. But when militaries occupy another state or people, they designate every male civilian of military age as a potential threat or a possible terrorist and the emasculation begins.

In Palestine's occupied West Bank, I met with Areem Hawari, the director of the Men's Project at the Women Against Violence Center in Bethlehem. He pointed out that the Israeli occupation forces Arab men to stay in the private sector, the home—the women's sphere. Occupation itself is Palestinian men's humiliation, which is why those men Hawari sees cannot even speak the term. After Israel cleared not just one house but the entire Jenin refugee camp, one Palestinian man said through his tears, "What hurt us the most was not the Israeli presence or their nuclear arsenal. What hurt us the most was to be impotent in front of a dying person, a child running in the road in a camp looking for her mother without the possibility of taking her along." That is how defeated men are humiliated. Their occupiers destroy their ability to be the protectors they were led to believe they are suppose to be. And the world turned away, "What hurt us the most is that we were abandoned to ourselves while the whole word was watching. Nobody defended us. Nobody! Nobody!"[13]

When men are made inferior their condition is reduced to that of women. That is intolerable to most men. Those men in turn force women's status to lower levels. In 2005, writing on the fate of Iraqi women during the U.S. War, Ghali Hassan remembered that, "prior to the arrival of U.S. forces, Iraqi women were free to go wherever they wish and wear whatever they like." Since the U.S. occupation, "the generation-old equality and liberty laws have been replaced by Middle Ages laws that strip women of their rights." Under U.S. occupation, the Iraqi Governing Council put Iraq's 1959 personal status laws under the control of religious clerics to interpret them from their religious groups' adherence to Islamic laws. That act "could affect women's rights to education, employment, and freedom of movement, divorce, children custody and inheritance."[14] Likewise, with the Soviet occupation of Aghanistan followed later by the U.S. war there, the Taliban rose to power and severely reversed the freedom women had experienced. And after Britain colonized Iran and then in a coup the U.S. brought down its first democratic leader, the Ayatollah Khomeini rose to establish Iran as an Islamic state and shred women's freedoms.

For many American soldiers empathy engages. But often it is not until they are home and away from the war that they stop to consider, "If it had been my home that foreign soldiers 'cleared,' how would I have reacted?" Something strikes a chord in some of their hearts. They identify with the complete vulnerability of the men whose homes they invaded. The soldiers who make that connection ask themselves, "How would I feel if this were my home?" That empathy, however, is usually filtered through *core masculinity*, one man feeling for another man because his manhood was violated. If a man makes that connection with another man, the problem becomes, how does he go out and clear houses again?

When a marine shouts "house clear" or "room clear," it means that human life in that area has been eliminated. On routine house-clearing missions, soldiers evacuate the inhabitants to an area outside of the house and keep them under guard until they are either allowed to return to their destroyed home or are taken away as prisoners. But by 2009, under President Obama's escalation of the war in Afghanistan, the CIA (Central Intelligence Agency), in conjunction with Afghan paramilitary forces, was increasing its secret night raids, using the advantage of surprising people when they are asleep. The civilian casualties were high. For example, in Kunar Province eight young students were handcuffed and then killed.[15]

In January 2010, a team of American and Afghan soldiers entered a remote village in Afghanistan, ostensibly to detain a Taliban commander, but they killed four males, including a boy. Villagers charged that those killed were innocent civilians and that they are actually trapped by the fighting. "We have no sympathy for the Taliban. We are poor people." The U.S. military issued a statement saying that "no innocent Afghan civilians were harmed in this operation," but a few days later, General McChrystal announced that the United States would cut back on night raids because they were unpopular among Afghans (as if they would be popular among other people!).[16] Over half of the 600 civilians killed in Afghanistan in 2009 were killed in night raids.[17] Although in 2010 U.S. General McChrystal issued orders to curtail night raids, and to have them led by Afghan soldiers, deadly force continued to be used.[18]

Evidence from Iraq shows that the invasion of private homes goes further. One soldier has testified that he was repeatedly ordered to return to people's homes "and put the screws to them." He paraphrased his commanding officer's reasoning—"The reason they are not talking to you is not because they are innocent or because they don't know anything, it's because you are being too nice to them. Treat them like shit." Even though that soldier knew that "the people I interrogated were honest and straightforward" and that they "knew nothing about terrorism, that they were barely surviving, terrified of what was happening," he would go back because "I was a soldier" and he would "be meaner to them and shittier to them."[19] The army demanded his depravity.

Military intelligence is usually about as accurate as that which is gained from torture when the victim will say anything just to get the torture to stop or as accurate as the intelligence that Bush used to claim that Iraq was ready to use weapons of mass destruction against the United States.[20] But if you are in the U.S. military and you believe in the validity of these draconian methods, you do not question the information you have received. In the arrogance of male American superiority, you could not possibly be deceived so you treat the intelligence you gained as authentic, pass it on to a military computer lab on a base back home that has no connection to what is happening on the ground in combat, and then a soldier technician sends the intelligence back through the chain of command. In the field, orders come down to a combat unit for another house clearing. And so house clearings go on nightly with intelligence that is as accurate as the so-called intelligence that got us into the war against Iraq. With the same demand for revenge that the U.S. president invoked after the 9/11 attack, when you are finished with one house you go on to the next.

One Iraqi spoke volumes for many when he hurled the most extreme insult you can pay another person in the Arab world by throwing his shoes at President Bush during a press conference in Baghdad in 2008. Iraqi journalist Muntazer al-Zaidi explained his actions in an article, "Why I Threw the Shoe," which revealed both the depth of humiliation and the despair that Iraqis have been driven to by the U.S. war. As the U.S. media has downplayed the Iraqis experiences of the U.S. war, most mainstream American newspapers did not reprint his article which appeared in the *Guardian*, published in England. But Al-Zaidi's statement is essential to a politics of empathy which requires that Americans in particular and Westerners in general understand the depth of devastation in lives lost and people humiliated.

Upon his release from prison, on September 19, 2009, Al-Zaidi wrote, "I am free. But my country is still a prisoner of war ... what compelled me to act is the injustice that befell my people, and how the occupation wanted to humiliate my homeland by putting it under its boot." He points to the devastation of Iraq and how "the invasion divided brother from brother, neighbour from neighbour. It turned our homes into funeral tents." Refusing the title of hero for standing up to and insulting the U.S. president, he explained, "It humiliated me to see my country humiliated; and to see my Baghdad burned, my people killed. Thousands of tragic pictures remained in my head, pushing me towards the path of confrontation." As a journalist, "I travelled through my burning land and saw with my own eyes the pain of the victims, and heard with my own ears the screams of the orphans and the bereaved. And a feeling of shame haunted me like an ugly name because I was powerless."[21]

Reporting daily on the war against his people in Iraq, humiliation grew inside him. "As soon as I finished my professional duties in reporting the daily tragedies, while I washed away the remains of the debris of the ruined Iraqi houses, or the blood that stained my clothes, I would clench my teeth and make a pledge to our victims, a pledge of vengeance." When he attended George W. Bush's press conference, "the opportunity came, and I took it. I took it out of loyalty to every drop of innocent blood that has been shed through the occupation or because of it, every scream of a bereaved mother, every moan of an orphan, the sorrow of a rape victim, the teardrop of an orphan."[22]

While some claim he offended journalism as well as Bush, Al-Zaidi brings us back to his subjective, felt experience of U.S. occupation, "I say to those who reproach me: do you know how many broken homes that shoe which I threw had entered? How many times it had trodden over the blood of innocent victims? Maybe that shoe was the appropriate response when all values were violated." His shoes that he flung through the air toward Bush expressed the humiliation and anguish of many Iraqis, and throughout the Arab world he was considered a hero. He had said what others dared not: "I wanted to express my rejection of his lies, his occupation of my country, my rejection of his killing my people. My rejection of his plundering the wealth of my country, and destroying its infrastructure. And casting out its sons into a diaspora...I didn't do this so my name would enter history or for material gains. All I wanted was to defend my country."[23]

Few humiliated Iraqi men would turn to this kind of symbolic, nonviolent means of expressing their refusal of American humiliation of them. It is easy to guess that many of those left alive after a typical night of house clearing by American soldiers will cheer or at least feel some vindication each time American soldiers are attacked. *Core masculinity* engages, and if you put yourself in the place of those terrified by these house raids, it is not a far reach of the imagination—you do not even need to be empathetic—to know that in ordering wanton violence against families, you will provoke men to take up arms against you. That is the logic of male domination everywhere and that is how the U.S. military made resisters of Iraqis.

Paul Wolfowitz, one of the masterminds of Bush's war against Iraq, noted that in planning the war, the White House never imagined an insurgency.[24] In other words, as he and Bush and other administration officials sat in their offices in Washington, D.C. planning an invasion with 150,000 U.S. soldiers on foot from Kuwait and with shock and awe bombing, as orders went out to destroy electrical plants, clean water facilities and means of sewage disposal, as U.S. soldiers were killing innocent Iraqis all along the way, the Bush administration never considered that the Iraqis would fight back. As soldiers occupied the country, stood by idly watching and sometimes participating in the looting and destruction of national treasures and precious artifacts from ancient Mesopotamia, or as Bremmer and his staff dismantled the Iraqi national health program, eliminated hundreds of thousands of Iraqi jobs, became the belligerent ugly Americans of the Emerald Palace, the Bush administration never imagined that the Iraqis would resist. That is more than failure of empathy. It is the devastating arrogance of American superiority that stems from the insulated position of power that makes its own blinders to the effects its actions have on others.

It could be tempting to view U.S. leaders' inability to foresee that they would provoke a reaction and a resistance in Iraq as their own stupidity. But the reality is more serious than that. Whether it takes the form of an abusive husband or an invading state, that power of masculinity—and the blinding macho that drives it—makes itself incapable of seeing the humanity of those it harms. That power severs itself from native intelligence and the knowledge that we normally derive from empathy. It blinds itself to human reaction to abuse and destruction. Its power is so heady that it is incapable of seeing that human beings will resist and struggle against their abusers.

Reporter Dahr Jamail came upon the Red Cross loading dead Iraqi bodies into an ambulance. "They were killed by Americans while they were walking down the road," an Iraqi man told him. "Do you think all these people, these innocent people being killed by the Americans, don't have families that are now joining the resistance?"[25] Ordinary Iraqi civilians were more knowledgeable about the consequences of U.S. war than the president of the United States, his cabinet, the U.S. military and the Americans who supported that war.

The men who are taken away from their homes after house clearings may return home from U.S. custody the next day, a week later or never. Why would anyone, especially the U.S. military, think that would be the last you would hear from them? You, the U.S. military, destroyed their homes, terrified and harmed their families, abused and humiliated them. That puts the U.S. military in the business of making enemies and invoking resistance. But when our military leaders report back to the Congress, the media, and the American people, they tell us that American troops are being attacked in Iraq by insurgents, as if that is unthinkable and without cause.

In war and under occupation, resistance is propelled by the collective human impulse for self-determination, the right of all people, as embodied in the UN charter and its International Covenant on Civil and Political Rights and on Economic, Social and Cultural Rights, to "freely determine their political status and freely pursue their economic, social and cultural development."[26] Affirming its position against human liberation, the United States ratified the Covenant on Civil and Political Rights with so many exclusions that it rendered the covenant meaningless. The U.S. Congress has never ratified the Covenant on Economic, Social and Cultural Rights.

Violated self-determination of a people brings about resistance. Resistance militias are built from the same *expendable lives* that enabled the U.S. military to invade and occupy them. The resistance militias opposing the United States were made up of aggrieved men who lost wives and children and brothers and parents, their homes, their jobs and their dignity. In the Arab world, violation of men's honor demands revenge. Americans can understand that. After all, it is the same irrational masculinist reasoning that supported George Bush's invasion of Iraq after the 9/11 Al Qaeda attack even though at the time Iraq had nothing to do with Al Qaeda or the 9/11 attack. If you know anything about masculinity anywhere in the world, you know that if provoked, many men will exact revenge, having learned the expectations of *core masculinity* when they were very young.

Iraqi or Afghan or any other people's anger and hatred from what you American soldiers have done to them turns you into *their* objects. They must get the soldiers out of their lives, out of their country. The drive of blinding macho that brought you soldiers to their country to fight and kill is the force behind their resistance to you. That resistance is born of their claim to their own self-determination. But the U.S. military refuses to recognize that it generates the resisters and instead treats them as insurgents and terrorists. For the United States, an insurgency is "aimed at the overthrow of a constituted government."[27] And under U.S. occupation, the United States constituted itself as that government.

It is always the case that some boys and men just see a fight coming and that stokes their own macho. They join the criminally minded and the sociopaths for whom fighting, harm, rape, and killing are part of the joyride of war. They are men in combat and they too will kill without remorse and with revenge. Some will become leaders of terrorist cells. If they prevail and gain power, they become the next psychopathic president, prime minister or ayatollah of their people. The war opened the way for Al Qaeda to move into Iraq, where it had not been before, and made it possible for other extremists to take center stage in the nationalist and religious fights against the US. Shiite-Sunni tensions unleashed their full fury on each other and the US. Others joined up with terrorists.

The forces on both sides of the fighting, Iraqi and American, are made up of men genuinely motivated to serve as well as criminals and sociopaths. Both are driven by the masculinity of their *expendable lives*. But the difference is that Americans are transgressing on Iraqi and Afghan homes, invading their personal and private lives. Iraqis are defending themselves, albeit through the masculinity of war. All of these people—resisters, macho men, criminals, sociopaths—this complex mixture of forces, was unleashed with the U.S. invasion of Iraq. Add to that mixture the fact that the U.S. soldiers could not tell an insurgent from an ordinary civilian, and you have the frightening mayhem that Iraq became to its people.

Not surprisingly, by 2006, according to a World Public Opinion Poll conducted by the Program on International Policy Attitudes, seven in ten Iraqis wanted a timetable for U.S. withdrawal. Half of them wanted that withdrawal within six months, believing that security for Iraqis would increase without the provocation of U.S.-led troops.[28] Quality of life had significantly degenerated for Iraqis with only "39 percent saying 'their lives are going well,' down from 71 percent in Nov. 2005."

A large majority of Shiites, Kurds, and Sunnis rejected Al Qaeda and Osama bin Laden but supported the resistance against Americans. An overwhelming majority believed that the U.S. military presence in Iraq was provoking more conflict than it was preventing. "If the U.S. were to commit to withdraw, more than half of those who approve of attacks on U.S. troops say that their support for attacks would diminish."[29] The United States remained and escalated its troop levels.

Revealing how far refusal of human empathy can distance soldiers from reality, many soldiers have said that they wouldn't have been angry and hostile toward Iraqis if they were welcomed by them as their liberators. The soldiers had given up time with their families, their jobs, and, for many, their dead-end lives, to come and fight in Iraq and make this sacrifice, as they saw it. Like their president and Congress, they too found the Iraqis ungrateful, and worse, they were trying to kill them.

House clearing, preventive and random killing, and the military tactics of the invading and occupying soldiers is how invader-occupiers make enemies. Provoking resistance and introducing the chaos of war insures job security for the U.S. military. It feeds the military industrial complex, keeping American factories buzzing and their CEOs raking in the profits of war. We know that these enemy-making actions are deliberate military tactics to perpetuate war because earlier in the war against Iraq some U.S. commanders refused to use them and their success was ignored.

By contrast, as journalist Thomas Ricks recounts the instructions that Colonel H.R. McMaster of the Third Armored Calvary Regiment in 2006 in northern Iraq gave to his troops, "Every time you treat an Iraqi disrespectfully, you are working for the enemy."[30] He ordered his soldiers to approach locals with dignity and respect. Then, "he met with sheikhs and clerics who had ties to the insurgency and apologized for past American mistakes." When McMaster took over, "Islamic extremists had begun to seep in from Syria and make contacts with local allies. By mid-2005 they had intimidated the locals with terror tactics and made the town a base from which to send suicide bombers and other attackers 40 miles easy to Mosul ... "[31] When McMaster attacked Tall Afar, a small city in northern Iraq, he brought his soldiers into neighborhoods to protect civilians. His approach worked. He began to be trusted by local sheiks and his soldiers were trusted by civilians. He had given them his word and followed through.

McMaster's more humanitarian approach did not catch on in the U.S. military until American public opinion turned against the war in Iraq when American military deaths passed the 4,000 mark. It took until 2007, four years into the war, after countless Iraqis were killed or had become resisters, for the U.S. military to consider "respecting Iraqis." General David Petraeus finally, chillingly admitted, "killing every insurgent is normally impossible." The *Counterinsurgency Field Manual* recognizes that attempting to kill every insurgent "can also be counterproductive in some cases, it risks generating popular resentment, creating martyrs that motivate new recruits, and producing cycles of revenge."[32]

Logically, by 2007 it was time for the United States to withdraw from combat and begin the reconstruction of the mess it had made of Iraq. But this was not to be. Counterinsurgency was less a military tactic than it was a public relations campaign that was meant to convince Americans that it was good for us and for Iraqis to have George W. Bush order a surge of 20,000 troops to Iraq to help Iraqis with *their problem*. Petraeus, in keeping with his penchant for dehumanizing language, introduced a new distinction to differentiate "reconcilable Iraqis from irreconcilable enemies," a start in redefining who was killable, if you could recognize irreconcilables and tell them apart from reconcilables.

Writing these words, disentangling terms like "reconcilables," revealing the mentality behind "killing every insurgent is normally impossible," as if you would kill them all if it were possible, takes my breath away. I sit at my desk and find my heart pounding as years of ghastly death and destruction are written off by U.S. commanders as the result of mistaken strategies. And then I see them take those strategies from Iraq to Afghanistan with the same consequences followed by the same acknowledgement of "mistaken strategies."

I feel shame creeping over me as an American, knowing not only that this war should not have been fought but that the U.S. military had no plans to protect the people of Iraq or of Afghanistan or the next state it decides to invade. Instead they turned them into enemies to perpetuate war and when that no longer worked, they turned them into reconcilables to not be killed. Instructions to soldiers vary; one day it is acceptable to shoot down Iraqis because they are driving too close to your Humvee, the next day, a soldier will go out on a "walk and talk" to make friends with them and show them that the U.S. forces are there to protect them and secure their village or their quarter of the city.

The occupier's arbitrary power over who will live and who will die reeks of depravity. On the occupier's own call, it will be murderous or beneficent or both. For those occupied, life can be safe and the authority over them respectful, not because that is a human right inherent in being alive but because today your occupier decides it will be so for you. With the new benchmark for U.S. military success in Iraq being a decrease in Iraqi civilian casualties, preventive, random and vengeful killing was to stop, as if by the snap of a finger.[33] That is how arbitrary killing in war is and how it requires that those living under that authority be thankful if their occupier decides not to try to kill all of them.

In counterinsurgency, as envisioned by Petraeus, the battle is for the hearts and minds of the people and is won by respecting them and providing them with security. That shift would require a major change in behavior among American troops and their command. The soldiers would no longer go out on the attack and then retreat to their barracks where they would remain until the next attack. They were sent to neighborhoods on patrol, for "walk and talks," to find out people's needs, to gain information on insurgents, to establish a security presence. The Iraqis' would-be "liberators" now were to become their friends. In Washington at military briefings, General Petraeus assured his audiences that of course they were still bombing. He would have it both ways.

Some marines found the "respecting Iraqis" strategy not to be at all to their liking. One marine near the end of his tour of duty admitted, "I didn't get what I wanted out of here." When asked what he wanted, he answered "Kill as many of the enemy as possible and don't look back." Instead he had to search out "high-value individuals," the irreconcilables in Petraeus's terms, such as Al Qaeda and other actual terrorists. To this soldier's disappointment, "we're not allowed to kill them anymore. We have to arrest them."[34]

Iraqi trust would not be garnered easily. In the first days of 2007, violence escalated to almost 180 attacks a day on U.S. forces. Baghdad saw, on an average, more than one car bomb attack a day. In one month, at least eight U.S. helicopters were shot down."[35] By the spring, roadside bombs became the favored means of attacking U.S. troops especially by Al Qaeda.

Marines in Alpha Company voiced their frustration to Gordon Forbes, a reporter embedded with them: "Part of the frustration is the fact that there are people here who are trying to kill us. And we haven't had the opportunity to kill back. For the marines, that balance, that justice is very important and when you don't have it, it wears on us quite a bit."[36] In 2008 on average, fifteen Iraqi civilians were killed daily. By February 2009 that rate had decreased to five a day. In other words, war as usual went on behind the military public relations claim of "winning the hearts and minds of the Iraqi people."

Television news reports began to show soldiers handing out candy and toys to children. It made for good human interest news in the media back home in the United States and around the world. But, by then the U.S. military and militias such as Blackwater were hated throughout Iraq. What we did not see on the evening news was the Iraqi boy, probably six or seven years old, who hit his little sister for taking candy from the U.S. soldier or the U.S. commanding officer who chased the boy down, lifted him two feet off the ground by his shirt, and, with his gun in the boy's face, threatened to kill him.[37] What Petraeus missed is that you have to have hearts to be able to win them. Those hearts are the ones that the military tried to wipe out of its soldiers in basic training and then stuffed away when pats on the back went out to any soldier for his first kill.

Despite the counterinsurgency, according to the Iraqi Center for Research and Strategic Studies which surveyed 3,000 Iraqis (62 percent men, 38 percent women) between September 25 and October 5, 2008, only 22 percent of Iraqis said they believed the United States could provide security to them, and that was a *15 percent decrease from the year before.*[38] Fewer than half the people of Iraq, 45 percent, even wanted their country to have strategic relations with the United States, while 77 percent wanted Iraq to have strategic relations with Syria, and 73 percent wanted them with Jordan.

All of the violence of making insurgents, becoming insurgents, fighting insurgents, and fighting Americans ultimately falls on the shoulders of Iraqi and Afghan and Pakistani women. The death toll of the Iraqi war has left one in ten Iraqi households to be headed by women, 76 percent of whom are widows who do not receive any form of pension and cannot go out to work. As there is no work for them, 87 percent of all women in Iraq are unemployed. The women and children in these households are immensely more vulnerable to food shortages and poverty than those in households headed by men.

By 2009, after six years of U.S. war and occupation, one-quarter of the women did not have access to daily drinking water. Half of them who had access to water found it was not potable.[39] About a quarter of the people of Iraq rated the availability of food rations, fuel, garbage pick-up, and the roads and bridges as very bad. For over one-half of the people, the availability of electricity was very bad.[40] One-third of the women had access to electricity for fewer than three hours a day; two-thirds had it for fewer than six hours a day. Women's income and their access to health services degenerated in 2008 from where it had been during the previous two years.

While more than half of all Iraqis, men and women, feel nervous, tense, and worried, and 42 percent have high blood pressure, significantly more women than men tire easily, often have headaches, are easily frightened, find it difficult to make decisions, have trouble with hands shaking, and cry more than usual.[41] Women are more vulnerable than men to mental health problems including depression, phobias, anxiety and post traumatic stress disorder.

What do many Iraqi women find happens after American soldiers finish house clearing and leave their homes in ruins? Their men—husbands, fathers, sons—leave to fight in the resistance. Men bring the war home, as they do from all wars, and that intensifies the subjection of women to violence and sexual abuse. Women do not leave their homes where 83 percent of them report controlling behavior from their husbands and 33 percent are subjected to emotional violence.

The U.S. war against Iraq displaced approximately 2.8 million Iraqis within Iraq while 2 million more have fled to other countries. That makes almost 5 million displaced people from a country of 29 million. About 17 percent of the population are refugees living in refugee camps or with relatives or in other makeshift quarters, most in Syria, Jordan and parts of Iraq that are not their homes. Most are in Syria and Jordan, and of these "some are ethnically or religiously mixed families that no longer fit into ethnically cleansed and homogenized neighborhoods. Many lack patronage links to ruling parties and so have no prospect of employment on returning to Iraq."[42]

In the United States, by 2008, interest in the U.S. war against Iraq had waned. By 2010, apparently buoyed by the promises of the Obama presidency, the ranks of the antiwar protestors had dwindled. If those same Americans were engaged in antiwar activism from a politics of empathy for Afghan people, the antiwar movement would be stronger than ever. Look to those Americans who remain in action such as CODEPINK, Women in Black and the Iraq Veterans Against the War among many others to see the activism that comes from knowing through empathy.

Ongoing War

In today's world, most wars are waged by the powerful, heavily militarized states that invade and occupy smaller, less-developed states or peoples. These bully wars may look like attacks on dangerous dictators or "terrorists," but in most cases, they end up making enemies where they were not before. The resulting ongoing wars have their own definitive cycles:

1. Presidents and prime ministers in remorseless disregard for human life provoke and bully other states and powerless peoples.

2. At the orders of the leaders in #1, armed forces wage wars terrorizing less powerful states and vulnerable peoples.

3. At the orders of leaders in #1 and the forces in #2, soldiers in combat wage war against relatively defenseless people, making enemies of humiliated men through their aggression and killings.

4. Men attacked and humiliated by the leaders of #1's militaries resist and fight back. (The leaders in #1 call them insurgents or terrorists to delegitimize their struggle and their claim to their right to self-determination against the occupation authorized by the leaders of #1 and enforced by the forces in #2.)

5. Leaders of the invaded, attacked, and humiliated men frequently invoke religion and culture to assert their domination, and psychopaths emerge from the ranks with terrorist tactics.

6. If the resistance prevails, its leaders will likely become the leaders in #1.

"If the resistance prevails," will the new leader who rises to power from the resistance forces begin the cycle again, turning into #1? Having been committed to fighting and killing, will the new leader become a president or prime minister with remorseless disregard for human life who then provokes and bullies other states and powerless peoples into conflict? Will they become state leaders of psychopathic proportions or will he or she fulfill the struggle for self-determination and engage in the liberation of its people as Nelson Mandela did when his rise to state leadership ended apartheid, and he turned the African National Congress to creating a democracy of South Africa? That success of the Mandela-led resistance, at least for a moment in history, cast a light that revealed the possibilities of a peaceful world and that contrasted to psychopathic leaders committed to ongoing war.

To justify ongoing war, state and military leaders conflate terrorism with self-determination as we have seen the U.S. military do in Iraq and Afghanistan. Likewise, both the United States and Israel identify Hizbullah and Hamas as terrorist groups, which in turn escalates people's fears and demands for protection from them. Meanwhile, neither the global community nor the United States have been able to arrive at a rational, legal definition of terrorism, that which the United States and Israel continue to fight against in ongoing wars.

In 1997 the United Nations General Assembly adopted a convention that defined a terrorist as any person who "unlawfully and intentionally delivers, places, charges or detonates an explosive or other legal device," in a public place "with the intent to cause death or serious bodily injury" or "destruction of such a place...where the destruction results in or is likely to result in major economic loss."[1] Would that definition not apply to the United States in its illegal (by UN standards of war) invasion of Iraq? Are resistance struggles against occupation that violates people's inherent, collective right to their self-determination illegal? Not if, according to the United Nations, all peoples have a right to their self-determination.

Since 1996, the United Nations has been deadlocked, unable to reach an agreement on a Comprehensive Convention on International Terrorism. While Israel and the United States refuse to recognize the validity of struggles for self-determination, the Organization of the Islamic Conference demanded that any international legal definition of terrorism exclude armed conflict against foreign occupation. This approach insists that military force exercised by a state, such as the United States in Iraq and Afghanistan or Israel in Lebanon in 2006 or Gaza in 2009 be in conformity with international humanitarian law.[2]

The U.S. Department of Defense has its own definition of terrorism as "the unlawful use of—or threatened use of—force or violence against individuals or property to coerce or intimidate governments or societies, often to achieve political, religious, or ideological objectives." By that definition, Al Qaeda is a terrorist organization aimed at destruction of the United States but so is the United States a terrorist regime that occupies Iraq and Afghanistan.

Noam Chomsky has been particularly articulate in exposing how the United States' aggressions against other states fit its own definition of terrorism. He paraphrases George W. Bush at the time of the 2001 U.S. invasion of Afghanistan when Bush said in effect to the Afghan people that "we will continue to bomb you, unless your leadership turns over to us the people whom we suspect of carrying out crimes." He then dismissed offers from Afghan leadership for negotiations about extradition. In distinguishing between Osama Bin Laden as a terrorist and U.S. state terrorism, Chomsky points out, "Its simple. If they do it, it's terrorism. If we do it, it's counter-terrorism."[3] I am not suggesting that Bin Laden is not a terrorist, but rather, that the United States is a terrorist state.

The CIA fixed the problem of defining a state such as the United States or Israel as terrorist by restricting its definition of terrorism to "subnational groups." Title 22 of the U.S. Code, Section 2656f(d) says that "the term 'terrorism' means premeditated, politically motivated violence perpetrated against noncombatant targets by subnational groups or clandestine agents."[4] The variations in the U.S. definition of terrorism result in an ad hoc approach where rational, humanitarian standards are required. But the CIA definition not only excludes the United States from its definition, it would exclude states like George W. Bush's "axis of evil" which named Iran, Iraq, and North Korea as state sponsors of terrorism.[5] As if making up a list for its ongoing wars, the State Department fixed that problem by issuing a list of "state sponsors of terrorism" that includes Cuba, Iran, the Sudan and Syria.

When Hamas in Gaza and Hizbullah in Lebanon shell Israel or when fighting breaks out on the border between Hizbullah in Lebanon and the Israel Defense Forces, Israel and the United States insist that these attacks arise from nothing, as if they have no cause. We are expected to believe that those aggressions are the work of terrorists who put Israel as a state and its people in imminent danger for no other reason than just to do so.

But charges of terrorism hide the roots of how Israel has made enemies of Palestinians and put its own people, the Jews of Israel, at risk in order to gain its people's acquiescence to their state's ongoing wars. With strong pressure from Britain, then the occupier of Palestine in 1947, the United Nations partitioned Palestine into two states, making of it a Jewish state, Israel, and an Arab state, Palestine. In anticipation of a state of their own, the Zionist leadership of the Jewish people had escalated immigration of Jews to Palestine in the preceding decades, establishing settler colonies among the indigenous Arabs and the Jewish minority who had always peopled the land. The UN partition plan designated 400 out of 1,000 Arab villages in Palestine for the Jewish state with the Jewish state to receive 56 percent of Palestine, an area that included almost a half millions Jews and 438,000 Arabs at the time. "The Partition Resolution incorporated the most fertile land in the proposed Jewish state as well as almost all of the Jewish urban and rural space in Palestine." [6]

One of the fundamental flaws of the partition, regardless of how much Jews needed and deserved a homeland, was that the United Nations, in violation of its own charter, turned over the land, farms, orchards, and homes of one people to another, dispossessing Arabs to make a state for Jews. It is fair to say that no place exists in the world where people, any people, can be driven from their homes and land without igniting their self-determination and causing them to fight back for what was theirs. That collective human impulse for survival and self-determination kicks in wherever people are displaced and dispossessed. Then men, in forming a resistance, usually turn that struggle into combat.

Why would United Nations leaders who were deciding the fate of the Arab people in Palestine, people who had no responsibility for the Holocaust, not expect them to fight back? Jews who had been in search of a homeland for decades, would even more fiercely fight for the land that was promised them, believing that they are in a state of their own where they would find protection from future Holocausts. No more powerful example can be found of how peoples are pitted against each other by the most powerful states in the world.

The Palestinians, made into a people by their displacement for a Jewish state, would be identified as the problem, instead of the European and American leaders who dispossessed them. Those white European and American leaders would then treat the conflict that resulted from their partition with the same racism that the U.S. military uses to disrupt the world of Iraqis, Afghans, and Pakistanis. Then those leaders throw their hands in the air when internal strife amongst warring factions escalates with a gesture that says "what can you expect of those people."

When neighboring Arab states came to the defense of Arabs in Palestine, they were resoundingly defeated by the Israel Defense Forces (IDF), the new Israeli military made up of the Zionist militias and gangs from Jewish settlements. From their War of Independence, Israel claimed more Palestinian land than it had acquired in the UN's partition plan. By July 1948, the Jewish state expanded to more than 78 percent of what had been Palestine, and the Israeli government refused to set actual boundaries, an expansionist policy that continues to this day with the Jewish settler movement. The act of creating a Jewish state and homeland simultaneously turned into the Palestinian Nakba or disaster of their ethnic cleansing by Israel.

Volumes of historiography shape our contemporary knowledge and debates over the founding of Israel. My concern here is not to review that history but to expose how the UN partition of Palestine led to cycles of invasions, occupations and resistance—that is, ongoing war in the Middle East. With the painful backdrop of Nazi aggression and its heinous death camps, not only had the United Nations taken from Palestinians their homes and land, but Israel with its new-found independence soon began to eliminate Palestinians themselves from their Jewish state.

Israeli historian Ilan Pappé has documented that ethnic cleansing. A month after the partition resolution was adopted in the United Nations on November 29, 1947, Israel began systematic ethnic cleansing of Palestinians. By January 9, 1948, Arab armies fought the Jewish military in small skirmishes, and by May 1948, and while ethnic cleansing of Arabs was in full swing, the British who had occupied Palestine since 1922 withdrew. In March 1948, before the British left, the leadership of Israel "openly declared ... it would seek to take over the land and expel the indigenous population by force."[7]

Israel's Plan Dalet, which was turned over to its military for execution, called for villages "to be expelled in their entirety either because they were located in strategic spots or because they were expected to put up some sort of resistance ... no village would be immune, either because of its location or because it would not allow itself to be occupied," according to Pappé's archival research. The result was "531 villages and eleven urban neighbourhoods and towns that were destroyed and their inhabitants expelled ... "[8] While massacres were not ordered by the plan, they went unnoticed by Israel and world authorities when those mass killings became part of depopulating Israel of its Palestinians.

Then, because men are marked for the expendability of their lives in combat, Palestinian males from age ten to fifty were rounded up and held in huge pens until they were removed to prison camps. Here are the origins of the house-clearing strategies that are used today by the U.S. military and continue to be employed by Israel against Palestinians in its Occupied Palestinian Territories. In carrying out Plan Dalet "Israeli troops would first put a place—a city or a village— under a closure order. Then intelligence units would start searching from house to house, pulling people out whom they suspected of being present 'illegally' in that particular location as well as any other 'suspicious Arabs.'"[9]

And the world did not notice these crimes against humanity? Pappé reveals that at the time, the *New York Times* and the Red Cross reported daily on the atrocities. The world, including the United Nations, did nothing to intervene. While Jewish people worldwide were welcomed to Israel, many being given emptied Palestinian homes, farms, and orchards, 750,000 Palestinians were systematically expelled from their *own* country. Israel denied Palestinians, most of whom peopled refugee camps of Lebanon, Syria, and Jordan, the right to return to their country or their homes—ever. Likewise, the state of Israel confiscated Palestinians' bank holdings.

In open air, before the entire world, the ethnic cleansing of Arabs to insure that Israel would be a Jewish state became a buried secret that since then has been sealed by censoring criticism of the state of Israel and charging its critics with anti-Semitism which I will discuss in Chapter 11. Palestinians who were evacuated from their land and rounded up in refugee camps of neighboring countries were to be recognized only as enemies of the Jewish people and the Israeli state—that is, as terrorists.

Since 1948 and the Palestinian disaster or the Nakba, provoked and unprovoked ongoing war with Arab states, conflict with the Palestinian territories, maintain Israel's image as a state beleaguered and besieged by Arabs. Without engaging in ongoing war, the state of Israel risks losing its status as a victim and when that happens, it will be left with acknowledging the legitimacy of Palestinian claims and admitting to the Nakba.

Most importantly, Israel keeps its Jewish population in a state of hypervigilence against terrorists. We already know the effects of manipulating Americans who in their relative protection from wars would support war crimes because their president had convinced them invading Iraq was essential to their security. Unlike Americans, Israelis are not geographically removed from wars. Every aggression by Israel against Hizbullah in Lebanon and Hamas in Gaza brings an attack on Israel, usually on its civilians and towns. Those kinds of attacks cannot help but invoke a collective traumatic identity in the people who have been repeatedly subjected to pogroms and genocide. Not only individual Holocaust survivors but the collective of Jewish people have internalized the trauma of their people's genocide.

Most peoples who have been subjected to collective trauma find that it resolves itself over time. Jeffrey Alexander is among the sociologists who have pointed out that once it is over and collective identity can be reestablished, there is a "calming down" period. The intensity of the original trauma lessens and emotions are less inflamed.[10] But many Jews understand that it would be dangerous for them to allow people to experience a 'calming down,' or less inflamed emotions about the Holocaust. Would that not put them at risk of another? Their history supports that fear.

Therefore, while genocide became etched in the Jewish collective identity, the Jewish people's fear from the original collective trauma would not be released. That collective traumatized memory is activated with all of the hypervigilance and adrenalin-rushing reactions that cause them to not only support their country's war but demand stronger protection, annihilation of anyone who might try to attack them. These traumatic symptoms, writ large in the collective consciousness, are extended to those who did not directly experience it; from there they are passed down through generations. Protection, it is believed, lies in never forgetting, never letting the world forget. Every attack on Israel can reawaken that original trauma or for those who are a generation or more removed from the Holocaust, the collective traumatized memory of it.

On the other hand, remembrance of the Holocaust has over time been used by Israel to silence the other remembering—of the Palestinian Nakba. As the world edges ever closer to recognizing the injustices, humiliations, and aggression against Palestinians, Israel, in 2010, was considering an anti-Nakba law that would forbid "marking Independence Day and the founding of Israel with mourning ceremonies and vandalizing or physical disdain towards the flag and State symbols."[11]

Criticism of the state of Israel is treated as if it is racial hatred of Jews. American politicians especially are manipulated by those charges of anti-Semitism into unqualified, unquestioning support for the state. That is why Barack Obama, during his presidential campaign, spoke to the American Israeli Public Affairs Committee (AIPAC), the most powerful lobby in Washington, and laid the blame for the Israeli war squarely on Hizbullah:

> We had to ask the world community, those who might have been critical during that summer, what nation in this world would not re-

spond when another nation crosses their borders, kidnaps their troops, and continues to rain down missiles on them. I don't know of any nation that would. We shouldn't expect Israel to do any less.[12]

His remarks included no acknowledgement of the devastating Israeli blockade of Gaza that prevents basic food and medicine from reaching people in need. Obama knew that if he did not support Israel's bloody war, he too would become victim of AIPAC which would have turned its powerful lobby against his campaign. So? He became part of the silence that has diverted most Americans from bothering to ask *why* Hizbullah captured those Israeli soldiers in 2006 or Hamas fires on Israeli villages.

After the forced evacuation of Palestinians from their homes and their country and their mass-murder through a preplanned strategy of ethnic cleansing in 1948, it would take another generation before Palestinians would rise up in resistance. The Palestine Liberation Organization (PLO) formed in 1964 with the goal of regaining Palestine through armed struggle. The original PLO charter called for the Palestinian right of return to Palestinian lands and for their self-determination. By 1974 the PLO called for Palestinian statehood in the original land that was granted to the Palestinians by the 1947 UN partition. From their bases in Jordan, Lebanon, and Syria, as well as from within the Gaza Strip and West Bank, the PLO used guerrilla warfare and terrorist tactics to attack Israel. In the 1970s, it was launching attacks on Israeli villages in northern Israel from Lebanon, while placing Lebanese in jeopardy of Israeli retaliation.

While the United States was fighting against Iraq in 2006, it was supporting Israel in a war against Lebanon to eliminate Hizbullah, a supposedly terrorist militia bent on the destruction of Israel. But where did Hizbullah come from? How did it become a militia? To answer that, we go back to 1982 when Ariel Sharon, then defense minister of Israel, led the Israel Defense Forces in a brutal invasion of Lebanon to do away with the PLO once and for all. From September to June 1982, the IDF killed almost 20,000 Lebanese, over 5,000 in Beirut alone bombing densely packed high-rise apartment complexes.[13] Backed by the United States, Sharon forced the evacuation of the PLO.

But Sharon did not stop there. He then orchestrated two days of rampaging rape and mass murder of mostly Palestinian refugees in the Sabra and Chatilla refugee camps near Beirut. He ordered the IDF to open the gates of the refugee camps to the bloodthirsty Phalange, a Christian Lebanese paramilitary, well known for its hatred of Palestinians. The Phalange flooded the Sabra and Chatilla refugee camps. Sharon then had his army seal off the camps so that the refugees could not escape and no one could get in to rescue them.

"Psychopaths are almost always rational," the psychologists Lilienfeld and Arkowitz tell us. Unlike people with psychotic disorders, they do not lose contact with reality, but instead "they are well aware that their ill-advised or illegal actions are wrong in the eyes of society but shrug off these concerns with startling nonchalance."[14] Ariel Sharon's leadership had another layer of psychopathy to it—a sadistic side. Sadists lie as an excuse to engage in physical cruelty; they use violence to establish dominance. They humiliate and demean others and take pleasure in the suffering they inflict. In private life, we condemn these kinds of sadistic and psychopathic actions as criminal. In war, sadistic violence is often obscured by patriotism that involves elevating one's own people above all others. Patriotism with religious triumphalism and its belief that one's religion and culture trumps all others gives sanction to the kind of sadism Sharon ushered into Sabra and Chatilla.

Fulfilling the military expectation that they behave as if they were uncaring sociopaths (the same expectation of American soldiers in Vietnam and later in Iraq), the Israeli soldiers sat in the trucks outside for two days, hearing the gunfire and screaming. Sharon ordered the Israeli soldiers to violate their own code of ethics, their doctrine, "Purity of Arms," which says that soldiers "will maintain their humanity even during combat" and are not to use their weapons "to harm human beings who are not combatants or prisoners of war." That would not be the last time Sharon's psychopathy would overrule the Israeli soldiers code of conduct to "act in a judicious and safe manner in all they do, out of recognition of the supreme value of human life."[15]

Israel is a militarized state. Military service is required of everyone when they reach the age of eighteen. Although both women and men are conscripted, Jewish men, especially Ashkenazi, the Jews who came to Israel from western and central Europe, are the "chosen" or elite of the military and therefore of the society. They form the top of the hierarchy of Israeli society to the extent that "whoever isn't a man, a fighter, a member of a fighting team, is simply worthless," according to Dr. Ruchama Marton, founder of Physicians for Human Rights. "There is a certain descending hierarchy. A man who doesn't serve in the army is worth less than a man who does," which of course leaves women at the bottom of the social order. Dr. Marton continues, "An Israeli Palestinian is worth less than that because he isn't allowed to be in the army at all."[16]

Extreme physical military training for combat is a mark of the Israeli soldier, his "chosenness" being a layer of his privilege, yielding him a better job or position and other marks of stature when he returns to civilian life. These are men who "must risk their lives and the lives of their children for the preservation of their faith and people," according to Israeli sociologist Meira Weiss.[17]

Their choseness effectively obscures the expendability of those Israeli soldiers lives. In war and massacres, they are no different than any other soldiers who are denied the protection of human rights that are supposed to be accorded to all human beings by the Universal Declaration of Human Rights. But their stature as military heroes, elevated even beyond the American worship of the "soldiers' sacrifice," hides the heinous acts they commit such as guarding Sabra and Chatilla to enforce the massacres Sharon had planned for which many soldiers would be haunted with post traumatic stress disorder.

In evacuating the PLO and engineering the Sabra and Chatilla massacre, Sharon made a new enemy in Lebanon—Hizbullah, the Party of God.* Hizbullah had been a nascent Shi'a organization somewhat linked religiously and militarily to Iran. But with Sharon's attack, it fought the IDF both with the force of self-determination and the masculinity that feeds almost every resistance when men are humiliated, their families violated, their homes destroyed, their people massacred. Israel then occupied Lebanon with U.S. military installations backing it there.

Hizbullah was determined to rid Lebanon of both of its occupiers—the Israel Defense Forces and the U.S. military. As Hizbullah could not match the U.S. backed Israeli military might, it turned to sacrificing its own, the ultimate in male expendability. Hizbullah re-

---

* I use the Lebanese/Shi'a spelling of Hizbullah instead of the Westernized Hezbollah.

peatedly targeted IDF forces and in 1983 attacked the U.S. Embassy in Beirut, which it followed with simultaneous truck bombings killing 241 U.S. marines and 58 French paratroopers. A year later, it again attacked the U.S. Embassy, which brought about U.S. withdrawal from Lebanon as its occupier.

Still Israel remained in Lebanon as their occupier. Hizbullah carried out twelve martyr missions or suicide bombings against the Israel military that were focused on military installations and movements while it shelled northern villages in Israel.[18] Its last martyr mission in December 1999 brought about Israel's withdrawal from Lebanon five months later.

As with every resistance force, Hizbullah had neither the manpower nor the armament to force the Israeli military out of Lebanon. Neither did the weak Lebanese military. But Hizbullah had the will of resistance and the fervor of religious fundamentalism. That is how it could take martyrdom where no other group had yet gone—to martyrdom missions, or suicide bombings.

In Islam, martyrdom comes from *jihad* which refers to one who "sees the truth physically and thus stands by it firmly, so much so that not only does he testify it verbally, but he is prepared to struggle and fight and give up his life for the truth," and thus becomes a martyr.[19] But Islam, as articulated in the *Qur'an*, forbids suicide. Allah says "And do not kill yourselves. Surely, Allah is Most Merciful to you," found in Surah An-Nisa Verse 29. In another verse of the *Qur'an*, Surah Al-Baqarah Verse 195, Allah says: "And do not throw thyselves in harm's way." *Jihad* is both struggle on behalf of Islam and surrender of one's conscience to God.[20]

Walking through the streets of Beirut, you find images of Lebanon's martyrs are everywhere—huge photographs mostly of men hang from almost every streetlight in the Dahiya, images of assassinated political leaders cover the sides of multistoried buildings, streets murals commemorate martyrdom, as do large banners with images of different martyrs on street posts.

Martyrs are those who have lost their lives in war; men who fight for Hizbullah and Lebanon, war victims of the many different sects or confessions that give Lebanon its diversity, and some women who having been condemned by their families for their "sins" are promised

atonement for sacrificing their lives.[21] Martyrs range from the assassinated to those who fall under stray bullets to those who sacrifice
their own lives. There is no equivalent in the United States, whose
country, city, village, neighborhood are not made into ongoing war
zones. Inhabiting the world where bombs are dropped, everyone is in
line for martyrdom.

In the Arab world, martyrs are the memory of humans sacrificed
and who sacrifice themselves in conflict and war. In the face of martyrdom in the Middle East, the West confuses resistance with terrorism
and self-defense with aggression. Ignoring the vast array of martyrs
and cultural sensitivity to the toll of wars which produce martyrdom
in the Middle East, Westerners' and particularly Americans' fears of
terrorism short-circuits their possibility for empathy for victims of
war.

Lebanese Professor Ibrahim el-Hussari through his study of the
Gulen educational movement in Turkey reveals how "Islam is a universal faith carrying a strong global message of peace and tolerance
in a world plagued by war."[22] Human rights has been a central tenent
of Islam for centuries before Europeans and Americans celebrated an
enlightened view of humankind. Gulen according to Hussari, developed an educational program to return to original Islam that teaches
how human rights are articulated in the *Qur'an*: "Islam approaches
human rights from the stance of the basic principles of freedom of
faith, life, reproduction, mental health, and personal property—all to
be preserved and observed even by the force of Islamic law."[23]

Hussari points to the "Islamic principle of universal mercy," and
shows how Gulen taught that "tolerance and dialogue ... are to be observed by true Muslims as prescribe by the *Qur'an*." That is why the
social welfare of people is a central feature of both Hizbullah in Lebanon and Hamas in Gaza. Hizbullah, according to American cultural
anthropologist Laura Deeb, "provides monthly support and supple-
mental nutritional, educational, housing and health assistance for
the poor; others focus on supporting orphans; still others are devoted
to reconstruction of war-damaged areas." In addition, Hizbullah provides schools and hospitals run mostly by women volunteers, these
programs serve local people, not a religious sect.[24] Hizbullah relies on
"individual donations, orphan sponsorships and religious taxes" paid

by Shiites as an annual tithe on their income while "much of this financial support comes from Lebanese Shiites living abroad."[25]

Hizbullah exploited the meaning of martyrdom in the Arab world. To force the withdrawal of both the United States and Israel from Lebanon, it took the growing Islamic *jihad* promoted by Iran and Al Qaeda to new lows in human desperation and depravity by turning human beings into bombs to kill Israelis and Americans. Suicide. Martyrdom. Self-inflicted martyrdom fully trumps the value of human life and defies the human urge to save and protect human beings whose lives are at risk. Hizbullah recruited boys and men to use their own bodies to blow up the invaders and occupiers. And the world asked, "How could this be?" as if martyrdom or suicide bombing were not predictable outcomes of that war that combines the seething lethal combination of blinding macho, men's humiliation and people's violation under occupation, and religious fundamentalism.

Most research on male suicide bombers comes to the same conclusion—that they are not from poverty, nor are they driven by depression or loneliness, they are mostly educated, between the ages of seventeen and twenty-eight, the same age group U.S. military recruiters focus on, the age when the male-as-protector role can be activated, the age by which young males have internalized their expendability.[26] Why do they choose to kill themselves and take as many of their enemies and its innocent civilians with them? That may be the wrong question.

Focusing on the martyr or suicide bomber obscures the reality that in every war military leaders plan for deaths of their own soldiers. Likewise "collateral damage" and "innocent lives" have become commonplace terms for expected civilian casualties in the wars of major powers. They count on soldiers being killed and that makes anyone else's death inconsequential.

In a meeting in Ho Chi Minh City in 1991 with General Giap, the mastermind of the Tet offensive against the U.S. military that was the turning point of the U.S. war in Vietnam, I saw how that calculation of death of one's own soldiers worked. Giap recalled, "we were determined to rid Vietnam of U.S. control. But we knew that we could not defeat the United States which had more guns, more planes and bombs, more tanks than we did." Giap's plan was to attack all military installations and civilian command posts in South Vietnam simultaneously and to catch the U.S. military by surprise by doing it on January 31, 1968, the first day of Tet that year.

Tet, a national celebration of the lunar new year, is the most important holiday in Vietnam, a time when everyone returns to their families and long celebrations take place. Americans, Giap reasoned, would think Vietnamese soldiers had gone back home. He planned a highly coordinated, countrywide offensive with more than 80,000 of his troops striking more than 100 towns and cities and the national capital. From January through August 1968 the Tet offensive cost the Vietnamese more than 75,000 dead and wounded.[27] "We knew we would suffer high casualties," General Giap told us.

As I sat listening to General Giap, I realized in a way that I had never thought of before that in planning the Tet offensive, he had already calculated and included in his plans the deaths of thousands of his own Vietnamese soldiers. Not unlike that, the 150,000 American soldiers preparing to invade Iraq had been told that one in three of them would die in the invasion. Like Giap in Vietnam, U.S. military generals planned for the death of 50,000 U.S. soldiers that day. That is what generals of every military do.

Marine officer Tyler Boudreau points out that to send your men down the road means to know that some will be killed and that you have to love your mission more than your men to do that.[28] Driven into the masculinity of war, resistance forces use human lives to make up for the lack of planes, bombs, and guns of their powerful enemies. Soldiers in combat know that they are facing death every day. It is their sacrifice, the measure of their manhood. Martyr missions or suicide bombings are the next step in war's depraved devaluation of human life.

Is this not really the same soldier's sacrifice that Americans demand of their men, that politicians laud in their soldiers? I suggest that only a short step, a hair-line fracture separates using your own life to take the lives of others and becoming a combat soldier in any military. That short step is between going into war knowing you likely will be killed and submitting yourself to a martyr mission knowing you will be killed.

Further, it is only a short step between being a mother of a martyr and a mother of a soldier sacrificed in war—in both cases your son or daughter is dead in combat, in both cases you are expected to honor their sacrifice, to accept their loss as patriotic or religious fulfillment and to support ongoing war so that your son will not have died in vain. When I watch the Americans vigorously waving their huge flags on the street corners opposite the Women in Black who are mourning deaths from war, I think of Americans who have lost sons and daughters in war and are proud of them for their sacrifice, and who believe the war must go on so that their son or daughter would not have died in vain. And when I heard Laura Bush while she was still first lady, on the eve of a trip to the Middle East, describe Palestinian mothers of suicide bombers as "uncivilized," I wondered how different are they really from those American mothers who proudly send their sons and daughter off to war.

Palestinian scholar and feminist activist, Nadera Shalhoub-Kevorkian studied "the trauma of losing a child in the context of the Palestinian-Israeli political struggle ... by focusing on the voices of mothers of martyrs." Shalhoub-Kevorkian helped mothers express and share their grief and trauma from losing a son. "Mothers not only felt the deep pain of the social/collective glorification of their son's acts while having to deny their personal agony, they also complained of being deprived of the chance of 'properly' saying goodbye to him."

Shalhoub-Kevorkian's work with mothers shows how "a woman's 'private' son became a nation's martyr." These mothers "not only lost their children/beloved ones during a bloody conflict. They were expected to react to the sudden death of their children with great pride, accepting the death as an act of God and for God, for it is the child's fate and destiny."[29]

One woman was not allowed to attend the funeral for her son: "My husband gave an order not to let me in. He did not want to be embarrassed by my reactions, and I failed to see him ... It has torn me apart. I was forbidden to kiss him and to cry, for the Sheik told me that my tears could bring him pain, and would make him impure."[30] She had gone from being some young boy's mother to a publicly recognized "mother of a martyr" which in Islamic fundamentalism elevates her to a higher status.

Mothers are not allowed to grieve or experience their feelings of loss. Forcing them to go against the human life force that seeks to protect and save human beings, they are required to embrace violent death. One Palestinian mother explained the reasoning of religion by saying, "Martyrdom is not death, it is an extraordinary death with a divine status, we should thank God for what he gave us, and refrain from crying or feeling sad."[31]

In Lebanon, when one woman was congratulated by a taxi driver on her son's martyrdom, she responded, "You congratulate me but it was a great loss. Nothing will compensate for my loss." But she is not allowed to express her pain. He corrected her saying, "You should be happy. You are the mother of a martyr. Your martyred son is in paradise."[32]

To encourage acceptance of their sons' martyrdom, families are granted a high status attributed to martyrs whose images and photographs adorn their neighborhoods. The secretary general of Hizbullah, Sayyid Hassan Nasrallah, who lost one of his own sons, Hadi, fighting in the Intifada, visits families of martyrs to convey to them their special status and recognition. Fatima el Issawi relates a story of one of Nasrallah's visits to "a family from Al Ashmar clan following the martyrdom of the second son of the family. As he walked into the house, he told the martyr's father, 'You have a higher rank than me. You carry two stars while I have only one,' in reference to the loss of his son while the other father had lost two sons."[33]

If we engage empathetically with mothers of martyrs, it should go without saying that mothers do not wish their children to be strapped with bombs and turned into human explosives. And indeed, Nadera Shalhoub-Kevorkian found in her work that "mothers stated that they did all that they could to prevent the death of their children." They kept them away from confrontations, used punishment to stop them, stopped letting them play in the yard in desperate attempts to protect them.

Like those Americans who want war to continue so that their sons will not have died in vain, martyrdom must be honored with the sacrifice of more lives. In the Arabic international daily paper *Asharq Alawsat*, Lebanese scholar Izzat Shararah Baydoun explains how a son's martrydom redefines the family. "The martyrdom becomes central to its affairs. It is a requirement that to honor the martyr, the war must continue. Peace is like betrayal to the martyr." The family will adopt, if they had not already, the politics of those who sent their son to martyrdom.[34]

Ariel Sharon and the IDF unleashed Hizbullah in Lebanon. Because of the Sabra and Chatilla massacres, Israel forbade Sharon from ever holding the post of defense minister again. But the United States, in its deadly alliance with Israel, blocked efforts to bring him before an international tribunal for crimes against humanity. Decades later Belgium began new criminal proceedings against Sharon, but Donald Rumsfeld in the Bush administration threatened to withdraw NATO (North Atlantic Treaty Organization) offices from Belgium. The trial was brought to an abrupt halt. Then, in 2001, just after the first inauguration of George W. Bush, Sharon was voted into office as prime minister of Israel, and Bush heralded him as a "man of peace," while providing to Israel the largest ever U.S. military aid.[35]

Leading up to his election as prime minister just four months after Israel withdrew from Lebanon in 2000, Ariel Sharon, as if ready to provoke another fight, insisted on visiting the Temple Mount Haram al-Sharif compound in Jerusalem's old city, a place holy to both Muslims and Jews. Only ten days before, the Palestinians had observed their annual memorial day for the Sabra and Chatilla massacre.[36] Sharon's visit to the Aqsa Mosque in September 2000 set off the Second Intifada.

Sharon evidently was making his bid to become prime minister of Israel. His visit to the mosque effectively demolished the Oslo peace accords in which Israel agreed to end its occupation of Palestine. Special elections were held in Israel five months after Sharon's visit to Temple Mount, and the man who had been forbidden to ever hold the post of defense minister in Israel again for his role in the Sabra and Chatilla massacres was elected prime minister of Israel in 2001. Three weeks earlier, George W. Bush had been inaugurated President of the United States and some months later Osama bin Laden launched the most powerful suicide bombing ever against the United States.

Meanwhile, by the year 2000, having succeeded in ridding Lebanon of both the United States and Israel, resistance was no longer Hizbullah's priority, nor Lebanon's necessity. Lebanese scholar Joseph Alagha, in his 2006 study, *The Shifts in Hizbullah's Ideology*, shows how Hizbullah changed its strategy to focus on participating in Lebanon's democratic government. With the 2005 Lebanese elections, Hizbullah had become a legitimate part of the Lebanese government winning 14 seats in the 128 member Lebanese Parliament and 58 seats by 2009, just short of the majority it had hoped to get.

Yet, the United States followed Israel in putting Hizbullah on its list of terrorists. Both states refused to recognize the change in Hizbullah's direction. Ongoing war that involves making and keeping enemies makes its own urgent case for global demilitarization.

Colluding in Preparatory War, Lebanon 2006

T hree years into the U.S. war in Iraq, on July 12, 2006, Israel invaded Lebanon, bombing all of the bridges and all electrical power stations that day. People fled; Israeli planes bombed anything moving on the ground. The bombing killed entire families in their homes and their cars. "Scores lay buried beneath the rubble of their houses for weeks, as the Red Cross and other rescue workers were prevented from accessing the areas by continuing Israeli strikes," according to Amnesty International.[1] The infrastructure that supports not only the country but the daily life of Lebanon's people was destroyed to the extent that by late 2009, with extensive rebuilding, most of Lebanon still had only eight hours of electricity a day.

The official Israeli reason for the 2006 war against Lebanon was that Hizbullah had "kidnapped" two Israel soldiers in a border raid. If we were to accept that as valid, we would have to believe that the capture of two Israeli soldiers at the border placed the state of Israel in imminent risk of war from Lebanon, an absurd assumption considering that boarder raids have been ongoing and provoked both by the Israel Defense Forces and Hizbullah in Lebanon for over two decades.[2] Israeli linguist and Professor Tanya Reinhart pointed out that Israel could have handled this border dispute as it did others, "with at most a local retaliation, or a prisoner exchange or, even better, with an attempt to solve this border dispute once and for all. Instead, Israel opted for a global war."[3]

According to Israeli political scientist Gerald Steinberg, "Of all of Israel's wars since 1948, this was the one for which Israel was most prepared." Speaking in mid-July 2006, during the war, he pointed out that "the military campaign that we're seeing now had already been blocked out and, in the last year or two, it's been simulated and rehearsed across the board."[4] Not missing a beat in the cycle of ongoing war, in 2000 Israel shifted from its occupation of Lebanon to planning a war against that country, paying no attention to the shift at that time in Hizbullah, due to Israel's withdrawal, from a warring militia to participation in the democratic government of Lebanon.

Israeli sociologist, Baruch Kimmerling, in his book *Politicide,* points to other preplanned IDF attacks on the Occupied Palestinians Territories. They were not unlike George Bush's preplanning of the U.S. war against Iraq from fall 2001 to March 2003 during which time Iraq posed no imminent danger to the United States. In the same way that Bush had preplanned the U.S. war against Iraq, in the spring of 2006 Prime Minister Ariel Sharon made operational plans to attack Lebanon the next time Hizbullah instigated a border attack.[5]

Months before the invasion of Lebanon, Sharon slipped into a coma and was in a persistent vegetative state. But his plans for war against Lebanon were in place. When Hizbullah captured two Israeli soldiers in early July 2006, Ehud Olmert who succeeded Sharon as prime minister of Israel picked up the mantle of his psychopathic leadership and put Sharon's plan into action. He proudly asserted to the Israeli commission investigating the war that he "behaved as Sharon would have."[6] When the first bombs dropped on Lebanon, one Israeli official said they would bomb Lebanon back twenty years. Others said that Israel would bomb Lebanon back to the Stone Age. For capturing two Israeli soldiers? Or because Hizbullah had forced Israel to withdraw its occupation in 2000? These questions do not even make sense. Why then?

Daniel Reisner, the former legal counsel to the Israeli military, the Israel Defense Forces, points out that Israel's objective is to change international law: "What is being done today is a revision of international law. And if you do something long enough, the world will accept it...That which is forbidden today can become permissible, if enough states do it."[7] And the state that matters because it has the most powerful military in the world has done it: in Vietnam in 1965, in Iraq, 2003, in Afghanistan in 2001, and Pakistan in 2009, and will do it against its next target. Will that be Iran?

Repeatedly committing war crimes normalizes them. As if to ridicule international law, Israeli policymakers treat humanitarian law as informal or customary law, the kind that develops and changes with local customs and cultural practices in simpler societies that usually do not have written legal codes. Reading humanitarian law as customary law effectively limits the universality of human rights, making rights culturally or nationally specific and therefore easily withheld from those who are not of your nation or ethnicity.

Hizbullah's reason for capturing the Israeli soldiers at the border was that it planned to use them to negotiate a prisoner exchange with Israel. It had not expected war in response, and during the 2006 invasion its leaders acknowledged that Hizbullah would not have captured the soldiers had they realized the extent to which Israel would retaliate. At the same time, in capturing those armed soldiers, Hizbullah recklessly endangered the Lebanese people, especially its Shiite Muslims. In the middle of that 2006 war, Professor Mona Fayad, a psychologist at the Lebanese University in Beirut, herself a Shiite, courageously contested Hizbullah's actions:

> To be a Shiite means that you do not question the meaning of resistance and pride, is it the fleeing from bombing and their stacking up on the tile floors of schools and their dust ? ...
>
> To be Shiite is to accept that your country be destroyed in front of your very eyes—with no surprise—and that it comes tumbling down on your head and that your family be displaced and dispersed and becomes "a refugee" at the four corners of the nation and the world, and that you accept standing up to the enemy with no complaints as long as there is a fighter out there with a rocket that he can launch at northern Israel and maybe even at its south without asking about the "why"? or about the timing? Or about the usefulness of the end result? ...
>
> To be a Shiite is to keep silent and not to ask what is the purpose of liberating a country. Is it to destroy it all over again and to make

it possible for it to be occupied once more? And not to ask about the leadership role: is it to preserve its military power and its men flush with arms without any care or concern for the normal human being?[8]

Who were these Hizbullah fighters? Terrorists to the United States and Israel. Resistance forces to the Lebanese and Palestinians. Journalist Nir Rosen had the opportunity to meet some of them when he attended a memorial service in a village near the Israeli border for the Hizbullah's soldiers there who were killed in the war. They were "men who between 18 and 25 years old and had never fought before." Of the 100 Hizbullah soldiers who fought in that village, sixty of them were local:

> The nine local martyrs who died in the 33 days of war were typi-cal of Hizballah's soldiers. They were a high school history teacher, a high school principal, a sweets shop owner, two high school graduates about to start university for engineering, a university student home on summer break. They were restaurant waiters, farmers, car mechanics, bakers. They had completed Hizballah's boot camp and training and returned to their normal lives, occasionally going for refresher courses, much like the U.S. Army reserves or National Guard.[9]

The White House denied that there was any connection between the United States and the Israeli war against Lebanon. Yet George W. Bush urgently sent a new shipment of satellite and laser-guided, smart bombs to Israel in the middle of July 2006.[10] He and U.S. Sec-retary of State Condoleezza Rice framed Sharon's war as an "opportu-nity." In her many visits to the Middle East, Rice intensified people's anger by repeatedly equating that war with bringing new life into the world: "This is the pain of labor. We are witnessing the birth of the new Middle East." She was commenting on the mass murder of civil-ians in southern Lebanon.[11]

In effect, George W. Bush was waging war against Lebanon through Israel while warring against Iraq, occupying Afghanistan, threatening war against North Korea, and planning a war against Iran. Business cannot get much better than it was for the military industries—the top six of which in 2006 posted these gross sales:

1. Lockheed Martin Corporation $74,308,716,610

2. Northrop Grumman Corporation $40,935,104,783

3. Boeing Company, The $34,015,348,659

4. Raytheon Company, The $27,973,206,383

5. General Dynamics $25,594,082,923

6. McDonnell Douglas (a subsidiary of Boeing) $22,495,637,931[12]

Of the U.S. military aid to Israel, 75 percent of it must be returned back to those same military industries as Israel is required to spend it on purchasing U.S. military armament and services.[13] Those and other military industries are the corporate arm of the U.S. military and the Department of Defense. War and its perpetual need for replenishing weapons, whether initiated by the United States or Israel, is profit making for those private companies. In the business of making arms and providing services to the militaries, their lobbying in Congress along with the military's strategies for making enemies join effectively to perpetuate war. They dictate more than they respond to U.S. government policy.

The Israeli war against Lebanon started with revenge. That first day of the Israeli invasion of Lebanon, on July 12, 2006, the Israel Defense Forces began bombing the southern Lebanon village of Zibqine at 7:00 in the morning. Its first target was the family home of Bezih, one of the Hizbullah fighters who had captured the IDF soldiers. That revenge attack killed twelve of Bezih's family—parents, brothers and sisters, other relatives. Their entire house was reduced to rubble.

Revenge killings are intentional and premeditated. Israeli soldiers from project "Breaking the Silence" have conducted over 300 interviews with Israeli soldiers and have documented the IDF strategy of "revenge attacks" as "a matter of policy that comes directly from the government." They site the example of the prime minister directly ordering an attack on a Palestinian village that had nothing to do with a shooting of an IDF soldier elsewhere in Palestine. The soldiers were told "This is revenge, we are going to revenge the blood of our own."[14]

While all of Lebanon was under attack, Israel focused its invasion on predominately Shiite Muslim communities, neighborhoods and villages. Other Lebanese—Christians, Druze, and people from the ten sects that make up the fabric of Lebanon—responded from that impulse to protect human beings when their lives are threatened, by opening schools, churches, and their individual homes in Beirut to those trying to escape. In the hardest hit areas, Hizbullah provided humanitarian aid to help organize the exodus of almost a million mostly Shiite Muslim refugees, or roughly one-quarter of the population of the country. Although the Lebanese government tried to help, it was inefficient and claimed it lacked the resources.[15]

Some weeks after the 2006 war, I found a tired familiarity with Israeli wars among the Lebanese. I realized that the question had been not whether Israel would attack Lebanon but whether this attack would be as bad as the 1982 Israeli war and whether Lebanon would again be occupied by Israel. When I went through south Beirut, in the Dahiya I saw Lebanese and Hizbullah construction crews rebuilding everywhere. Little rubble remained and I saw few signs of the bombings.

"There" I was told to look. "There" is where the buildings were. But I saw only empty space. And again, "there!" I was told that several high-rise buildings had been there. I had my camera ready but I saw no ruins. Nothing. Maybe the rubble had already been cleared away, I thought. No.

Those bombs, smart as they are, when they were dropped on densely packed, multistoried apartment buildings in Beirut, hit the top of the buildings, descended fifteen or twenty floors into the basement, into and through the bomb shelters below ground to implode the buildings so that each one violently collapses inward on itself. The implosion (not outward explosion) reduced everything—walls, toys, steel girders, furniture, clothing, refrigerators, and any human beings inside—to grey powder, which descended into a lump of dust within the rectangle that had been the foundation of the building.

Later that day, when looking at aerial photographs taken after the bombing in this predominately Shiite and very poor community, my guide pointed, "There, there, and there, . . . one, two, three, . . . eleven, twelve . . ." As these images of the bombings filtered through my consciousness, they dispelled any vestiges of the fiction that in combat militaries do not intentionally kill civilians or that civilian deaths are merely unavoidable collateral damage. On July 30, 2006, when Israel bombed a three-story building in the village of Qana killing twenty-six civilians who had taken refuge there from surrounding bomb attacks, Israel's excuse was that Hizbullah had taken shelter there and that the IDF had warned civilians of Qana to leave. Kenneth Roth, Executive Director of Human Rights Watch, pointed to the inhumanity of this reasoning, "Through its arguments, the Israeli military is suggesting that Palestinian militant groups might 'warn' all settlers to leave Israeli settlements and then be justified in targeting those who remained."[16]

How did Israel decide on which buildings to bomb? If it was trying to rout Hizbullah, which ones were Hizbullah fighters in? One in this building? Three in that one? Likely none. Hizbullah fighters do not make themselves publicly known. Israel really does not know and cannot count or specifically locate those resistance fighters so it bombs all of the buildings, kills everyone left inside just in case. Or perhaps Israel does this just because it can, just because the United States is its supplier of unlimited bombs and bullets.

For public relations, as with the bombing in Qana, Israel claimed that the people had been warned ahead of time. On the ground in Lebanon, I asked almost everyone I met about those Israeli warnings until I realized that people were looking at me incredulously as if I had been duped. I realized that it was not flyers but the 1982 Israeli war against Lebanon that took 20,000 lives with bombings at the same location in Qana and the ten storied buildings in Beirut that caused the massive exodus of Lebanese when the 2006 invasion began.

Finally, my vision cleared, and I saw the rectangular frames of what had been a dozen high-rise apartment buildings, the cramped living spaces of this mostly Shiite Muslim population in south Beirut. There in the photos, I saw mounds of grey dust filling in the rectangular foundations that had supported the apartment buildings, the same dust that filled the air to the extent that while I was in Lebanon the seashore was never distinctly visible, the same dust to which Lebanese were attributing the tremendous increase in hospitalization from severe respiratory flu.

Lebanese writer, singer/composer, poet, and Professor Emerita, Evelyne Accad has known repeated wars in her homeland. She voiced the desperation that issues from such destruction:

How to speak of you, Lebanon? How not to speak of you?

How to express the unbearable suffering when faced with destruction repeated a thousand times, more violent and more cruel each time? With more capacity for total extermination of humankind each time, the earth crying out its strangulation through suffocating pollution?

How to express our earth bleeding from all its wounds?

How to find words to describe the carnage repeated *ad nauseam*, bodies buried under buildings smashed with fragmentation bombs, phosphorus bombs, depleted uranium bombs, all made in the USA, stones reduced to ashes, sea reduced to a pool of fuel and tar, fish and birds dying with children desperately clinging to their mothers till their last breath.

How can one explain the land taken hostage by men filled with bitterness, thirsty for vengeance, leaving no space for dialogue, no room for negotiation, no prospect for productive exchange with the Other, the different? How to express the struggle between the desire to respond to violence with violence and the deep conviction that such violence will only lead to more revengeful violence until total extermination of humankind?

How to speak of the tearing apart of a beloved country attacked, destroyed, asphyxiated? How to convey the feeling of powerlessness and anger while realizing that the forces of death and destruction had planned this scenario months, perhaps years before, this long procession of deaths and irreparable physical and mental destruction?

I mourn the utter waste of all these lives, amputated, torn apart, killed, sacrificed, but for whom, for what, all these broken lives of a million Lebanese, displaced and fleeing on the roads ...[17]

The cowardice of *core masculinity* and blinding macho writ large by the state—killing 1,200 human beings, 30 percent children under the age of thirteen—for what? By Israel's own admission, it was to demonstrate Israel's strength to its Arab neighbors and to Iran. The war against Lebanon was not about Lebanon at all. In order to clear the way for another war, one against Iran, it was a *preparatory war*.

I define *"preparatory war"* as invasion by one country that bombs and kills human beings, destroys homes and the other country's infrastructure and reduces millions of human beings to homeless refugees not because their counrty has threatened imminent attack, but to prepare for another war against yet another country, in this case

Iran. Ephraim Sneh deputy defense minister told Trita Parsi author of *Treacherous Alliance* halfway through the war, "Lebanon is just a prelude to the greater war with Iran."[18] Journalist Seymour Hirsch reported that "the White House was more focused on stripping Hizbullah of its missiles, because, if there was to be a military option against Iran's nuclear facilities, it had to get rid of the weapons that Hizbullah could use in a potential retaliation at Israel."[19] The United States in collusion with Israel, made *preparatory war* to eliminate Hizbullah in order to attack its ally, Iran.

As war crimes go, you cannot get much more removed from the United Nations charter which requires that war be engaged only for self-defense from an imminent attack than to make a *preparatory war* against a state in order to pave the way for invading another state. Undermining the United Nations charter that was put in place after and because of the Holocaust, opens the way for powerful states and leaders to make any war against any people it chooses.

In defending its actions which otherwise would be considered war crimes, Israel, like the United States, uses the language of preemptive war which has gained acceptance. The former legal counsel to the Israel Defense Forces, Daniel Reisner, explains that "we invented the doctrine of the preemptive pinpoint strike, we had to promote it, and in the beginning there were protrusions which made it difficult to fit it easily into the mold of legality. Eight years later, it is in the middle of the realm of legitimacy."[20]

Israeli rehearsals of air attacks on Iran, backed by Israel's own stockpile of nuclear weapons and combined with repeated "or else" threats from American leaders, in fact, could be construed by Iran as imminent threat of war. That provocation could be just the excuse that the tyrannical leadership in Iran is looking for to develop and deploy nuclear weapons. The United States would defend Israel, and as Hillary Clinton indicated in her presidential campaign, she would "obliterate Iran." The whole world would be subjected to a nuclear catastrophe. Still, the world remained silent while Israel escalated tensions and continued its provocative rehearsals of air attacks on Iran.

Lebanon took its demand for a ceasefire to the UN Security Council where in accordance with helping Israel prepare for a war against Iran by warring against Lebanon, John Bolton, the belligerent U.S.

Ambassador to the United Nations, used the one U.S. vote to veto every cease-fire resolution that Lebanon had introduced. U.S. intransigence seemed like blind loyalty to Israel, but it was much more and worse than that. Bolton was stalling on a cease-fire resolution in the United Nations "in order to give Israel time to defeat Hizbullah."[21] That would give the United States and Israel the green light for their next war—against Iran. Prime Minister Ehud Olmert thanked George Bush for his support in quashing every cease-fire resolution. The United States increased its already hefty military aid to Israel to $30 billion over the following decade which would be funneled back into military industries to purchase more weapons.

Finally, when Israel found it could not defeat Hizbullah, it decided it had to withdraw. Only then did France and the United States draft cease-fire plans at the United Nations. Lebanon, reduced to the child of the authoritarian parent, the David to the U.S. Goliath, was not even consulted on the cease-fire resolution until Israel was satisfied with all of the provisions of Security Council Resolution 1701, which was signed August 11, 2006.

Reminiscent of Ariel Sharon's sadism in the 1982 war against Lebanon, Israel was not yet finished targeting Lebanese civilians. After signing the UN cease-fire, in the last days and into the last few hours and minutes, when Israel had already prepared to withdraw from Lebanon, it slammed southern Lebanon with millions of made-in-the-USA cluster bombs. From those bombs, hundreds of particles—bomblets—spread over vast areas where people live and farm, where children play. They remained unexploded on the ground to kill and maim Lebanese people.

By 2009, 250 more Lebanese, mostly children, had been killed by those cluster bomblets, and 900 people, again mostly children had been injured.[22] Under pressure from the United States who supplied the cluster bombs, Israel later provided Lebanon with a map of where cluster bombs were dropped. By 2009, 250,000 had been removed, leaving 2.75 million.

How can we understand this defiance of the universal value of human life other than as crimes against humanity? How much of their own humanity must they, those soldiers, have lost to carry out those orders? These are not merely postwar rhetorical questions. We cannot change the conditions of war as long as male expendability remains unchanged and produces those cold, remorseless sociopathic soldiers.

Under U.S. law, it is illegal for foreign military aid to be used in violation of U.S. law, which includes the treaties and conventions to which the United States is a party. At the end of the war against Lebanon, George W. Bush said he would look into the question of whether any U.S. law had been violated by the Israeli use of U.S. military aid. Previously, after the 1982 Israeli war against Lebanon when Israel used U.S. cluster bombs, President Reagan put a six-year ban on the sale of cluster bombs to Israel.[23] In January 2007, the State Department sent a report to Congress detailing Israel's violation of U.S. law. In collusion with Israel, Nancy Pelosi and Joe Biden decided to take no action against Israel's violation of U.S. law.[24]

Aside from the United States, most of the rest of the world was aghast at Israel's use of cluster bombs. In May 2008 one hundred nations agreed to *forever* abandon the use of cluster bombs, to destroy any arsenals they hold, and to require that the United States remove its arsenals of cluster bombs from their countries. The United States, Israel, Russia, China, and Pakistan were absent. Even without them, decommissioning weapons of war was underway.

Yet in large part because of the U.S. collusion with Israel's war against Lebanon, tensions remained high. After a month of war against Lebanon, when Israel was not close to succeeding in its objective to eliminate Hizbullah, support for Hizbullah in Lebanon had risen to 87 percent of the entire population,[25] eight percentage points higher than Americans support of Bush when he went to war against Iraq. The war game of making enemies had escalated once again.

Meanwhile Hizbullah turned to addressing the humanitarian needs of the Lebanese returning refugees many of whom found their homes and businesses destroyed. While I was still stinging from the sight of African Americans and poor whites wading through streets of waist high water with dead bodies floating by for days and days on end after Hurricane Katrina had hit New Orleans only a year before, I watched in astonishment as Hizbullah managed the return of Lebanese refugees to their homes with dignity and speed. I gulped with shame as I watched some Lebanese find unexploded mortars stamped "Made in the USA" in the ruins of where they had lived.

Victims of Katrina in New Orleans had faced only disregard from George W. Bush, and days passed with no relief, no emergency food and water shipped in, and it was almost a week before Bush activated the National Guard. While the U.S. and Israel were preoccupied with sustaining the image of Hizbullah as a terrorist organization, Hizbullah's humanitarian efforts far out-distanced those of the United States for its own people.

In the summer of 2006, Hizbullah workers, clipboards in hand, with fists full of money, organized the Lebanese return home, some to homes that soon would be rebuilt, others to shelters with money for emergencies until housing could be provided for them. One, two, three years after Katrina, George Bush's administration, preoccupied with warring against Iraq, had failed to provide housing to those who survived and were displaced. Charity has done more than the people's own government of the wealthiest country in the world to save human lives in New Orleans.

Hizbullah also retained its fighting force. In 2006, during the month-long war with Israel, Hizbullah retaliated by launching rockets that hit Israeli towns and killed civilians. Israel reported forty-three Israeli citizens and twelve soldiers were killed in the 2006 war by Hizbullah rockets inside Israel. During the course of the thirty-four-day conflict, thirty-three civilians suffered serious physical injuries, sixty-eight suffered moderate physical injuries. Between 300,000 and 500,000 Israelis were displaced.

According to Israeli Professor Tanya Reinhart, "The Israeli government knew right from the start that launching its offensive would expose the north of Israel to heavy Katyusha rockets attacks." She pointed out that "This was openly discussed at this government's first meeting on Wednesday: 'Hizbullah is likely to respond to the Israeli attacks with massive rocket launches at Israel, and in that case, the IDF [Israeli military] might move ground forces into Lebanon.' One cannot avoid the conclusion that, for the Israeli army and government, endangering the lives of residents of northern Israel was a price worth paying in order to justify the planned ground offensive."[26]

The 2006 war against Lebanon, a carefully disguised collusion between Israel and the United States, was a *preparatory war* that perpetuated destabilization of the Middle East. In turn, naming resistance forces like Hizbullah as terrorists deflected attention and resources from actual terrorist groups such as Al Qaeda. And when they are falsely labeled and then attacked, it is more difficult for Lebanese to challenge the regressive force of Hizbullah's fundamentalism.

"No One Understands!"

T he other side of Israel intentionally killing Lebanese civilians was that it intentionally provoked attack on its own people, the Jews of Israel. Why? According to Tanya Rienhart, Israel knew that once it invaded Lebanon Hizbullah would fire its rockets on Israeli villages. Was Israel relying on Hizbullah rocket attacks eliciting deep-seated fear in Israelis?

I am invoking the politics of empathy here to explore what those fears might be with the awareness that any group of people under attack and taking recourse in their own group for safety will resist others' interpretations of their experiences. When I first became conscious of the oppression of women, I strongly resisted generic terms like "human beings" or "people" that could obscure women's subordination in the universality of language once again. But I also came to realize that we cannot extend or receive empathy from others outside our group unless we can find larger ground for our common humanity. In thinking about Israeli fears that come from being under attack, I assume that those fears would be stronger and deeper than the fear Bush manipulated Americans to feel after the 2001 attack, as it would ignite in many Jews traumatic memories of the Holocaust that have been passed down through generations. That genocide of 6 million Jews left a collective trauma with "indelible marks on group consciousness, marking their memories forever and changing their future identity in irrevocable ways."[1] That awareness forces the question: "Is that fear what the Israeli government relies on to maintain support for its ongoing wars?"

Human Rights Watch condemned Hizbullah's rocket attacks into northern Israel and noted that the rockets were old and without guidance systems. Israel, it appears, was drawing fire from Hizbullah to some of its northern villages. Journalist Jonathan Cook was told by a member of the Israeli Knesset that, "I saw Israeli tanks shelling Lebanon from the two [Israeli] towns of Arab al-Aramisha and Tarshiha."[2] Hizbullah would try to aim its rockets at the source of Israeli fire.

Numerous Israeli and American organizations like Jewish Voice for Peace in the United States have been deeply critical of Israel' occupation of Palestinians. In Israel, significant discontent is voiced by Israelis who are sustaining long and courageous campaigns against their government for its attacks on Palestine and for its wars against Lebanon. Among the groups are Jeff Halper's Israeli Committee Against House Demolition; Shministim, the high school seniors who are refusing their state's mandatory military conscription and serving jail time; Physicians for Human Rights; Israeli soldiers in Breaking the Silence and the determined Israeli feminist antiwar movement, New Profile, which is "prioritizing life and the protection of life. It condones painful compromises in the interests of preserving life."[3] Its members counsel war resisters, support victimized Palestinians, and expose Israel's crimes against Palestinians.

Still, especially in the United States, any criticism of the Israeli state is equated with anti-Semitism against Jewish people anywhere. In the silence that results from that censorship, the continual occupation, humiliation of, and Israeli attacks on Palestinians go by mostly unnoticed. To get underneath those silencing allegations of anti-Semitism that block criticism of the state of Israel, I began by first analyzing the war strategies of the state of which I am a citizen, the United States. Identifying U.S. war crimes is more than just criticism of the state. It establishes a moral baseline using the United Nations charter and Declaration of Human Rights for confronting that state's war crimes. For me that moral baseline cannot be different from that which I use to analyze and criticize any other state's involvement in committing war crimes.

When I turn to the politics of empathy, I realize that I need to understand how genocide, ethnic cleansing, wars and occupations construct a people subjected to them to the extent that may lead many to absolve their state from wrong-doing. Writer Jean Améry, a Jew and Holocaust death camp survivor and a member of the Belgian resistance, was most eloquent in his exploration of personal identity and the ethnic identity imposed on a people by crimes against their humanity. Because Améry grew up without either ethnic or religious identity, and because he shared neither cultural heritage nor religious ties with Jews, he pinpointed with astute clarity how the Nazi state constructed Jewish identity.

In 1935 Améry studied the Nuremberg Laws, the anti-Semetic laws introduced by the Nazi Party which deprived Jews of citizenship in Germany and forbid them to marry Germans. "After I had read the Nuremberg Laws I was no more Jewish than a half hour before," he said, but simultaneously that was the moment when he knew himself as a Jew.

He observed that it is the state that grants both citizenship and dignity to human beings and that to be a human being one must be located in a state. He recognized in the Nazi withdrawal of German citizenship from Jews that "the denial of human dignity sounded the death threat."[4] Death became life for Jews. In Auschwitz, where the inmates sole fate was death, he realized "we were not afraid of death," and no one talked about it. But "dying was omnipresent." And the prisoners had nowhere to turn. Thus "I became a person not by subjectively appealing to my abstract humanity but by discovering myself within the given social reality as a rebelling Jew and by realizing myself as one."[5] That identity was framed in the awareness that one had only their own people to turn to which was not enough to prevent the extermination of 6 million Jews.

One of the long-term consequences of persecution of any people is their isolation. Turning within their own communities for protection, they necessarily close ranks against the outside world. In those conditions of isolation imposed by persecution, it is not unlikely that those people will conclude that their suffering is the worst suffering ever experienced by anyone. In being assigned the Nazi identity of a Jew, Améry, when he looked to the future, recognized that the mass extermination of Jews "cannot be ruled out as a possibility." When the states control people's destinies, it is neither the characteristics of those people, such as those associated with Jews nor their religious beliefs that cause their oppression, only society and the state can do that.[6] Protection then could come only from having a Jewish state which was fortified by internal cohesion and the recognition that outside themselves "no one can understand!"

Self-protection through a state has its own dangers. It can, as it has in the case of Israel, insulate itself from justice for crimes the state commits against others. That insulation is held in place by silencing criticism of the state for those crimes with charges of anti-Semitism. We have seen the result as the world looked away when the newfound state of Israel adopted the policy of ethnic cleansing of Arabs in Palestine.

The conviction that "no one can understand" because almost no one did when genocide ruled the day for European Jews, led to the belief that the Holocaust was the worst violation of humanity ever. The problem is, of course, that as soon as there is agreement that the suffering and victimization of any one people is the worst ever, the violation of any other people becomes less significant. The Holocaust reminded Jews that when their people were violated the world stood by watching without intervention. Enforced isolation left them with only themselves to rely on.

In a conversation with an African American friend, the subject of the Holocaust came up and I mentioned the reactions I had received for my criticism of Israel's 2006 war against Lebanon. He took recourse in his racial identity against the implication that his people had not suffered as much as another people, asserting that never in history has there been anything worse than black slavery. Although at that point we had been friends for over ten years, that was the first time he spoke this way about slavery. It came from his reaction to a sensed diminished significance of his people's oppression in relation to that of another people. Both his reaction and that of my Jewish-American friends reminded me of my first trip to Ireland.

On that trip the taxi driver on the way in from the airport to Dublin asked me if I had any "connections" in Ireland. No, I told him, at that time, I knew no one there. But I did not yet truly understand the Irish meaning of "connections"—that ancestry from the diaspora, connection to the land, the people, the culture that had been flung throughout the world as the Irish escaped impoverishment and brutality under British occupation. When I figured out what he was asking me, I gave him my name as evidence of my Irishness, careful to spell out "Barry" so that he would not think it was the English "Berry." He turned to me in dead seriousness and proclaimed, "Did you know that Britain is the cruelest country on the face of the earth?" There it was again—the protection of ethnic, national identity from a history of murderous occupation. "Cruelest country!" There was nothing worse in history than the brutal 700 year occupation and devastation of Ireland by the British! And presumably, only we, the Irish could understand that.

Which crime against which people is the worst? Genocide of Jews? African-American slavery? British occupation of Ireland? Or the Palestinian Nakba? In fact, that is the wrong question, for those acts of inhumanity all are the worst. If you and your people are systematically subjected to barbaric violation and murder over so many generations it becomes your history, there is nothing worse.

Throughout history people have suffered similar experiences: the Native American's experience of European settlement of what is now the United States, the Aboriginals when Australia was settled, and peoples all over the world colonized by Britain, France, Spain, Belgium, Portugal, Holland. My point here is that *each* is the worst, *each* is the most abhorrent. Each invader and occupier the most cruel. Each death, each heap of mounting deaths, the most deadly. In other words, slavery, genocide, ethnic cleansing are indeed crimes against humanity, whatever our race, ethnicity, national origin, gender, or sexual orientation. They are crimes because they are leveled against human beings.

Comparing one oppression to and elevating it over another was the failed intellectual exercise that characterized the American Left in the 1960s in their reaction to feminists when we launched a movement for our own liberation. They ironically were mostly white men who told us women that we did not fit into their who-is-the-most-oppressed hierarchies. Ignoring them, feminists built a global movement while the Left retreated at the time.

Whether they are Lebanese or Palestinians under attack by Israel or Jews under attack by Nazi Germany or Iraqis dying in the hundreds of thousands at the hands of the U.S. military, or women raped in their homes, their bosses' offices, or in a war zone, the isolation of victims from everyone else coupled with the failure of others to come to their aid to stop the attacks usually makes them feel that "no one can understand!" Suspicious of universal terms such as the human being, Améry concluded, "Let others not be prevented from empathizing. ... Their intellectual efforts will meet with our respect, but it will be a skeptical one ... "[7]

Globalization puts new responsibilities on us to engage our shared human consciousness beyond state and even regional boundaries. In this book I argue for a politics of empathy from which everyone can understand if we choose both to be empathetic because we are human beings and simultaneously to deeply engage with each other's diversity of race, ethnicity, and gender. Rather than assuming that we cannot possibly know and therefore cannot empathize with another who is so different from oneself, diversity insists on us the necessity of learning the objective conditions that frame others racial, ethnic and gendered experiences. Then we have the context, the situation in which to empathize. It is unrealistic to assume that in combining the universality of being human with the diversity of our identities, there will be others who can understand. But that idealism is already a work in progress around the world.

Since the Holocaust, the United Nations Declaration of Human Rights set the standard—that all human beings are born with dignity and rights. Each and every act against any and all people is as heinous and repugnant as any other. Only the likes of John Yoo and George W. Bush and Dick Cheney occupy their time determining how much torture is too much, which dead are the most dead, or how to torture up to just before the moment of death, showing us the deadly coldness of psychopathic minds.

Yet, "no one can understand" was our inheritance from wars, from those who terrorize women and children in private. It is the experience of soldiers sent to fight other men's wars. The realization of what they have done to others and to themselves under orders isolates them apart from their families and the caring world at home. Rather than facing the world where no one understands, it drives some to suicide and leads many others to reenlist even though they are facing their own deaths every day.

Isolation was not my only experience of harm when I was raped in my twenties; it sealed my pain with silence, trapping me inside of it. The first person I told was my roommate. Her response was remote and disconnected. Her failure of empathy left me with that feeling that no one would understand, that I would have to get through that trauma alone, which is likely why I did not bother to tell anyone else. Instead, I wrapped myself in that terrible isolation that becomes a constant reminder that because I was raped, I was different from any-one who mattered. Then feminism happened and I found an internal strength just waiting to be tapped.

Perhaps that is why I cannot ignore the misogyny in which the 2006 war against Lebanon and the Middle East crisis were discussed in Russia that October. I was returning home to California from Paris after a trip to Lebanon when I heard a news report on the radio as my taxi sped through the streets of Paris to Charles De Gaulle Airport. I gleaned something about the Israeli police against the President of Israel. The news bulletin passed too quickly, like the cars around my taxi, for me to fully comprehend, but it sounded dire. I asked the driv-er, a Nigerian man, "What happened in Israel? A *coup d'etat*?" which seemed highly unlikely.

"*Ce n'est pas ca,*" he disconfirms, telling me that the president "*avoule.*" I did not understand and repeated his words. He immediately corrected me, pronouncing slowly and enunciating clearly so that I would not miss "*a viole*"—rape—several women—the president of Is-rael, Moshe Katsav, is charged by the police.

My mind bounced from the news in this taxi to the bombs that Israel dropped on Lebanon during the summer under a pretense of destroying Hizbullah while Israel's president, a largely ceremonial and symbolic position, is charged with raping women in his office. I blurted out "*Incroyable!*" "But why would I think that a president of any state raping women is unbelievable," I asked myself. Then I real-ized that what was so incredible to me was that this made the news. Of course, I had not yet left France where criticism of Israel is less censored than in America. The unsaid became known—at least that is what I thought that morning in Paris.

My taxi driver, obviously stung by the news, uttered with deep gravity, "*C'est affreux!*" Yes, this is horrible. Repulsion is the human reaction to the crimes of a psychopath in high office. I estimated the hours until I would be back in the United States where I would get more detailed news. I noted with amazement, not for the first time, at how the premise of this book that I was writing was being instantaneously fed by the human catastrophe made from the masculinity of war.

In the subconscious of the unsaid, for that is where our genuine knowledge of reality goes when it cannot be spoken, our minds make all of these connections even before we are consciously aware of them. As those connections started springing to the surface of my consciousness, I began wondering if the president of Israel would be removed from office, which, of course at the time, made me wonder— would the Democrats in Congress dare to impeach George W. Bush and Dick Cheney?

I turned back to the news I had just heard. Criticism of Israel is suppressed and censored in the United States by charging its critics with anti-Semitism, to insulate the state from potential charges of war crimes. I began to wonder, "Will the collective exact penalties for speaking against the president of Israel just as Islamic fundamentalists reacted violently to the Pope's discourse on Islam or the Danish anti-Islamic cartoons? No. I am sure that this news is too big to be contained. Those women who took their cases to the police are too brave to be ignored, I tried to believe.

Finally, I arrived at the Philadelphia airport to clear customs and change planes for California and rushed to the television—and waited and waited. When it became evident that CNN was not reporting news of the Israeli president's alleged rape of several women, I proceeded to my connecting flight. This was beginning to feel like the United States quashing Lebanon's cease-fire proposals over and over again at the United Nations. This was beginning to feel like the isolation of being a rape victim. News that had blared from the radio in Paris this morning was silent in the United States this evening. The dirty secrets airing in Europe were to be kept from Americans. The usually scandal-driven

American media once again is protecting the U.S.-Israeli alliance with silence, I realized.

This entire issue likely would have passed into silence had Israeli feminists not fought for and won a new sexual harassment law in 1998. Dina Kraft of Tel Aviv, correspondent for the Jewish Telegraphic Agency, a global news service, points out that "for decades it was widely accepted that some of Israel's top military officers and government ministers considered sexual encounters with female employees a seigniorial right."[8]

Obviously, the president of Russia, Vladimir Putin, did not have the difficulty I had in getting those news reports as evidenced by what happened next. Psychopathic cold indifference to human life feeds misogyny and together they form the context in which world leaders met immediately after the 2006 war against Lebanon to discuss the "Middle East crisis." When Russia hosted a meeting in Moscow that October, Putin greeted Israeli Prime Minister Olmert with a message for the president of Israel with "Say hello to your president," and then, "He really surprised us." Instantly, Putin's microphone went dead and reporters were immediately ushered out of the room. Some news organizations reported that Putin's next words were, "We did not know he could deal with 10 women." The Russian newspaper *Kommersant's* reported Putin's remarks differently: "He turned out to be quite a powerful man." Andrei Kolesnikov, the paper's reporter in the official Kremlin pool, quoted Putin as saying. "He raped 10 women. I never expected it from him. He surprised all of us. We all envy him." The *Post* reported that Olmert responded by saying, "I wouldn't be jealous of him."[9] Laughter from the Russian and Israeli diplomats present launched the meeting on the Middle East crisis.

Later, Putin was confronted with his remarks during a call-in television show. Attempting to make of himself a protector of women's rights, he responded that "using instruments such as protecting women's rights to resolve political issues that are unconnected with this problem is absolutely inadmissible. And this is because it actually discredits the struggle for women's rights." He never denied making the comment.[10]

Here is some of what they were laughing at: The story of the woman allegedly raped by the president came out in court. She was identified as "A," and testified that she was called into his office, that the president pushed her onto the corner of his desk and forced her hips on to the table. She said his hands were over hers on the desk and how she felt immobilized. As he was pulling up her skirt, she said she was certain that he would stop. She told him that she was leaving, that she quit. She said that he continued and penetrated her and that when it was over, she pulled up her panties, left and went to a nearby public garden where she sat in her isolation for hours, smoking one cigarette after another, before taking a taxi home. Like many rape victims, she then faced her own self-blame asking herself if she struggled enough and ultimately, that unanswerable question "why me?" She felt like her life was ruined and taking a shower at home she tried to wash away the rape.[11]

The Israeli police can be credited for taking her and other women's stories seriously, determining them credible and referring them to the attorney general. Charges against Moshe Katsav included "two counts of rape; one count of committing an indecent act, using force; one count of committing an indecent act; two counts of sexual harassment; one count of harassing a witness and one count of obstructing justice."[12] Denials, deals, and diplomatic maneuvering ensued until Katsav finally stepped down from office. Even with postponements and delays, the victims and the police have been steadfast. The trial was continuing in mid-2010.

Sexual violence against women is intricately involved in every aspect of war: women soldiers, wives of soldiers, women working for presidents and prime ministers and even in demilitarized countries like Costa Rica associated with world peace. Rape was a Nazi tool in the Holocaust and it has been used by men in United Nations peace keeping forces. Uncovering and exposing these crimes against women is not enough. The politics of empathy, from a feminist paradigm, speaks into the void of silence as it transcends all borders humans wrap around themselves separating themselves from each other. It breaks victims' isolation and fuels human rights campaigns around the world, more so today than ever before.

Unmaking War

Without consent of the governed, a basic condition of any democracy, the United States has made of itself the government of the world. The United States determines which countries will receive economic and military support for making war, which will be sanctioned or have to submit to costly and often humiliating requirements, which will be punished, which will be "protected" and which will be violated, which regimes should be supported and which will be set up to fall or be overthrown out-rightly, which will be armed with nuclear weapons and which will not be permitted to have them. No other state and not even the United Nations has the power to stop U.S. attacks on others states and wars of aggression.

As the most powerful state in the world, the United States will allow no state or world body to hold it accountable. The United States has refused to even recognize the International Criminal Court (ICC) established in 2002 to investigate and prosecute cases of war crimes, crimes against humanity, and genocide. Although 110 states are members of the ICC, George W. Bush asked the UN Security Council to make U.S. nationals *exempt* from jurisdiction of the ICC in 2003. However, when torture of prisoners at Abu Grahib was exposed in 2004, the United Nations did not extend to the United States an exemption from jurisdiction of the ICC. That led the United States to demand immunity agreements to gain exemption from criminal conduct on a state-by-state basis. Through these agreements, 102 states have excluded U.S. citizens and military personnel from extradition by the ICC and given them free reign to conduct war crimes and crimes against humanity. Because of its power, with or without UN approval or state agreements, U.S. leaders are answerable to no legal authority that would make judgments on its commission of war crimes and render punishment for them.

The United States extends its immunity from scrutiny and prosecution for war crimes and crimes against humanity to its allies, particularly Israel, as long as they are useful. When Hamas, the militant Islamic resistance to Israeli occupation of the Palestinian territories, was elected to govern in Gaza after the Israeli withdrawal, Israel imposed an economic and political blockade on the Gaza strip in 2006. It cut off imports of goods and food, and closed off entrances thereby disconnecting families and preventing people from going to their work outside Gaza. The blockade cut fuel and electricity to the area, leaving Palestinians to live in a perpetual state of emergency due to unsafe health and water conditions. Hamas retaliates with random rocket strikes on Israeli villages.

Hamas reacted as Hizbullah did in Lebanon by firing missiles on nearby Israeli towns, which in December 2008 Israel used as justification for launching a land, sea, and air attack on Gaza for one month. In an attack not unlike its 2006 war against Lebanon, in the siege of Gaza, the Israeli military took nearly 1,400 Palestinian civilian lives. Three Israeli civilians and ten soldiers were killed.

Nine months later South African judge Richard Goldstone, himself a Jew and strong supporter of Israel, reported to the United Nations high commissioner on human rights the result of an investigation he had been asked to conduct. He found that hospitals were intentionally targeted with white phosphorus, which burns fiercely and creates intense blankets of smoke, and that Israel had no basis for its claim that terrorists or Hamas soldiers were firing from within them.[1] His report confirmed the cries we saw from Gaza in media reports on the siege.

Further, in descriptions reminiscent of the Israel attack on Lebanon in 2006, the Goldstone report found "several incidents involving the destruction of industrial infrastructure, food production, water installations, sewage treatment plants and housing" as well as "destruction by the Israeli armed forces of private residential houses, water wells, water tanks, agricultural land and greenhouses there was a specific purpose of denying sustenance to the population of the Gaza Strip."[2]

The report found that Israel deliberately destroyed non-military targets, citing a flour mill, a chicken farm, and water pumps, and further found that Israel's wider policies toward Gaza over the last two years, "including a border blockade imposed after the 2007 Hamas takeover of the territory, 'might justify' a court finding of crimes against humanity."[3] It also noted that in its indiscriminate firing on civilian populations, Hamas had committed crimes against humanity. The Goldstone report recommended that Israel be required to pay reparations to Gazans for property damage and that it be referred to the United Nations Security Council for possible action by the International Criminal Court.

Immediately upon publication of the report and its scheduled consideration by the UN Security Council, the Obama administration through Secretary of State Hillary Clinton pressured Mahmoud Abbas, president of the Palestinian Authority to defer United Nations action on the report. Although President Obama earlier in 2009 had indicated that he would reverse U.S. policy of not recognizing the International Criminal Court, he used the power of the U.S. presidency to protect Israel from being brought before that court for crimes against humanity.

In order to sustain ongoing global warfare, the United States has mortgaged its own country with more than a $12.8 trillion debt as of May 2010, which is expected to climb to at least $20 trillion by 2020. In 2010, the People's Republic of China and Japan held approximately 42 percent of the U.S. debt with the balance distributed among other states and institutions.[4]

A 2008 Global Trends report from the National Intelligence Council (NIC) report predicted *before* the 2009 U.S. economic meltdown, that America's global preeminence would gradually disappear over the next fifteen years—in conjunction with the rise of new global powerhouses, especially China and India." Writing about the report Michael Klare pointed out that, "as a result of the mammoth economic losses suffered by the United States over the past year and China's stunning economic recovery, the global power shift the report predicted has accelerated. For all practical purposes, 2025 is here already."[5]

The decline of U.S. power in the world under its own self-destruction provides a possible space, an opportunity, for a paradigm shift from ongoing war and crimes against humanity to a world governed through upholding human rights with a politics of empathy. If those states holding American debt were in a position to call in their loans, the United States would no longer be able to exert its lethal military control of the world. But the question remains—which state would take over and rise to the level of power the United States exercises now?

A better question is: how will we grab hold of this historical moment to manifest our life force in our collective conscience in order to humanize the world? The question before us is not which state will rise to power, but rather how will we reshape power relations by unmaking war, disabling its machinery, disavowing psychopathic leadership, and rejecting patriarchal power?

Unmaking war. Idealistic? Utopian? Fantasy? Yes. Genuine change begins with envisioning a different kind of world, one that is governed through a politics of empathy. We are taking a long view to a world that barely seems possible in the present. That is the kind of view abolitionists took early in the nineteenth century when they refused to accept the belief that slavery was so integral to the U.S. economy, so deeply ingrained in the American way of life, that it could not be dislodged. That kind of idealism fueled decades of struggle for the liberation of blacks from South African apartheid.

Today feminist movements from CODEPINK to the Revolutionary Association of Women of Afghanistan to Women in Black struggle against both patriarchal domination over women and foreign occupation of people. We can chart progress in women's liberation, for people's self-determination and with global peace and environmental movements. In Israeli and American wars those who refuse to fight are giving us courageous new models of masculinity. The means of change that will remake the world are all around us. That will be more likely if our goals are clear and fueled by both global feminist consciousness and the politics of empathy.

Demilitarization—eliminating state militaries and militias and decommissioning weapons—is a work already in progress. Consistent with the movement toward global interconnection of all human beings, in Prague in April 2009 President Barack Obama made this announcement: "Today, I state clearly and with conviction America's commitment to seek the peace and security of a world without nuclear weapons. I'm not naive. This goal will not be reached quickly—perhaps not in my lifetime." Not mere rhetoric, he has a plan in which, "we will reduce the role of nuclear weapons in our national security strategy, and urge others to do the same."[6]

It was a bold move, although one that was compromised by his simultaneously escalating the war against Afghanistan; and one that can have only limited effect as long as states must provide for their own defense with their own state militaries. "Make no mistake," he told us emphatically, "as long as these weapons exist, the United States will maintain a safe, secure and effective arsenal to deter any adversary, and guarantee that defense to our allies." Nevertheless, he initiated a global effort to "begin the work of reducing our arsenal."[7]

Furthermore, President Obama did an about-face that would re-enter the United States into global peace initiatives: "To achieve a global ban on nuclear testing, my administration will immediately and aggressively pursue U.S. ratification of the Comprehensive Test Ban Treaty." He added that, "if we are serious about stopping the spread of these weapons, then we should put an end to the dedicated production of weapons-grade materials that create them. That's the first step." And the second step would be to "strengthen the Nuclear Non-Proliferation Treaty as a basis for cooperation. The basic bargain is sound: Countries with nuclear weapons will move towards disarmament, countries without nuclear weapons will not acquire them, and all countries can access peaceful nuclear energy."[8]

In that speech, for a moment, we saw nationalistic American arrogance and presidential macho dissipating in front of our eyes. Indeed, we could see the possibility of a world opening to shared human consciousness in this dramatic departure from his predecessor. But Obama's approach did not level the nuclear war playing field. He would have the United States hold on to enough nuclear weapons to destroy the globe many times over and would insure that Israel's stockpile of nuclear weapons remain unexamined.

Until all states decommission all of their nuclear weapons and no state develops new ones, the United States, Russia and Israel will continue to militarily dominate the globe and determine who else can and who cannot have them. Demilitarization of all nation-states is essential to world peace. But even that long-term goal is not sufficient to get us to world peace.

At this point, I would like to be able to argue for a military-free world. But because I know that psychopaths will always be attracted to power and will have the ability to rise to state leadership, to shun state and international law, and to con the public to follow them into making war, I am convinced that a peaceful world will still require a military. As long as psychopaths can rise to positions of power in our communities and nations, the world cannot afford to be free of military protection. But we need a different kind of military.

I propose a global peacemaking military comprised of women and men from each nation-state who are trained to use the minimum force necessary. Such a military would identify the individual hardcore leaders who perpetrate actual terrorism. In short, a peace force would, if necessary, attack hard-core fighters, not an entire nation. Such a global peacemaking force would draw women and men from every state to serve and would, importantly, replace state militaries. It would intervene to stop crimes against humanity but leave nation-states' internal security to be handled by their own police, firefighters, and coast guards. But in the event of genocide or ethnic cleansing or terrorism, if efforts at peaceful negotiation fail, the global peacemaking force would be deployed to immobilize, capture, and refer to trial those responsible for crimes against humanity.

Some who are currently serving in state militaries are people who are drawn to serve in the way most firefighters serve. Those firefighters enter the ranks from a sense of calling to serve. In a global military soldiered by those called and committed to service, women and men would be sworn to uphold the Universal Declaration of Human Rights and would have as their first responsibility upholding human rights and protecting human life in all instances—for civilians and soldiers, states and ethnic groups. No more human lives would be marked as expendable for war.

Most significantly, a global peacemaking force is not oriented toward large-scale combat because *there would be no state militaries.* Where terrorists emerge, either in public office or throughout the land, they would be fought with the precision of special forces that are highly trained and expertly skilled to take out pockets of danger where terrorists have menaced people and disrupted peace, but without putting civilians in harm's way. Such a force would have as its standard of success achieving peace and protection of peoples rather than victory over enemies.

Who would serve? The bar for qualification would be set high in order to rule out those aching for a fight, to rule out sociopaths for whom killing is without remorse, and to rule out racists and misogynists. Recruitment would emphasize that the jobs are for those who have a calling to serve and protect people. It would recognize that the desire and willingness of people to serve is an honorable human pursuit and that fighting for international peace is substantially different than wanting victory over an enemy. It would, therefore, proportionally recruit an international peacekeeping military from all nation-states.

How would they be trained? First and foremost the recruit's training would focus on understanding international human rights to build in them a reverence for human beings. Instilling in them respect for human beings would begin with the value of their own lives and the need to protect others as they would their own if it comes to combat. The training would neither degrade nor dehumanize soldiers but would treat them according to the humanitarian standards that they are expected to uphold in combat. This would provide a new standard for military training for soldiers. Each state would be required to contribute financially to maintain the global peacemaking force. The amount would be significantly less than the cost of maintaining states' militaries around the globe.

The lesson I take from recent agreements to decommission nuclear weapons, is that the only way to eliminate the problem of each state holding on to enough power to deter another state's military is to eliminate all state militaries and establish a world body through which each state would be protected by the global peacemaking military. Returning to the vision of a global peacemaking military, we are left with the problem of how such a force would be operated.

When I originally began to think about this, all of these proposals pointed in the direction of a world government, one that would have the force of law to govern over demilitarized states with a peacekeeping military. Demilitarization of states and replacing state militaries with a global peacemaking military obviously requires a world body to monitor crimes against humanity and deploy forces. It should have as its function to:

- Address all crimes against humanity and war crimes to the International Criminal Court for adjudication.

- Decommission all nuclear weapons—not only in Iran but those held by the United States, Russia, Israel, Pakistan, India, etc.

- Deliver armaments of war from nation-states to a newly constituted world body for destruction or, if usable, for the new global peacemaking force.

In its present form the United Nations cannot serve that role. With the elite, powerful states controlling the Security Council that has power over the General Assembly of the represented states, and with representatives appointed by governments rather than being elected by people, it cannot function as a representative democracy. Nor does it have the power to implement its decisions.

Knowing that this proposal would seem idealistic—even improbable—to many, I persisted writing about the possibilities of an overarching world body that leaves states free to police within their borders but would have the power to intervene against crimes against humanity whether they be ethnic cleansing or genocide. Such a world body is already envisioned by peace activists who are organizing globally under a Constitution for the Federation of the Earth. Its broad functions are:

- To prevent war, secure disarmament, and resolve territorial and other disputes that endanger peace and human rights.

- To protect universal human rights, including life, liberty, security, democracy, and equal opportunities in life.[9]

Globalization is a difficult concept, and feminists themselves disagree on its utility. Some, like political scientist Susan Hawthorne, have exposed how present-day globalization is an abuse of power that attempts to homogenize the diverse peoples of the world. This important and critical view recognizes the economic power particularly of Western states to menace the developing world economies with structural adjustment programs. Those programs force developing countries to conform their economies to capitalist markets and in turn drive more people into poverty by diverting their meager resources from people to markets.[10]

Other feminists consider both the negative aspects of globalization such as militarization and wars, climate change and economic exploitation with positive forces such as global feminism and the global environmental movement.[11] My study of masculinity and war made clear to me that global demilitarization is an essential next step, and that would require a global monitoring body such as a world government. That is the direction of unmaking war in which I planned to take this book until I went to Costa Rica to see what an actual demilitarized state looks like.

The tiny Central American country of Costa Rica became the first successful example of demilitarization in 1948 when it recovered from a bloody coup that brought down the government. To prevent future coups, its president, José Figueres, supported the proposal of his Minister of Security Edgar Cardona Quirós to disband the military.[12] Breaking out of the paradigm of war that sees escalating armament and militarization as the only route to protecting one's people, Figueres insured that his country would never suffer a civil war or participate in an international war again. Since 1948, fifteen other states have followed Costa Rica's example. But unlike Costa Rica, they rely on military backing of the giants—Australia, Great Britain, France, or the United States—for their security. Some other states have shifted from a combat-focused military to a peace-keeping military.

Since its demilitarization, during the years 1977 to 1979 Costa Rica suffered some attacks on its soil from neighboring Nicaragua under the brutal dictator General Somoza who threatened to invade the country. Venezuela and Panama came to Costa Rica's defense under the 1947 Inter-American Treaty of Reciprocal Assistance, or the Rio treaty that was originally ratified in 1947 by all twenty-one American republics. In that treaty, all states of the Americas, from the North Pole to the South Pole pledged to protect each other, to "prevent and repel threats and acts of aggression against any of the countries of the Americas." In the Inter-American treaty, all states agreed "not to resort to the threat or use of force in any manner inconsistent with the provisions of the Charter of the United Nations or of this Treaty." As a treaty of mutual defense, the states agreed that "an armed attack by any State against an American state shall be considered as an attack against all of the American States," which would lead the other states to "assist in meeting the attack in the exercise of the inherent right of individual or collective self-defense," as guaranteed by the UN charter. Further, "no state can use force without the unanimous consent of the other states."[13]

Many Americans falsely assume that the United States, with its mighty military, provides defense for Costa Rica. That myth surfaces whenever Costa Rican demilitarization is mentioned. Worse than not being true—the United States is the only country to have breached Costa Rican peace. The CIA under the Reagan administration set up bases there, paying the Costa Rican government handsomely, so that from those bases it could train and arm Contra (counter-revolutionaries) forces to overthrow the Sandinista government that had deposed Somoza, the U.S.-backed dictator of Nicaragua. In order to fund its war against the Contras and in violation of the 1947 Inter-American treaty, during the 1980s, the CIA secretly (so as to keep the CIA activities from the U.S. Congress and public) funded, armed and trained Contras in Nicaragua through narcotic-trafficking and sales of arms to Iran.

The Sandinistas had undertaken agrarian reform with a more equitable redistribution of land and had extended education and health care to the poor. In 1986, Oscar Arias, the newly-elected president of Costa Rica, intervened against the U.S.-supported Contras on Costa Rican territory and engaged neighboring state leaders in a peace plan that led to a peace accord and for which he was awarded the Nobel Peace Prize.

The problem with treaties is that they leave us with "Peace by Luck" where we need "Peace by Law" as Hungarian writer Emory

Reves, showed in his classic study "The Anatomy of Peace" written at the end of World War II. Treaties, including that which formed the United Nations, he pointed out, do not lead to lasting peace because "conflicts are inevitable as long as sovereign power resides in individual members," that is, states.[14] Instead, peace is only possible in a legal order with a democratically controlled government. "A legal order is a plan laid down by the common consent of men [sic] to make their individual lives, their families and their nations secure."[15] If we are separated into sovereign national units, peace, Reves argued, is a mere dream. As the United States and other states' violations of the UN charter and the Rio treaty show, treaties and diplomacy do not lead to lasting peace.

In fact, the United States in its defense of corporate interests abroad has repeatedly violated the Rio treaty with crimes of aggression. It warred against Guatemala in 1952 and 1954, Cuba in the Bay of Pigs invasions in 1961, the Dominican Republic in 1965, and Panama in 1958, 1964, and 1989; overthrew the elected Chilean government in 1964 and 1973; waged a contra war against Nicaragua from 1981 to 1990; invaded Grenada in 1983 and invaded Haiti with the forcible eviction of President Aristide first in 1991 under George H. W. Bush and again in 2004 under George W. Bush.

The problem is not simply that the United States continually violates state sovereignty throughout the world, sovereignty itself is the problem. State sovereignty, the supreme authority of a state to control itself, is the basis of state independence and its right to govern itself. Most states require a standing military to protect their sovereignty. Economic sanctions and war are the only remedies available to states when their sovereignty is threatened. Professor Glen Martin, actively promoting the Constitution for the Federation of the Earth, points out with respect to sovereignty, "An entire people, most innocent, none protected by due process, must be attacked because of the absurdity that international law applies to states, not to individuals."[16]

Global protection of vulnerable peoples is impossible as long as sovereignty rests in separate states. After World War II, Albert Einstein foresaw that the need for security cannot be met by states. He formulated security as a human right in an argument to the United Nations at its inception: "Security is indivisible. It can be reached only when necessary guarantees of law and enforcement obtain every-where, so that military security is no longer the problem of any single state."[17]

State sovereignty that is backed by a military makes the state with the most powerful military, ipso facto, the ruler of the world. That is why a world body to oversee a global peacemaking military seemed to me a necessary means to demilitarization and world peace. The prob-lem remains, in a world driven by blinding macho not only in war but in homes and on the streets, in a world where psychopaths too easily find their way into leadership, in a world where women from Condo-leezza Rice to Hillary Clinton rise to power by conforming to male norms for aggression and violence, who will lead?

I was looking for answers in Costa Rica where, without a military and with more than sixty years of peace, generations of men are no longer made expendable for war. But in this, the most peaceful of all nation-states in the world, men war against women. More than one in every two Costa Rican women are victims of wife abuse. Sociologist Lori Suddereth has reported that 58 percent of all Costa Rican women will be beaten by a spouse or partner at least once in their lifetimes, only one in ten reporting it to the police.[18]

Costa Rica's rates of violence against women does not differ sig-nificantly from other Central American countries that are militarized such as Nicaragua and Panama where at least 50 percent of women suffer at least one incidence of martial or intimate violence in their lifetimes.[19] Statistics are higher for women with higher educational levels, likely a result of them being more informed of their rights, but also revealing that economics is not the driving force of domestic vio-lence. Neither is culture. Although it is tempting for Westerners to think of these statistics as unique to Latin cultures and their machis-mo, around the world at least one in three women is beaten, coerced into sex, or otherwise abused during her lifetime.[20]

Moreover, in Costa Rica in 2004, eighteen women died at the hands of spouses or friends, a figure that rose to thirty-five in 2006.[21] This femicide follows a pattern of increased violence in Central Amer-ica where between 2000 and 2006 male homicides increased by 40 percent. But femicide, mostly perpetrated by husbands and partners, increased by 111 percent.[22] Femicide in Costa Rica takes the lives of almost one in every 100,000 Costa Ricans, making it third only to heart diseases and cancer as the cause of death of Costa Rican women, according to Costa Rican researcher on history Ronald Castro Fernández. He points to the *guaro* culture of liquor from sugar cane over which the government has exercised a monopoly since 1857 as a prominent contributing factor. Men turn their blinding macho on women in private. The fact that men are not called up for war or ever expected to fight and sacrifice their lives, limbs, or sanity, has not diminished their misogyny and contempt for women at home or in the streets.

Costa Rica has not turned its back on its women. Stiff laws with substantial prison terms for wife abuse have been on the books since 1995 but with little effect. Its 1996 law against domestic violence provides women with protective measures that will order out of the home anyone who inflicts psychological, physical, or sexual violence on a relative and bar that person from caring for, raising, and educating any underage children. Aggressors will have their weapons taken from them and will be ordered to pay for the family's food, medical care, and any property that was damaged during the assault. In the year after the law went in effect, over 7,000 legal actions involving domestic violence were reported. Domestic abuse hotlines were established, and a decade of heightened awareness of the problem followed.

But a large number of Costa Rican men still turn their backs on the laws and their families. Young girls escape violent homes, and in a state where women earn only 40 percent of men's wages in the labor force, they marry young. Of girls between the ages of fifteen and nineteen, 20 percent have been married and divorced or widowed according to a 2004 UN report. Deadbeat dads are so much of a problem that Costa Rica adopted laws allowing women and girls who are pregnant to identify the father with DNA testing, a law that is slowly beginning to show positive effects for women. And the sex tourism industry picks up on and exploits women's desperation. Western men, particularly Americans with their retirement or tourist dollars in hand, easily find Costa Rican women less than half their age through sex tours and romance holidays. Eliminating militaries, dissolving the need to reduce men to *expendable lives* for combat, has had no impact on men's wars against women in private. Demilitarization does not reduce men's misogyny, which reigns in the most peaceful state in the world.

Terrorism against women and families by men in demilitarized Costa Rica led me to turn from the proposal I was developing for a world body that would monitor a global peacemaking military back to the problem of undoing *core masculinity*, dissolving blinding macho and remaking men from the ground up, from the personal to the political. It further convinced me that the failure of global movements to achieve world peace comes from the fact that in demanding change, they do not cast their nets wide and far enough. World peace will remain an illusion as long as women are still subjected to masculine violence. Men's violence against women in Costa Rica seriously compromises that country's reputation as a leader in world peace.

For a moment, it seemed that Barack Obama might be a national model for the new kind of manhood that we urgently need. During his campaign for the U.S. presidency, he showed to the world the kind of empathetic manhood that I consider central to men remaking themselves. As president, on a trip to Ghana and a visit to the former slave ports, he spoke of wanting his daughters to "engage in the imaginative act of what it would be like if they were snatched away from Mom and Dad and sent to some place they had never seen before." He showed them how others have suffered and wanted them "to make sure that they are constantly asking themselves questions about whether they are treating people fairly and—and whether they are examining their own behavior and how it affects others."[23]

In the first months of his administration, during the debates on health care, he showed how empathy does not conflict with strength, how it enhances rather than diminishes leadership. Initially, in facing down the health insurance industry with the memory of how his mother suffered at their hands, we saw him bring his empathy to a woman at one of his health care forums who through her tears told him of how her insurance company was denying her life-saving treatment. He went to embrace her, assuring her that she was not alone. What a relief after the coldness and emotional disengagement of the Bush-Cheney era!

In his April 2009 speech to the Arab world in Islamabad, he said that he has "no sympathy and no patience for people who go around blowing up innocent people," ignoring the fact that U.S. forces were blowing up Afghan people even as he spoke. But a glimmer of empathy shown through on May 9, 2009, in a rare gesture by an American president, when he apologized to President Hamid Karzai in Washington a few days after the U.S. military killed an estimated 140 Afghans in Farah, 94 of them girls under the age of 18 who had gathered in a compound to take shelter from the fighting. Some villagers said the strikes hit an area that the Taliban had already left and where there was no fighting.

Although Obama apologized he did not stop the bombing. In fact, drone strikes on Pakistani villages three days later in South Waziristan killed eight people. Four days after that, U.S. forces killed 25 civilians in a village in North Waziristan. None were Taliban, none were Al Qaeda. And the drone attacks continue, weekly—daily sometimes. What were his daughters learning from his empathy?

Eleven months later Barack Obama, in all seriousness, as if he was not lying, told Afghans, "I want the Afghan people to understand— America seeks an end to this era of war and suffering. We have no interest in occupying your country," although the United States was occupying Afghanistan and had been since 2001.[24] In November 2009, while we were anticipating his decision on war in Afghanistan, I wrote an open letter to President Obama. He had already escalated war there shortly after his inauguration, an act that was a refusal of empathy for Afghans.

> While you were telling Americans that you wake up every morning and go to sleep every night thinking of how to keep America safe, you were denying that safety to the families of Afghanistan and Pakistan. Mr. President, you know that the empathy that you so highly value cannot be selective. When you engage it for some, say Americans, and refuse it to others, like Afghans and Pakistanis, you are telling the world that only Americans' lives are of value and that everyone else's lives can be put at risk to protect American lives.
>
> You have expressed your pain and sorrow in phone calls to families of American soldiers who have lost a son or daughter, a husband or wife. But what about the soldiers still there in combat? If you are truly pained by the loss of American soldiers in this war, bring those who are

still there in combat home and give them the support to put their lives back together. . . .

Mr. President, before announcing your decision, please think hard and long from that place of empathy within you of what it would feel like to receive that call telling you the fate of one of your daughters, the kind of call that far too many Afghans have received about their boys and girls who are with them no longer.

While Secretary of State Clinton credits the United States for freeing Afghan women, the U.S. war there gave control to the warlords of the Northern Alliance which has been responsible since then for widespread rape and abuse of women. In fact, Afghan women are struggling for their own liberation against both the U.S. ally, the Northern Alliance and its enemy, the Taliban. The United States has a long history of support for those criminal warlords in Afghanistan. That history extends back to the Soviet invasion and occupation of Afghanistan when Osama bin Laden, who also was supported by the United States, was initiating his wars to rid the Muslim world of infidels. After the Soviets withdrew from Afghanistan, the Afghans found that the CIA and U.S. Special Force "handed out millions of dollars in cash and weapons to Northern Alliance commanders." As soon as the U.S.-sponsored Northern Alliance took over, "the warlords started a new wave of crimes and brutalities."[25]

In 2009 a spokeswoman from the Revolutionary Association of Women of Afghanistan (RAWA) named Zoya said that the power of the warlords is so fierce that most families do not send their children to school from fear that they will be beaten, raped, or have acid thrown on them, the work of the warlords of the Northern Alliance. "Today," Zoya said in late 2009, the situation of "Afghan women is as bad as [it was] under the Taliban."[26] She pointed out that rape, early, forced marriage, and wife abuse are driving increasing numbers of women and girls to self-immolation.

To appease the warlords, in July 2009, President Karzai sold out women in exchange for warlord votes in the election that month when he approved the new Shia personal status law which, among other things, "permits Shia men to refuse to give food to their wives if they do not have sex with them."[27] While the Obama administration was pressuring Karzai for open, honest elections, the United States remained deadly silent about Karzai's plan to legalize marital rape and torture.

Then, instead of empathizing with Afghans, on December 1, 2009, Barack Obama escalated the war in their country ordering 30,000 more U.S. troops under the fiction "that our security is at stake in Afghanistan and Pakistan." A few days later, Secretary of Defense Robert Gates, speaking as if the United States was doing a favor to Afghans by intensifying war there, said, "We want to communicate a sense of urgency to the Afghans of their need to accept responsibility" for "We will not provide for their security forever,"[28] with a ring of George W. Bush talking about Iraqis and the violence in their country as "their problem." Gates's words, however, were meant not so much to assuage the Afghan people as to convince Americans that he was not doing in Afghanistan what George W. Bush had presided over in Iraq.

That is when General Petraeus again waved his counterinsurgency banner, the military's public relations campaign: "our forces and those of our Afghan partners have to *strive to secure and serve the population. We have to recognize that the Afghan people are the decisive 'terrain.'* And together with our Afghan partners, we have to work to *provide the people security...*" (Emphasis mine.) All of this while the United States was bombing and raiding Afghanistan.

We can do better than Obama's selective empathy and concessions to the rule of the military generals in the United States. Afghan feminists point the way as they know better than any U.S. general, and certainly better than the U.S. president, a viable route to peace. But first they want Americans to invoke our empathy. "Do you not think our blood is red like yours?" Zoya asked. Sending her personal condolences to the American "families who have lost sons and daughters in my country," she asked them to "please change your tears to a strength and raise your voice against your government."[29]

RAWA and most Afghans want the U.S. military to leave their country and allow them to handle their own problems. That is their own self-determination; they want neither Taliban nor the Northern Alliance, nor the warlords and certainly not the United States to control their government. Turning to Afghan women's demands of U.S. withdrawal from their country, RAWA wanted the United States to "stop supporting the Northern Alliance criminal groups...who were [after Soviet withdrawal] the first criminals to rape" beat and murder fellow Afghans.[30]

Neither the entire U.S. military command nor the presidents of the United States and Afghanistan have been able to arrive at a humanitarian proposal to end the war; but some Afghan feminists have proposed that as long as the U.S. military is still in Afghanistan, it disarm the Taliban and then leave. Instead, the U.S. military escalated combat in order to defeat the Taliban. If defeat over them is the military goal, how could they think of disarming the Taliban? Their solution instead requires sacrificing more soldiers and killing Afghans all along the way.

In 2009, according to Zoya, by RAWA's count fewer than 100 hard-core Taliban were fighting in Afghanistan, and media reported the same number of Al Qaeda operatives at the border. After John Kerry returned from Afghanistan in October 2009, he numbered the hard core Taliban at 1,000, likely a U.S. military over-exaggeration. But even if Zoya was underestimating and Kerry's figures are inflated, the rest of the Taliban, not unlike most of the U.S. and international soldiers, are their country's *expendable lives*, young men who cannot find work, who have lost family to U.S. bombings and attacks and are paid by the Taliban to fight with them.

The Taliban fight in small guerilla groups. The most effective strategy for fighting them would be with small but highly skilled special forces. Instead of sending in small group of fighters, Obama escalated the war, so that by mid 2010 there were 98,000 U.S. troops in Afghanistan, almost 1,000 for every one Taliban fighter as if bigger is always better.

Rather than escalating armament, a plan to decommission weapons would save lives, civilians as well as soldiers, Afghan as well as American. In late October 2009, Barack Obama signed a defense bill that went part of the way by authorizing payment to Taliban fighters to switch sides but not to stop fighting. No mention was made of disarming the militants and no specific amount was set aside for the soldiers who renounce violence against the Afghan government in favor of "re-integration into Afghan society."[31] In contrast to a life-saving approach, by October 6, 2009, 813 American soldiers died in Afghanistan that year.

Obama had emptied his leadership of the empathy he so prized. His ability to send American soldiers to their death, to order U.S. forces to bomb and kill throughout Afghanistan again puts a glaring spotlight on the arbitrariness of power—the power of the United States over the world, the power of a man to shift from empathy to authorizing the killing of others when expediency calls for it.

The model of masculine empathy Obama promised was in fact selective and not universal, tied to power and not committed to peace, and could be abandoned when he preferred the expediency of practical rather than moral commitments or the opportunism of political calculations. His leadership and the failure of demilitarized states to reduce violence against women when men no longer are expected to be expendable in combat argue strongly for the work of remaking men. Our struggles for demilitarization can only lead to world peace if men abandon *core masculinity* and its violent standards of manhood.

Remaking Men,
Reknowing Ourselves

What if someone were losing her or his life such as the drowning man on the beach near Bodega Bay, but it was happening in Fallujah in Iraq, in the Farah province in Afghanistan, or during the siege of Gaza or the shelling of Sderot in Israel? What if we wandered with our Frisbees not to the beach but to the scene of another's violent death in the lands where violent death has turned into a way of life under American and Israeli wars and occupations?

You do not have to have been with me on the beach that day to feel what we who experienced that man's drowning felt. We do not need to travel to a war zone to feel the pain of war's victims. With almost instant media reporting, from the killing fields of American- and Israeli-made wars, we do not have to be there in those countries to actually witness the violent deaths and the killing carried out by our states, ordered by our militaries—killings that are most often "mistakes" for which our generals sometimes apologize while another drone is being loaded with bombs for its next killing mission. Empathy is possible.

Why then, do we not see in war what those of us saw and felt that day near Bodega Bay? How do so many of us watch these reports and, in a manner of speaking, act as if we are at the beach where the drowning is taking place, but turn our backs, picking up our Frisbees and continuing to play? Worse, how are we able to refuse to know, to intentionally not turn on the news or to turn it off when it comes to war reporting? Because we feel impotent? Unable to make a difference? Incapable of producing change? Or, worse, do we turn away because—as some people said to me after asking what I was writing about when I was completing my first book, *Female Sexual Slavery*— "that's a downer!"?

It could be tempting to think "How dare we write off human suffering in favor of sustaining your own positive vibes!" But that approach will get us nowhere. Righteous indignation is easy. The work of unmaking war is found elsewhere. For some it will begin with facing that point when you want to turn away from the loss of others' lives. Unmaking war requires that we be present and face the atrocities our country commits. It means that we cannot avoid being hurt, steeped in sorrow, and even enraged when we are faced with today's reports of killing in war.

If you have read this book to this last chapter or looked into some of the antiwar websites and followed accounts and calls to action, you are already at that point. You know that it is not necessary to be steeped in media reports of killing and war to be a witness to and empathetic with war's consequences for people far away. We need only locate the present moment of wars' and occupations' realities, and open our hearts to that suffering, and allow our emotional knowledge to take us into empathy. We do this because that is where we begin to make change by valuing human lives.

Had we at that moment, on the beach near Bodega Bay, picked up our Frisbees and started playing again, the most immediate statement our actions would have made in front of the grieving family is that this man's life had no value, no meaning, no significance to us. When we engage our collective grief for the lives of those who have just been killed by U.S. or Israeli forces or by resistance militias or terrorist cells, we connect the value of their lives to our own and disown the valuing of one human life over another. That is when we as citizens of a country that commits such crimes, begin to change the energy and consciousness of our own states away from killing.

By facing the emotional knowledge that can flood in on us when we witness loss of life in war, we bring that death close into ourselves.

True, I do not want it there in me. I do not want corpses made from war littering my world or my consciousness. But there are ways to handle pain and suffering. Buddhists call it mindfulness, living in the present moment. Taking on the realities in front of us, breathing, being present, knowing that the pain will pass and that it will not last forever, we arrive in a new place with that painful knowledge we've acquired. Mindfulness is not withdrawal; it opens us to new choices: to face those deaths and turn them into a collective refusal of war, to feel the pain of those living in states our country has devastated and from that felt connection insist on our state paying reparations.

By refusing war and killing, we become part of a collective response that could become so powerful that we, people of aggressor states, could use it to bring down those politicians and leaders, not to mention the generals and CEOs who make their livings off of war. When I feel that sorrow and pain and allow my political anger to rise, whether it leaves me standing alone or it is rising collectively, from all around me, I am in a new kind of political space that is constantly under construction daily turning the raw emotions of fear and sorrow into meaningful political action.

This new kind of political space needs every kind of presence—from the silent witnessing of Women in Black to the activism of CODEPINK watchdogs in Congressional hearings, from the exposure by New Profile of Israeli attacks on Palestinians to sending support to the Revolutionary Association of Women of Afghanistan; from writing letters, e-mails, and making phone calls to talking to your son or daughter or high school seniors about deselecting military service.

The shared human consciousness I found that day on the beach near Bodega Bay is ruptured every time we refuse to be grounded in our interconnections with each other. Our human interconnection carries within it responsibility—to others and to live from, not against, our human life force that is driven to save, protect, and value all human lives, that is the source of our souls, that is the spirit through which we are all connected with each other.

If we insulate our lives and refuse to know the pain of war and the suffering that our state and militaries inflict on the planet, we are more likely to not see war's corruption here at home in our society, our communities, and our daily lives. There are four corrupting consequences of that isolation: First, we become one of those who cannot understand the trauma of American soldiers returning home from combat. The military training that created remorseless killers does not disappear when soldiers get their discharge papers. But many find that they have to hide their trauma from us. When they do, the violence of war is obscured; we cannot see how it reaches deep into our society and silently but surely shapes all of our lives. Along with their unrecognized, untreated trauma, soldiers bring home the violence of war. It can surface in wife and partner abuse, rape, unprovoked fights, and murders.

The violence of wars turns against soldiers, if not during the war, then when they return home, where too often their trauma is not understood, their stories are left unheard.

It is estimated that "more than half of all Vietnam veterans, about 1.7 million, have experienced symptoms of PTSD."[1] In a U.S. government-funded study of veterans of the wars in Afghanistan and Iraq, review of the records of 103,788 veterans who were first seen at veterans affairs facilities between September 30, 2001, and September 30, 2005, show that a quarter have been diagnosed with a mental disorder.[2]

Unless they connect with Service Women's Action Network, Iraq Veterans Against the War, Veterans for Peace, or other consciousness-raising veteran groups, or unless they go through withdrawal from war alone or with the support of a loved one until they can free themselves of it, these soldiers have to stuff the pain and ugliness of their combat experiences deep inside them when they come back home. They sense the insularity of their society, they see our willingness to thank them for their service and sacrifice. But they also know that American appreciation too often is accompanied with refusal to know what it is the soldiers did in combat or the loss of a soul that comes home with them and disrupts theirs and our lives.

Military personnel testify to Congressional hearings on all that they are doing to help soldiers with PTSD yet that too is a public relations campaign designed to camouflage the denial of health services to our vets. The National Veterans Legal Services Program (NVLSP), made up of lawyers who take on difficult medical entitlement cases for soldiers free of charge, has uncovered cases where doctors reveal that they were under pressure from the military not to diagnose traumatic brain injury and PTSD in soldiers. VoteVets.org exposed an e-mail from a Texas psychologist at a veterans affairs facility in which she said, "Given that we are having more and more compensation seeking veterans, I'd like to suggest that you refrain from giving a diagnosis of PTSD straight out." Instead, she proposed that they "consider a diagnosis of Adjustment Disorder," a temporary condition, that typically does not qualify for disability payments from the government.[3]

Second, racism attached to banners of patriotism leads to further corruption of our own lives here at home. Anti-Arab, anti-Islamic racism has reached epidemic proportions in the United States abetted by a media and the politicians who see terrorists lurking behind every Arabic name. Americans have hardly begun to acknowledge the depth of the anti-Arab racism that was unleashed in our society to sustain in us a fear of terrorists. It not only invites harm to people because of their race or ethnicity, it pollutes our environment, our lives, the very air we breathe with racial hatred. The ugliness that America had sunk into with its racism before the 1960s civil rights movement has returned in full force. We see it in the extremists' reactions to the first-ever African American president. And we find it in American security being tied to fear of Arabs. Whether it is the Fort Hood massacre or denying entry to the U.S. to some, an Arab name is sufficient for many politicians and the media to associate it with terrorism.

Third, the war paradigm shifts state and national resources away from people's needs and redirects them to support fighting and killing. By March 2010, the cost of the U.S. wars to Americans was over $123 billion. In a country where people are still losing jobs and homes from the economic crash of 2008 and where healthcare costs have skyrocketed leaving medical treatment a privilege of higher classes, in 2009 those war costs amount to 26.5 cents per U.S. taxpayer dollar.[4] Conscientious political activists unrelentingly expose the waste of military spending and the deprivation at home that results from it. But until that kind of activism spreads wide and far and is fed by a politics of empathy, we remain victims of our state.

Fourth, having learned to expect lying, fraud, and psychopathic behaviors from our leaders, the White House and Congress suffer from diminished standards of leadership. Whether from feelings of impotence or apathy, most Americans who care have come to accept that their leaders' crimes will go unpunished, that justice will not be called upon to restore our governing bodies. Only a few voices continue to demand that Bush and Cheney be charged with war crimes. The bar has now been set even lower.

Returning soldiers' violence and trauma, escalation of violence throughout our society, patriotic racism, economic priorities shifted away from people's well-being and toward the military to fight wars, diminished standards of leadership—these all fold together into a collective thinking that is driven not by facts but by a *dogmatism*. Peoples of oppressor states hide behind strong beliefs about the superiority of their own people. These beliefs are then expressed in American patriotism and Israeli nationalism. Their feelings of impotence are places from which it is impossible to reach genuine shared, human consciousness.

Dogmatic patriotic beliefs turn into effusive praise for "the soldier's sacrifice" and thanks to soldiers for their "service to our country." That service was to fight in a war that never should have been waged, that constitutes a war crime. No wonder some soldiers returning from combat will tell us, when they are given the opportunity to speak, instead of being overwhelmed by our patriotism, that they do not like to be thanked, that "you don't thank people for the kinds of things we did." Thanking them becomes yet another way of not seeing what they did, of not seeing what it did to them, of staying inured to the pain and suffering our country's wars invoke daily.

To get to that point where we can act from and through interconnections with each other, where our collective thinking is born from a politics of empathy, I return to the issue of consciousness with a classic statement from Karl Marx and Frederick Engels: "Life is not determined by consciousness but consciousness by life."[5] That is, our consciousness is formed by the actual events and realities before us and how we respond to them. Consciousness is not some prefabricated feeling-good state that comes from spiritual or other kinds of forces. Rather, our genuine ability to feel good with spiritual energy running through our being is not only possible but spontaneous when we engage our consciousness with the actual reality of life around us. I have often wondered if the proliferation of feel-good, how-to spiritual programs are not evidence of the extent to which, when in denial of painful realities, we destroy the spontaneity of our own spirit.

"Life is not determined by consciousness but consciousness by life" means that action is the cornerstone of consciousness. As we feminists have shown, the materialism of Marx must be fed by feeling and emotions as well as facts, thoughts, analysis. From the feminist-human rights paradigm, empathy is central to our consciousness. Through empathy we arrive at reverence for the dignity of human beings. Necessarily that which violates human dignity, the power of masculinity and its extension into the power of states, demands our attention and leads to *critical empathy*.

Critical empathy engages our objective knowledge that questions, challenges, and sets right the distortion and disinformation that we receive through presidents and their generals with our subjective knowing that we receive from feeling, emotional awareness, and intelligence. *Critical empathy,* further, refuses selective empathy, that identification with the suffering of some, refusing to acknowledge it in others.

The kind of objective knowledge that fuels the struggles for self-determination of violated and occupied people yields a consciousness that combined with subjective knowledge insists on turning away from violence. In *critical empathy* such as that of the Iraqi journalist who exposed the humiliation of his people by throwing his shoes at Bush, we see a new force for liberation that breaks from the cycles of ongoing war.

For those of us whose states are the occupiers, the warring aggressors, critical consciousness requires our own awareness of our state as an oppressor. With critical consciousness we challenge the chorus of those who see U.S. aggression as benevolent, as they must in order to accept and promote the fiction that Afghanistan is such a mess with its tribal warlords and extreme poverty, that somehow the U.S. occupation is an improvement for the country or that Americans will lead Afghanistan to a better life. Those beliefs only mirror the occupier's version of reality.

Almost everyone who has freed themselves from being subordinated by another, whether that other be a spouse or a state, knows the personal experience of liberation. In breaking away from our state's grasp on our minds and hearts, we discover ourselves in a collective that has the power to remake our society and state.

Still we are left with the question: "Why do wars persist in the face of the human urge to save and protect life?"

Of the many ways to address this question, I turn to that which I believe to be the most fundamental—*core masculinity* and men's distancing and disengagement from other people as well as from their own feelings and emotions. Distancing and disengagement may well be survival mechanisms that kick in when one is made expendable for war or is expected to risk one's life to protect others. But they also drive the machines of war. Through their distancing and disengagement, men disconnect from shared human consciousness.

True, we know of men who care and comfort, who rear their children with nurturance and love, who live in the present moment. In over forty years of teaching, I saw a dramatic change in younger generations of men, many of whom build their lives around equality and diversity, and in young women, who expect that kind of empathy from men as they forthrightly claim their own rights in the world and in relationships. Since writing this book, I have seen the most powerful possibilities of this new masculinity in many of the men who make up groups like the Iraq Veterans Against the War, the Courage to Resist, and Veterans for Peace and other men who stand on the front lines to reject the masculinity of combat.* I've seen this masculinity in men who organize programs to help men confront their misogyny and turn off their violence against women. I've seen it in American men in Vietnam who have returned there to build hospitals and orphanages. Taking responsibility for the acts committed under the sociopathic conditions of war is a move into this new masculinity.

As encouraging as it is to see these men remaking themselves and redefining masculinity, *core masculinity* is still firmly in place. The arbitrary power of *core masculinity* ushers in control. Or it does not. Either way, control is in the hands of those who disengage to a place where they are required to take few or no emotional risks. We have already

---

*   In this and previous chapters I refer to organizations that I know are making a difference by addressing the issues covered in this book. These references are not meant to be an exhaustive list but only an indication of the kind of groups that represent the values presented in this book. I encourage readers to search the Internet and their communities for similar organizations and movements.

seen how the military uses the disconnect of core masculinity to make soldiers into ruthless killers.

How do we get back? To reconnect? To feel? Again I turn to our most fundamental of all human acts, interpretive interaction, the way we make meaning in each and all of our interpretations of the acts, gestures, words, behaviors of others. I have already taken my approach to interpretive interaction further than most sociologists are willing to go, and I will now go a step further. By putting oneself in the place of the other and feeling empathy, we experience our own humanity. We are empathetic because we are human. That is, goodness is writ into our humanity.

But can we emotionally afford to be empathetic all of the time? Would it not be an enormous emotional overload to empathize every time we see a report of killing in war, of trauma for killing in war, of violence that reaches into families from killing in war, just to name a few of the violations around us every day? There is another way to pose these problems: we might consider the intolerance for killing, violence and trauma-making that could occur if most of us were to engage in that kind of empathy. Rather than being a personal drain on our own emotional resources, empathy could become a source of energy for action, to make changes such as championing state demilitarization.

Critical empathy takes us to human dignity which is inherent in all human beings. It is the source of our goodness. Dignity—being worthy of respect, that feeling of esteem one has for someone else— comes first from self respect, holding *oneself in dignity*. It is not inconsequential that the UN Declaration of Human Rights begins with the assertion that all human beings are inherently protected in dignity and in rights. The words "in dignity" do not appear in the U.S. Constitution, nor in the Declaration of Independence, which established Americans' right to "life, liberty and the pursuit of happiness." Human dignity, missing from the U.S. definition of rights, is neither assumed nor rejected. It simply is not there. And if we look carefully at the resistance to providing health care for everyone, to the disregard for Iraqi and Afghan loss of life in U.S. wars, we will see that valuing human dignity is not prized in American society.

It is not enough to ask soldiers to refuse to kill others. Men must insist on their humanity if they are to regain their will to live in shared human consciousness and to refuse to allow their own lives or those of any men to be rendered expendable. Self-respect in human interconnection is where men will find the strongest, most powerful, and most valid basis to stop tolerating the killing of others.

Men, we ask you not to refuse to kill that human being because she is a child or because she is a woman. If those are your reasons, then killing men is still acceptable and women and children will still be your unavoidable collateral damage in your fighting. Decide not to kill those women and children because you are a human being and recognize in them your humanity. Then you can recognize other men, not as *expendable lives*, but through your own humanity. We cannot fully value any human life as long as that of our own, our brothers', fathers', husbands', sons', and now also our daughters', mothers', sisters' lives are devalued, expendable everywhere—in Palestine and Pakistan, Afghanistan and Iraq, the United States and Rwanda, Australia and Lebanon, China and Tibet.

But after you've been through basic training with its glorification of killing, once you have cleared houses and taken lives in Iraq, Afghanistan, Pakistan, Lebanon, Palestine, how do you return to yourself, the human being you were before the military or a militia reduced you to a remorseless killer? Moreover, how do you go back further, dig deeper, and undo that *core masculinity* that set you up for killing in war by making you expendable in the first place? That is the question that hung over me through writing every page of this book.

While I knew I could suggest possibilities for regaining one's humanity, and while I have seen profound examples of change in combat veterans who have come home to challenge and stop war, until I was writing this last chapter, I had not yet seen verifiable evidence of new models of masculinity, men who have remade or are remaking themselves. Now I can introduce you to two such men.

Meet Josh Stieber and Connor Curran who in 2009 bicycled the United States to talk to anyone who would listen about their path to peace, the Contagious Love Experiment.[6] Beyond their powerful antiwar message, coming directly from their own horrific experiences in combat, theirs is a story that defuses *core masculinity* and sparks the creation of something new.

Josh was in the barracks one night, somewhere in Iraq, not liking at all who he had become and especially not liking how he had no room in his life to maneuver a change in who he was. His awareness, born in a moment of self-reflection, was enough for him to decide to make different interpretations of his experiences, which meant he had to create different experiences. When no one was watching, he decided he would take out the trash, a small act to clean up the barracks. But it was a huge move for Josh who, without orders to do so, was about to do something useful, even helpful. If he could do it, he knew that gesture would enable him to regain some of his own self. So he took out the trash. Nobody noticed, so he did not get in trouble for doing it. And it felt good to do something useful. He began to look for other helpful acts he could do, on his own, without orders, to "build up internal change" within himself. As his story unfolds, you see that in the accumulation of small acts, Josh began to regain his own initiative, that personal drive in our human life force that the military tries to expunge. He was literally remaking himself step by incremental step.

Small acts of individual initiative for the good of everyone reignited in him his own empathy. "I started imagining what if another country did this [house clearing] to us, and somebody took my Dad away and treated him like we treated them." He was on the road of return to his own humanity. But he was without direction and without support, and he was still angry. When he went home on leave, he thought of returning to the military the money it had paid him. That would show the military that he refused to be rewarded for doing what he had been ordered to do in Iraq. His parents, seeing his suffering, did some research and suggested that he look into filing for conscientious objector status. He had never heard of that.

Filling out the forms to become a Conscientious Objector was an act of soul searching. He returned to his unit in Iraq and refused orders to go out on missions because he was waiting for approval of his application. His commanding officer was angry. Josh knew that anger well. It had controlled him since before he went into the military. There in that interaction with his commanding officer, "I decided not to match his anger," Josh said, another small but significant act that not only built his own transformation but changed his commander. By the time he left the military, he had transformed not only his own self but his commanding officer who sent him off with a good-bye hug.

Listening to Josh talk about this experience was seeing transformation of consciousness in action. He connected the personal to the political and asked himself, "if that could change, what else could change too?" That question launched him and his buddy Connor on a cross-country bicycle trip for peace.

Connor remembers being on patrol in Iraq one time when not much was happening, no orders were coming in. He and his unit were passing by one Iraqi home with a beautiful garden in its walled compound—that was too good to let stand, they thought. Connor, who was in command, led the guys in his unit inside the compound. He scanned the ground with a metal detector and began to tear up the garden while others in his unit went inside and tore up the house, a sort of impulsive house clearing. They found not only several guns but a box of money. Surely signs of an insurgent or terrorist, they assumed.

While they were tearing the garden apart, the Iraqi man who owned the home came out with a tray of tea and personally served a cup of tea to Connor and each of his men. Confronted with kindness from a man whose home and garden he was destroying, Connor, who had gone into the military from a life of drugs, found his anger slipping away from him. It was that one human contact, the decency that refused to accept the humiliation the Americans were provoking that touched Connor's heart in a place that had not been reached in a long, long time. Later, he learned that the man was in training to be a police officer and that was why he had been given the guns and been paid the money that Connor's unit had found.

When he returned home from the military, Connor was diagnosed with PTSD. While struggling through that, he found that "you have to face yourself, you have to forgive yourself, you have to forgive those who helped you get on the wrong path." His return to himself began with forgiveness. He remembered that Iraqi man and his tea. "I would want to live my life in a way, and with the love that this Iraqi showed me." He turned to his mother for support and began to practice small acts of kindness.

Connor created in himself a new basis for interpreting meaning in his interactions with other. This made him even more aware of his anger and how he was making terrible judgments of people he did not even know, strangers he passed on the street. There in making interpretations we can make new and different choices. Change begins there. Connor decided to see if he could get through the day without judging others. Day added to day and Connor found his fear and anger dissipating. "I came back to myself," he says and he was not being controlled by others. Actually, in coming back to himself, he was not being controlled either by *core masculinity* or military brainwashing.[7]

Josh and Connor model the new masculinity that I have in mind in what must become a human project of men remaking themselves. Not only have they each found a path back to their own humanity and created a means to come together to encourage others on that route through their Contagious Love Experiment, but, in taking responsibility for remaking their lives, they are not expecting women to do that for them or to take care of them. I see that as an enormous, quantum leap from the generations of men, who if they even think of making a change, turn to women for attention, support, congratulations and energy. My guess is that numbers of women will support men like Josh Stieber and Connor Curran precisely because they come free of the self-centered male ego emboldened by *core masculinity*.

Josh and Connor found their way to their own humanity through small human interactions, just as the bumper sticker that advises us to "Commit Random Acts of Kindness." They prove that in our interactions with each other, even in the harshest conditions humans are subjected to, even if your life has been made expendable, the goodness of the human spirit can bring you home to yourself. But ways of igniting that spirit are not always evident.

Attending one of the hearings of Iraq Veterans Against the War, one young man, probably about twenty-four years old, a marine veteran, who sat quietly waiting for his turn to speak. He had a greyish pallor about him as if his life force had been sucked from him. He was introduced, and he said that this was the first time he was speaking in public and that, while he was diagnosed with PTSD, the veteran's hospital could not see him for eight more months. Would we have patience with him as he tried to tell his story, he asked? He spoke haltingly, his thoughts and words disrupted by his blank stares and then he would return to what he was saying. A deeply respectful and supportive hush came over the room. Still, his eyes darted rapidly in one direction and then another, almost randomly. He seemed as if he was startled, even in the silence, from something that was not there in that room. Bravely, he persisted and told his story.

Afterward I spoke with him about a new technique called tapping. The procedure is simple and involves releasing blocked energy on meridians, lines of energy that run through the body. According to a theory of Chinese medicine, specific points on those lines hold energy that can be released through acupuncture. But instead of needles and acupuncture, tapping involves using one or two fingers on a sequence of acupuncture points on the head and upper body while recounting a negative experience in brief phrases and then following those phrases with positive ones. The process has the effect of releasing traumatic memory, hence leading to emotional freedom.

I was taught tapping to address the PTSD I suffered after barely escaping a fire in my condo building a few years before, and in a few sessions, recurring images of the fire and the anxiety that came with them dissipated and never returned. When I did some research, I found that tapping is being used successfully with veterans either with the help of a trained practitioner or anyone can do it on their own. Gary Craig, founder of the Emotional Freedom Technique has worked with the Iraq Vets Stress Project to successfully release trauma from combat in veterans.[8]

Tapping acupuncture points on the body does more than release blocked energy. It frees one's vital spirit or *chi* to flow again, making one more fully alive in oneself and with each other. That is the life force through which we are interconnected, in which we find the source of what I think of as the goodness of being human. We experience our most vital spirit immediately in the present moment, that point of time and timelessness that is always new, always filled with possibilities.

One way to describe the experience of spirit in timelessness is through meditation, a technique for clearing the mind. I use a mantra, a word or sound that has no meaning, which I say to myself every time I become consciously aware that my mind has wandered into thoughts. Saying a mantra silently to myself takes me away from my thoughts to a realm of timelessness. One does not see or feel timelessness for one is in a realm that is beyond thinking. You know that something beyond usual consciousness has occurred when the meditation is over and you experience a quiet joy or special silence. That is where we experience the value of human life. There in spirit, soul, or whichever language speaks to your own understanding of that which gives us life, is where the "final arbiter" that Hannah Arendt was looking for to take us beyond war, will be found.

In the present moment, we touch possibility that can break through feelings of impotence or inadequacy. In the present moment we can change the direction of our states committed to ongoing war. Vietnamese Buddhist monk Thich Nhat Hahn during the U.S. war against his country began a practice of "engaged Buddhism" through which he encouraged Vietnamese people in nonviolent, civil disobedience against the war. He was exiled from Vietnam by both the Communist and U.S. controlled governments, but then he turned to working with veterans from that war. Seeing how stuck they were in suffering over the harm they had committed during war, Thich Nhat Hahn offered a different perspective to them, one that emanates from the present moment:

> I would say to the Vietnam war veteran, okay, you did kill five children. We know that. But here you are, alive in the present moment. Do you know that you have the power to save five children today? You don't have to go to Vietnam or southeast Asia. There are American children who are dying every day; they may need only one pill to be saved from their illness. . . .
>
> You are here; you can do something. Why do you let yourself get caught in the past? You can save children in the here and now. You can use your life in a very useful and intelligent way. You can very well transform that negative energy into a positive energy that empowers you and makes life meaningful.[9]

Following Thich Nhat Hahn's teachings, writer Maxine Hong Kingston started a writing group for veterans that has been continuing for over twenty years and has expanded throughout the country.[10]

Bringing the present moment into our interactions with each other, discovering that our life force is full with possibility and that it is up to us to create from it, we find our own ways of breaking out of and refusing to be complicit with a state committed to ongoing war, aggression, and occupation and turn our energies toward making peace a reality. As men are remaking themselves, we can find among all of us the leadership and drive to demilitarize the world. When the time comes that we ask of soldiers that they make that change from being remorseless killers because all of us can stand with them, then we will be fully invoking our humanity toward saving the lives of others. We must ask nothing less of ourselves.

Postscript

I was writing the last pages of this book amidst rallying calls for war against Iran from both Israel and the United States. While the menacing language of war has changed from the threat of WMD's in Iraq to the threats of nuclear terrorism from Iran, the tactics are the same. U.S. leaders continue to garner support at home for another war by provoking fear in its people. The possibility of breaking out of these repetitive cycles lies with us, the people of aggressor states who insist on another approach. Engaging the politics of empathy to turn ongoing war into diplomatic solutions would have to begin by insisting that state leaders address empathetic questions that can change their tactics and policies.

With Iran we would begin by recognizing the reaction of Iranian leaders to Israel and the U.S. for having concurred with Israel's ethnic cleansing of Palestinians in 1948. We would have to ask why we would expect Iranians to trust the U.S. government, which manufactured the overthrow of its first elected democratic leader Mohammad Mossadegh in 1953 in support of the British Petroleum Company's control of Iran's oil until Mossadegh nationalized it? Why would we not expect Iran to be suspicious of the U.S. when at their doorstep, the U.S. waged war against Iraq that had no justification? Why would we expect Iranian leaders to not reject insulting humiliations such as Secretary of State Hillary Clinton's derision of them as adolescents?

With Israel pressuring the U.S. to attack Iran and dramatizing their own intentions with rehearsal airstrikes, why, we could ask, would Iran be willing to give up its development of nuclear energy that may or may not lead to nuclear weapons while the U.S. and Israel retain more than enough of those weapons to destroy Iran and the world? These questions, far from a defense of Iranian leadership, are meant to direct us to the situation of Iran or any state the U.S. is threatening to attack.

Knowing the other's position, from their likely point of view, is the beginning of making reasonable interpretations that should lead to diplomatic solutions rather than sanctions and attacks that serve mainly to harm the people. The politics of empathy does not require that the U.S. or any state let down its guard when faced with threats of attack. The purpose of defense is to protect one's state. But aggression against other states in the form of preventive wars with their massive death tolls and destruction only invites more threats and increases the possibility of attack on invading states.

By the time this book is published or you are reading these words, our states may have taken their bully wars to other relatively defense-less lands. We, those of us who insist on our own humanity, *can* be the arbiters who change the direction of our states.

Kathleen Barry
May 15, 2010

Notes

Chapter 1 The Value of Human Life

1. The 4.6 million estimate is higher than previously reported by other sources. It is based on additional information provided to Human Rights Watch by soldiers who fired cluster munitions from multiple launch rocket systems. Human Rights Watch, *Flooding South Lebanon: Israel's Use of Cluster Munitions in Lebanon in July and August 2006*, 20, no. 2(E) (February 17, 2008), http://www.unhcr.org/refworld/docid/47b943b12.html (accessed 24 March 2010).

2. Science for Human Rights, "Lebanon," Amnesty International USA, http://www.amnestyusa.org/science-for-human-rights/lebanon/page.do?id=1650023 (accessed March 16, 2010).

3. Malalai Joya speaking at an event held by Grandmothers for Peace. Berkeley, California, November 7, 2010.

4. Cynthia Enloe, *Globalization & Militarism: Feminists Make the Link* (Lanham, MD: Rowman and Littlefield, 2007), p. 84.

5. United Nations, Fourth Geneva Convention relative to the Protection of Civilian Persons in Time of War, 1949.

6. Universal Declaration of Human Rights, Articles 1-3. December 10, 1948.

7. Peter Lehu, "War Games in Northeast Philadelphia," The World Can't Wait, February 18, 2009, http://www.worldcantwait.net/index.php/features-main-menu-220/the-war-of-terror/5390-war-games-in-northeast-philadelphia (accessed March 16, 2010).

8. Craig A. Anderson, "An Update on the Effects of Violent Video Games," *Journal of Adolescence* 27 (2004): 113. See also Craig A. Anderson "Violent Video Games: Myths, Facts, and Unanswered Questions," *Psychological Science Agenda* 16, no. 5, (2003), http://www.apa.org/science/psa/sb-anderson.html (accessed March 16, 2010).

9. Lehu, "War Games."

10. Kathleen Barry, *Prostitution of Sexuality: The Global Exploitation of Women* (New York: New York University Press, 1995).

11. See for example: American Coalition for Fathers and Children (ACFC: http://www.acfc.org), dedicated to "the creation of a family law system and public awareness which promotes equal rights for ALL parties affected by issues of the modern family;" the CIRCLE Brotherhood Association (http://www.math.buffalo.edu/~sww/circle/circle.html), a "group of African American men practicing, and dedicated to, the quality of life, successful manhood and parenting, economic growth and development, and the pursuit of excellence and spiritual

development;" R.W. Connell, "Politics of Changing Men" ("presents a pro-feminist analysis of masculinity politics") *Australian Humanities Review*, http://www.australianhumanitiesreview.org/archive/Issue-Dec-1996/connell.html (accessed March 16, 2010); Michael Flood, "Homophobia and Masculinities among Young Men (Lessons in Becoming a Straight Man)," XY Online, http://www.xyonline.net/content/homophobia-and-masculinities-among-young-men-lessons-becoming-straight-man; American Psychological Association, Division 51: The Society for the Psychological Study of Men and Masculinity (SPSMM, http://www.apa.org/about/division/div51.html): Promotes the critical study of how gender shapes and constricts men's lives in the following ways:

- Committed to an enhancement of men's capacity to experience their full human potential.
- Endeavors to erode constraining definitions of masculinity, which historically have inhibited men's development, their capacity to form meaningful relationships, and have contributed to the oppression of other people.
- Acknowledges its historical debt to feminist-inspired scholarship on gender, and commits itself to the support of groups such as women, gays, lesbians, and people of color that have been uniquely oppressed by the gender/class/race system.
- Contends vigorously that the empowerment of all persons beyond narrow and restrictive gender role definitions leads to the highest level of functioning in individual women and men, to the most healthy interactions between the genders, and to the richest relationships between them.

12. John Stoltenberg, *Refusing to be a Man: Essays on Sex and Justice*. (New York: Routledge, 2000).

Chapter 2 Making Men Expendable

1. *Encarta Dictionary* English (North America), online dictionary, s.v. "coward."

2. Tim O'Brien, *The Things They Carried* (New York: Broadway Books, 1990), p. 41.

3. Ibid., p. 42.

4. Ibid., p. 44.

5. Ibid., p. 52.

6. Ibid., p. 57.

7. Ibid., p. 57.

8. Ibid., p. 59.

9. Erich Maria Remarque, *All Quiet on the Western Front*, trans. A. W. Wheen (1929, New York: Random House, 1957), pp. 87-88.

10. I am referring to the unconscious as a location in the mind and do not include or even accept Freudian theories of its formation from sexual repression. Useful to my discussion of the unconscious is psychoanalyst Jacques Lacan in *Four Fundamental Concepts of Psychoanalysis* (W. W. Norton & Company: 1998),

who speaks of the unconscious as the gap between symbol and significance where meaning is not fixed.

11. According to an article by Helen Benedict, by 2007 there were at least 160,500 American female soldiers serving in Iraq, Afghanistan, and the Middle East since the war began in 2003. They constitute 15 percent of active duty forces. In Iraq seventy-one had died. Helen Benedict, "The Private War of Women Soldiers," Salon.com, March 7, 2007. http://www.salon.com/news/feature/2007/03/07/women_in_military (accessed May 5, 2010).

12. Enloe, *Globalization & Militarism*, p. 84.

13. From the citation for the Silver Star reported by Sgt. Sara Wood, US Department of Defense: "Woman Soldier Receives Silver Star for Valor in Iraq American Forces Press Service." http://www.defense.gov/news/newsarticle.aspx?id=16391(accessed May 3, 2010).

14. Michael Moore, *Will They Ever Trust Us Again? Letters from the War Zone.* (New York: Simon and Shuster, 2004).

15. Ibid., p. 39.

16. David Goodman, "A Few Good Kids," *Mother Jones*, August 31, 2009.

17. Aimee Allison and David Solnit, "Top Military Recruitment Lies" (Posted online with permission of the publisher, Seven Stories Press, AlterNet, September 20, 2007). See also Aimee Allison, David Solnit, *Army of None: Strategies to Counter Military Recruitment, End War and Build a Better World* (New York: Seven Stories Press, 2007). http://www.alternet.org/world/62945/ (accessed May 5, 2010).

18. "Military Bonuses Explained," Military.com. http://www.military.com/recruiting/bonus-center/resources/military-bonuses-explained (accessed May 3, 2010).

19. Allison and Solnit, "Top Military Recruitment Lies."

20. Ibid.

21. Pierre Bourdieu, *Masculine Domination*, trans. Richard Nice (Stanford, California: Stanford University Press, 2001).

Chapter 3 Remorseless Killers: Military Training

1. Testimony, Bay Area Iraq Veterans Against the War, University of California, Berkeley, Goldman School of Public Policy, Berkeley, California, March 11, 2009.

2. Ibid.

3. Steve Hassna, conversations with author, Santa Rosa, California, August, 2007.

4. Testimony, Bay Area Iraq Veterans Against the War.

5. Thomas Ricks, *Making the Corps* (New York: Scribner; Touchstone edition, 1998), p. 29.

6. This is the same process I describe in *Prostitution of Sexuality: Global Exploitation of Women,* (New York: New York University Press, 1995) that is used by pimps to put women into prostitution and keep them there.

7. *American Heritage Dictionary*

8. U.S. Army, *Soldier Life, Living Army Values* http://www.goarmy.com/life/living_the_army_values.jsp (accessed May 3, 2010).

9. Ibid.

10. Hassna, conversations with author.

11. Harold Garfinkle, "Conditions of Successful Degradation Ceremonies," *American Journal of Sociology* 61, no. 5 (March 1956): 420-424.

12. Professor William Cross, conversations with author, Syracuse, New York, June, 2008.

13. Dave Grossman, *On Killing: The Psychological Cost of Learning to Kill in War and Society* (Boston: Little, Brown, 1995), p. 87.

14. SLA Marshall, *Men Against Fire* (Gloucester Mass: Peter Smith, 1978).

15. Catherine Ryan and Gary Weimberg, Captain Pete Kilner, Interview, *Soldiers of Conscience, POV*, PBS, October 16, 2008, www.pbs.org/pov/soldiersofconscience (accessed March 18, 2010).

16. Testimony, Iraq Veterans Against the War.

17. "Tyler Zabel on How He Became a Conscientious Objector," Iraq Veterans Against the War, October 30, 2009, http://www.ivaw.org/node/5528 (accessed March 18, 2010).

18. Ricks, *Making the Corps*, p. 150.

19. Ryan and Weimberg, *Soldiers of Conscience*.

20. Based on observations made by Medea Benjamin and reported at San Francisco CODEPINK meeting, February 13, 2010, upon her return from Haiti.

21. As quoted in Captain Pete Kilner, "Military Leaders' Obligation to Justify Killing in War," Paper, The Joint Services Conference on Professional Ethics, Washington, DC, January 27-28, 2000, from Frontline interview, "Ambush in Mogadishu."

22. Marshall, *Men Against Fire*.

23. Twentieth Century Atlas, "Death Tolls for the Major Wars and Atrocities of the Twentieth Century," http://users.erols.com/mwhite28/warstat2.htm (accessed March 18, 2010).

24. Ricks, *Making the Corps*, p. 192.

25. Ibid., p. 193.

Chapter 4 First Kill: The Soldier's Loss of Soul

1. Philip Zimbardo, *The Lucifer Effect, How Good People Turn Evil* (New York: Random House, 2007), p. 265.

2. Christopher Browning, *Ordinary Men: Reserve Police Battalion 101 and the Final Solution in Poland* (New York: Harper, 1992), p. 184-5.

3. Professor William Cross, conversations with author.

4. 'Weapons of Mass Destruction' Quotes, ZFacts.com. http://zfacts.com/p/581.html (accessed May 5, 2010).

5. Ibid.

6. John W. Dean, "Is Lying About the Reason For a War an Impeachable Offense?" Special to CNN.com, June 6, 2003, http://www.cnn.com/2003/LAW/06/06/findlaw.analysis.dean.wmd/ (accessed March 18, 2010).

7. Sgt. John Bruhns, interview by Amy Goodman, *Democracy Now*, "The Other War: Iraq Veterans Speak Out on Shocking Accounts of Attacks on Iraqi Civilians," July 12, 2007, http://www.democracynow.org/2007/7/12/the_other_war_iraq_veterans_speak (accessed March 18, 2010).

8. Hassna, conversations with author.

9. Since its appearance on May 9, 2007, this video has been removed from the Internet.

10. Grossman, *On Killing*, p. 115.

11. Ibid, p. 116.

12. Testimony, IVAW, University of California Berkeley, March 12, 2009.

13. Iraq Veterans Against the War, "Winter Soldiers: Iraq & Afghanistan, Eyewitness Accounts of the Occupations," March 15, 2008, http://www.ivaw.org/wintersoldier/video, (accessed March 15, 2008).

14. Peter W. Chiarelli, United States Army, Vice Chief Of Staff, The House Armed Services Committee Subcommittee On Readiness, First Session, 111th Congress On United States Army Reset, July 9, 2009, PDF, http://armedservices.house.gov/pdfs/Joint-CHIARELLI.pdf (accessed May 9, 2010).

15. As reported by Steve Vogel, *Washington Post* Staff Writer, *Washington Post*, August 10, 2009.

16. Judson Berger, "The Number of Soldiers Seeking Opiate Abuse Treatment Skyrockets," Fox News, May 6, 2010. Report on Michael Moore.com. http://readersupportednews.org/off-site-news-section/46-46/1666-us-soldiers-in-opium-land-feeling-the-addiction, (accessed May 6, 2010).

17. David Bellavia, interview by *Booknotes*, Cspan 2, October 28, 2007.

18. Camilo Mejía, *Road from Ar Ramadi, The Private Rebellion of Staff Sergeant Camilo Mejía* (New York: New Press, 2007), p. 213.

19. Gorden Forbes III, "Wilderness of Zaidon," *Alpha Company: Iraq Diary*, Documentary on the Military Channel, 2005. http://military.discovery.com/tuneins/alpha-company.html (accessed March 19, 2010).

20. Ryan and Weimberg, *Soldiers of Conscience*.

Chapter 5 Preventive Killing

1. Brian Turner, "What Every Soldier Should Know," in *Here, Bullet* (Farmington Maine: Alice James Books, 2005), p. 9.

2. Michael Moore, *Will They Ever Trust Us Again? Letters From the War Zone* (New York: Simon & Schuster, 2004), p. 24.

3. Aaron Glantz, Iraq Veterans Against the War, *Winter Soldier: Iraq and Afghanistan Eyewitness Accounts of the Occupation* (Chicago: Haymarket Books, 2008), p. 17.

4. Ibid., p. 47-49.

5. Iraq Veterans Against the War, http://www.ivaw.org/wintersoldier/video (accessed March 19, 2010).

6. Glantz, Iraq Veterans Against the War, *Winter Soldier*, p. 22.

7. Iraq Veterans Against the War, Winter Soldier Hearing.

8. Glantz, Iraq Veterans Against the War, *Winter Soldier,* p. 20.

9. Ibid.

10. Wikipedia, s.v. "The Iraqi Insurgency," http://en.wikipedia.org/wiki/Iraqi_insurgency (accessed, March 19, 2010). The insurgency includes:

- "Ba`athists, the supporters of Saddam Hussein's former regime including army or intelligence officers, whose ideology is a variant of Pan-Arabism.

- Nationalists, Iraqis who believe in a strong version of Iraqi self-determination. These policies may not necessarily espouse a Pan-Arab ideology, but rather advocate the country's territorial integrity including Kuwait and Khusestan. Historical figures of this movement include the pre-Ba`athist leader of Iraq Abd al-Karim Qasim and his government.

- Iraqi Sunni Islamists, the indigenous armed followers of the Salafi movement, as well as any remnants of the Kurdish Ansar al-Islam: individuals with a Sunni-only policy opposed to non-Sunnis though not aligned to one specific ethnic group. Though opposed to the U.S.-led invasion, these groups are not wholly sympathetic towards the former Ba`ath Party as its members included non-Sunnis.

- Shi'a militias, including the southern, Iran-linked Badr Organization, the Mahdi Army, and the central-Iraq followers of Muqtada al-Sadr. These groups have Shia religious theories and as such, neither advocate the dominance of a single ethnic group, nor the traditional ideologies behind the Iraqi state (eg. these particular Shi'ites do not support the capture of Khustestan or other border areas with Iran, but rather promote warm relations with Iran's Shi'ite government).

- Foreign Islamist volunteers, including those often linked to al Qaeda and largely driven by the Sunni Wahhabi doctrine (the two preceding categories are often lumped as "Jihadists")

- At least one socialist revolutionary (such as the Iraqi Armed Revolutionary Resistance).

- Nonviolent resistance groups and political parties (not part of the armed insurgency).

11. The United States Department of the Army, *The U.S. Army/Marine Corps Counterinsurgency Field Manual* (Chicago: University of Chicago Press, 2007), p. 161.

12. Dahr Jamail "Iraq Has Only Militants, No Civilians," Common Dreams. org, November 26, 2007.

13. "Collateral Murder," Wikileaks, www.collateralmurder.com (accessed May 6, 2010).

14. Josh Stieber and Ethan McCord, "Soldiers in 'WikiLeaks' Unit Apologize for Violence," truthout, Statement, April 19, 2010. http://www.truthout.org/soldiers-wikileaks-company-apologize-violence58714 (accessed May 5, 2010).

15. "US-NATO Bans Media Coverage of Taliban Except for Approved Propaganda Reports," March 2, 2010, http://www.thewe.cc/weplanet/asia/afghanistan/afghanistan.html (accessed March 22, 1010).

16. Paul Wiseman, "Cluster Bombs Kill In Iraq, Even After Shooting Ends," *USA Today*, December 16, 2003.

17. "Afghans Demand New 'Rules of Force'," Al Jeezera.net, August 26, 2008.

18. Pentagon Report of May 2007, survey conducted by Office of the Surgeon General of the U.S. Army Medical Command, as reported in Chris Hedges and Laila Al-Arian, "The Other War: Iraq Vets Bear Witness," *The Nation*, July 30, 2007.

19. Justin Rood, "Blackwater Chief Accused of Murder, Gun-Running, Company Calls Allegations 'Offensive'," ABC News, August 5, 2009.

20. "More Than 1,000,000 Iraqis Murdered," Opinion Research Business. PDF report, September 2007.

21. In the study by Opinion Research Business of London in conjunction with the Iraqi Independent Institute for Administration and Civil Society Studies, the estimates were derived from a nationwide household survey of 1,849 households throughout Iraq conducted between May and July 2006. The results are consistent with the findings of an October 2006 study of Iraq mortality conducted by the Hopkins researchers. Also, the findings closely reflect the increased mortality trends reported by other organizations that utilized passive methods of counting mortality, such as counting bodies in morgues or deaths reported by the news media. The study was published in the October 14, 2006, edition of the peer-reviewed scientific journal, *The Lancet*. Johns Hopkins Bloomberg School of Public Health study of October 11, 2006 estimated that over 600,000 Iraqis had been killed as a result of the invasion *as of July 2006*. Iraqis have continued to be killed since then. The death rate is at least ten times greater than most estimates cited in the U.S. media, and this number is based on the only scientifically valid study of violent Iraqi deaths caused by the U.S.-led invasion of March 2003. Yet U.S. politicians and the media continue to cite the smaller numbers that do not account for random killing.

22. Sinan Salaheddin, Associated Press writer, "Government Says 85,000 Iraqis Killed in 2004-08," Yahoo News, October 14, 2009.

23. According to Nancy A. Youssef, "US Paid Nearly $31 Million in Condolence Payments to Iraqis, Afghans," McClatchy Newspapers, reprint: Common Dreams.org, June 1, 2007, "The military makes condolence payments for killing or injuring a civilian or for damaging property. Generally, Iraqis and Afghans received up to $2,500 for property damage or death. In April 2006, military officials in Iraq raised the maximum payment to $10,000. In addition, U.S. officials began paying the relatives of Iraqi soldiers and police who were killed because of U.S.

operations, the report states." http://www.informationclearinghouse.info/article17809.htm (accessed May 5, 2010).

24. Rod Powers, "U.S. Military, Active Duty Death Entitlements," *Your Guide to U.S. Military,* About.com; also paid a "death gratuity" which is "a lump sum gratuitous payment made by the military to eligible beneficiaries of a member who dies on Active Duty (AD), Active Duty for Training (ADT), or Initial Duty Training (IDT), or full-time National Guard duty. Its purpose is to help the survivors in their readjustment and to aid them in meeting immediate expenses incurred. The death gratuity payment is $12,420, and is non-taxable."

25. "The United States Department of Veterans Affairs Offers Servicemembers' Group Life Insurance (SGLI)." The SGLI payment is $400,000 unless the member elected a lesser amount or declined coverage in writing. Monthly premium payments for the level of coverage selected by the member are automatically deducted from the member's pay. http://www.insurance.va.gov/sglisite/sgli/sgli.htm (accessed August 5, 2008).

26. Michael Carey, "Anti-Arab Racism in the Military," *Harvard College Student Middle East Journal,* September 7, 2007.

27. Ibid.

Chapter 6 Grunts: From Soldier to Sociopath

1. Tyler E. Boudreau, *Packing Inferno: The Unmaking of a Marine* (Port Townsend, Washington: Feral House, 2008), p. 2.

2. Ibid., pp. 54-55.

3. Hassna, conversations with author.

4. Iraq Veterans Against the War, Winter Soldier Hearing.

5. Camilla Mortensen, "Back to Iraq? A Eugene Soldier Fights Killing," *Oregonian Weekly,* May 22, 2008, http://www.eugeneweekly.com/2008/05/22/coverstory.htm (accessed March 22, 2010).

6. Mortensen, "Back to Iraq?"

7. Adam Szyper-Seibert, Courage to Resist e-mail message to Kathleen Barry, October 20, 2009.

8. "Desertion Not as Fashionable as It Used to Be," *Strategy Page,* July 17, 2008,

   http://www.strategypage.com/htmw/htatrit/articles/20080717.aspx (accessed March 21, 2010); And "You Wouldn't Catch Me Dead in Iraq," *Sunday Times,* August 27, 2006, http://www.timesonline.co.uk/tol/life_and_style/article612898.ece (accessed March 21, 2010).

9. In January, 1971, Vietnam veterans met in a meeting called Winter Soldier which was chaired by John Kerry, who is now a U.S. Senator, to expose the war crimes they participated in during the Vietnam War. In March, 2008, Iraq Veterans Against the War sponsored a Winter Soldier hearing for the same purpose in Iraq.

10. Iraq Veterans Against the War.

11. Ibid.

12. Ryan and Weimberg, *Soldiers of Conscience.*

13. Zimbardo, *The Lucifer Effect.*

14. Cited in Reading Eagle, McClatchy-Tribune News Service, July 13, 2008   http://news.google.com/newspapers?nid=1955&dat=20080713&id=-8zMxAAAAIBAJ&sjid=saIFAAAAIBAJ&pg=1221,4411927 (accessed May 5, 2010).

15. Jane Harman, "Rapists in the Ranks," *Los Angeles Times,* March 31, 2008.

16. Security Council, United Nations, Resolution 1820, June 19, 2008, http://ods-dds-ny.un.org/doc/UNDOC/GEN/N08/391/44/PDF/N0839144.pdf?OpenElement (accessed May 6, 2010).

17. Ann Wright, "Is There an Army Cover Up of Rape and Murder of Women Soldiers?" Common Dreams.org, April 28, 2008.

18. Ibid.

19. Susan Griffin, "Rape: The All-American Crime," *Ramparts,* September, 1971.

20. Ann Scott Tyson, *Washington Post,* May 13, 2005.

21. Anne Sadler, with Brenda Booth, Bradley Doebbeling, "Researchers Study Women's Risk of Rape in Military," University of Iowa News Release, March 11, 2003; see also *American Journal of Industrial Medicine,* March, 2003.

22. Department Of Defense, Report on Sexual Assault in the Military Fiscal Year 2009, Washington D.C., p 2.

23. Suzanne Goldberg, "Woman Soldier Claims Sex Harassment in Iraq" *The Guardian,* June 20, 2006, http://www.guardian.co.uk/world/2006/jun/20/usa.iraq1 (accessed May 5, 2010).

24. Lizette Alvarez and Dan Frosch, "A Focus On Violence by Returning G.I.s," *New York Times,* January 2, 2009.

25. Harman, "Rapist in the Ranks."

26. As reported in Christine Hansen, "A Considerable Service: An Advocate's Introduction to Domestic Violence and the Military," *Domestic Violence Report,* 6, 4 (April/May) 2001.

27. Ann Wright, "Military Town Newspaper Challenges U.S. Military on Murder of Military Women," Truthout.org, October 17, 2008.

28. Wesley Autrey, Wikipedia.org, http://en.wikipedia.org/wiki/Wesley_Autrey (accessed March 17, 2010).

29. Daniel Goleman, "The Instinct for Altruism," *Shambhala Sun,* November 2006, p. 74.

Chapter 7 Psychopathic Leadership Versus the Politics of Empathy

1. Alexander DeConde, *Presidential Machismo: Executive Authority, Military Intervention and Foreign Relations* (Boston: Northeastern University Press, 2000), p. 286.

2. Sociologists refer to this construct as an *ideal type* not because it is ideal or even average but because it is a construct that represents a recurring phenomenon in social life, in this case, a particular kind of leadership, in which psychopaths are

attracted to power and they effectively con people into believing that through them the people will have security, safety, or whatever goal the psychopath has convinced people they need from them.

3. Martha Stout, *The Sociopath Next Door,* (New York: Broadway Books, 2005), pp. 1-2.

4. Robert Fisk, *The Great War For Civilisation: The Conquest of the Middle East* (New York: Knopf, 2005).

5. CounterPunch Wire, "Weapons of Mass Destruction: Who Said What When" Counterpunch, ed. Alexander Cockburn and Jeffrey St. Clair, May 29, 2003, http://www.counterpunch.org/wmd05292003.html (accessed March 22, 2010).

6. Ibid.

7. Mary Ellen O'Connell, "The Myth of Preemptive Self-Defense," Moritz College of Law and the Mershon Center for International Security and Public Policy, The Ohio State University, August 2002, p. 6.

8. President George W. Bush, (Graduation Speech at West Point United States Military Academy, West Point, New York, June 1, 2002).

9. Ibid.

10. Article 51 of the UN charter asserts that "nothing in the present Charter shall impair the inherent right of individual or collective self-defense if an armed attack occurs against a Member of the United Nations."

11. Hans Blix, Executive Chairman of UNMOVIC, "The Security Council, January 27, 2003: An Update On Inspection," United Nations.

12. Bush, (Graduation Speech at West Point).

13. *Uniform Code of Military Justice,* Sec. 809, Art. 90 (20), Sec. 891, Art .91 (2), Sec. 892, Art. 92 (1), Sec. 892, Art. 92 (2).

14. Ibid.

15. Rod Powers, "Oath of Enlistment," About.com. http://usmilitary.about.com/od/joiningthemilitary/a/oathofenlist.htm (accessed May 9, 2010).

16. West Point Graduates Against the War, http://www.westpointgradsagainstthewar.org/laws_and_treaties_violated_by_pr.htm (accessed March 22, 2010).

17. Robert Hare, *Without Conscience: The Disturbing World of the Psychopaths Among Us* (New York: Guilford Press, 1993).

18. Impeach Bush, "Impeachment for Violating International Laws," http://www.impeachbush.tv/impeach/treaties.html (accessed March 22, 2010).

19. As reported in Telegraph.co.uk, July 10, 2008.

20. To study psychopaths in leadership, I have relied on the expertise of prison personnel whose clients are most frequently clinically diagnosed psychopaths. Prison social worker David Barry and prison psychologist Dr. Roger Kotila have independently confirmed to me the parallels between U.S. leadership in the White House under Bush and criminal psychopaths' behaviors.

21. See Medea Benjamin and Nancy Mancias, "Did You Hear the Joke About the Predator Drone That Bombed?" AlterNet, May 5, 2010, http://www.alternet.

org/world/146739/did_you_hear_the_joke_about_the_predator_drone_that_ bombed_ (accessed May 8, 2010).

22. A Gallup poll conducted on behalf of CNN and the newspaper *USA Today* concluded that 79 percent of Americans thought the Iraq War was justified, with or without conclusive evidence of illegal weapons. Only 19 percent thought weapons were needed to justify the war, May 2003.

23. In Diane Bell, "Good and Evil: At Home and Abroad," the author captures and records the intolerance of critique and demand for blind patriotism in the U.S. at that time; *September 11, 2001, Feminist Perspectives,* ed. Susan Hawthorne and Bronwyn Winter, (North Melbourne Australia: Spinifex), 2002, pp. 432-439.

24. Kathleen Barry, "Non-Selective Compassion, 14 September 2001," in *September 11, 2001, Feminist Perspectives,* ed. Susan Hawthorne and Bronwyn Winter, p. 16.

25. Refugees International, "Afghanistan," http://www.refintl.org/where-we-work/asia/afghanistan 2009 (accessed March 22, 2010).

26. See Rajiv Chandrasekaran, *Imperial Life in the Emerald City: Inside Iraq's Green Zone* (New York: Knopf, 2006) for a thorough account of Bremmer's rule and Iraq's decay under him.

27. Ibid.

28. Hare, *Without Conscience,* p. 21.

29. The United States House of Representatives, A Resolution: Articles of Impeachment of President George W. Bush, exhibited by the House of Representatives of the United States of America in the name of itself and of the people of the United States of America, in maintenance and support of its impeachment against President George W. Bush for high crimes and misdemeanors, introduced by Dennis J. Kucinich of Ohio, Washington, June 10, 2008, http://kucinich.house.gov/News/DocumentSingle.aspx?DocumentID=93581 (accessed March 23, 2010).

30. U.S. Code, "War Crimes," Part I, Chapter 118 § 2441.

Chapter 8 Making Enemies—Humiliating Men

1. Amnesty International, "Trapped by Violence: Women in Iraq," March 2009, p. 3.

2. I have drawn this description from hundreds of accounts of military house-clearings including videos made by reporters embedded with military units who accompany them. This is a "thick description," as sociologists and anthropologists refer to this method written from the perspective and experience of men who are its victims and typifies the general practice.

3. Lance Cpl. Geoffrey P. Ingersoll, "Urban Fighting Skills Honed as Part of a Specialized Camp Pendleton," *Marine Corps News,* March 22, 2007.

4. Jim Garamone, "Special Forces Soldiers Train Iraqis in Qaim," *American Forces Press Service,* U.S. Department of Defense, June 12, 2006.

5. Chris Hedges and Laila Al-Arian, "The Other War," *The Nation,* July 30, August 6, 2007, p. 13.

6. Ibid., p. 15.

7. Dahr Jamail, interview with Josh Simpson, *The Will to Resist* (Chicago: Haymarket, 2009), p. 38.

8. This is a repeated theme in testimony from Iraq Veterans. See also, Chris Hedges and Laila Al-Arian, "The Other War."

9. Gordon Forbes III, "Wilderness of Zaidon," *Alpha Company: Iraq Diary*, Documentary on the Military Channel, 2005, http://military.discovery.com/tuneins/alpha-company.html (accessed March 19, 2010).

10. Grammatically "machismo" is the correct word but it has a Spanish/Latin American ring to it. I choose the term blinding macho, which is less suggestive of race or ethnicity.

11. Rhonda Hammer, *Antifeminism And Family Terrorism: A Critical Feminist Perspective* (Lanham, MD: Rowman and Littlefield, 2002); See chapter 4, "Family Terrorism," which establishes the gendering of masculine violence in private life that is not conveyed in language such as "intimate partner violence" as if both parties are likely to be equally responsible, p. 133.

12. Joshua Goldstein, *War and Gender: How Gender Shapes the War System and Vice Versa* (Cambridge: Cambridge University Press, 2001), p. 295.

13. *Jenin Jenin*, VHS, directed by Mohammed Bakri (Arab Film Distribution, 2003).

14. Ghali Hassan, "How the U.S. Erase Women's Rights in Iraq," Canadian Global Research Institute, Global Research, October 7, 2005, www.globalresearch.ca/index.php?context=va&aid=1054.

15. "The CIA's Shadow War," *Mother Jones* as reprinted from TomDispatch website, January 11, 2010.

16. Dexter Filkins, "Loyalties of Those Killed in Afghan Raid Remain Unclear," *New York Times*, January 22, 2010, http://www.nytimes.com/2010/01/22/world/asia/22afghan.html.

17. Iason Athanasiadis, "Is Afghanistan War, a Kinder, Gentler Night Raid?" *Christian Science Monitor*, April 20, 2010, http://www.csmonitor.com/World/2010/0420/In-Afghanistan-war-a-kinder-gentler-night-raid (accessed May 13, 2010).

18. Dion Nissenbaum, "Afghanistan War: US Night Raid Sparks Protest Over Civilian Deaths," *The Christian Science Monitor*, McClatchy Newspapers, April 29, 2010, http://www.csmonitor.com/World/2010/0429/Afghanistan-war-US-night-raid-sparks-protest-over-civilian-deaths (accessed May 13, 2010).

19. Dahr Jamail, *Will to Resist*, p. 38.

20. Peter Finn and Joby Warrick, "Officials: Torture Confessions Not Proven Useful, *Washington Post*, March 30, 2009.

21. Muntazer al-Zaidi "Why I Threw My Shoe," Comment, Guardian News, September 17, 2009 http://www.guardian.co.uk/commentisfree/2009/sep/17/why-i-threw-shoe-bush (accessed March 24, 2010).

22. Ibid.

23. Ibid.

24. Paul Wolfowitz, The Hudson Institute, April 28, 2008.

25. Dahr Jamail, *Beyond the Green Zone: Dispatches from an Unembedded Journalist in Occupied Iraq* (Chicago: Haymarket, 2007), p. 21.

26. Charter of the United Nations and the International Covenant on Civil and Political Rights and the International Covenant on Economic, Social and Cultural Rights, Common Article 1, paragraph 1 of these Covenants.

27. United States Department of Army, *Counterinsurgency Field Manual*, p.2.

28. WorldPublicOpinion.org, "Poll of Iraqis: Public Wants Timetable for U.S. Withdrawal, but Thinks U.S. Plans Permanent Bases in Iraq," Program on International Policy Attitudes, January 31, 2006, http://www.worldpublicopinion.org/pipa/articles/brmiddleeastnafricara/165.php (accessed March 24, 2010).

29. WorldPublicOpinion.org, "Most Iraqis Want U.S. Troops Out Within a Year," conducted by the Program on International Policy Attitudes, September 27, 2006, http://www.worldpublicopinion.org/pipa/articles/brmiddleeastnafricara/250.php?nid=&id=&pnt=250 (accessed March 24, 2010).

30. Thomas Ricks, *The Gamble, General David Petraeus and the American Military Adventure in Iraq, 2006-2008* (New York: Penguin, 2009), p. 60.

31. Ibid., p. 60.

32. United States Department of the Army, *Counterinsurgency Field Manual*.

33. Ricks, *The Gamble*, p. 156.

34. Forbes III, *Alpha Company*.

35. Ricks, *The Gamble*, 166.

36. Forbes III, *Alpha Company*.

37. Iraq Veterans Against the War, Winter Soldier Hearing.

38. Iraq Poll, February 2009. This survey was conducted for ABC News, the BBC, and NHK by D3 Systems of Vienna, Virginia, and KA Research Ltd. of Istanbul, Turkey. Interviews were conducted in person, in Arabic or Kurdish, among a random national sample of 2,228 Iraqis aged 18 and up, from 17 to 25 February 2009, news.bbc.co.uk/2/shared/bsp/hi/.../13_03_09_iraqpollfeb2009.pdf (accessed March 24, 2010).

39. Oxfam International "In Her Own Words: Iraqi Women Talk About Their Greatest Concerns and Challenges," Survey, 2009.

40. Iraq Center for Research and Strategy Studies, Poll, face-to-face interviews with 3,000 Iraqis between September 25 and October 5, 2008.

41. "Iraqi Family Household Survey 2006/7," Table 21, Iraq Ministry of Health and Ministry of Planning with the World Health Organization, http://www.emro.who.int/iraq/pdf/ifhs_report_en.pdf (accessed March 24, 2010).

42. Juan Cole, " Iraq Refugee Crisis," Informed Comment, Thoughts on the Middle East, History, and Religion, http://www.juancole.com/2008/08/iraq-refugee-crisis.html (accessed March 24, 2010).

Chapter 9 Ongoing War

1. International Convention for the Suppression of Terrorist Bombings, United Nations: Entry into Force, 23 May, 2001.

2. United Nations General Assembly, *Report of the Ad Hoc Committee established by General Assembly Resolution 51/210 of 17 December 1996*, Sixth session (28 January-1 February 2002), Annex IV, art. 18.

3. Noam Chomsky, "Is the U.S. a Terrorist State?" This is an extract from an interview with Noam Chomsky on the Canadian Broadcasting Corporation program *Hot Type* with Evan Solomon, April 16, 2002, as edited by Sunil Sharma and published July 28, 2002, in *Dissident Voice* as "Noam Chomsky on the Middle East and the U.S. War on Terrorism."

4. United States Department of State, Office of the Coordinator for Counterterrorism, *Country Reports on Terrorism*, April 30, 2007, http://www.state.gov/s/ct/rls/crt/2006/82726.htm (accessed March 25, 2010).

5. George W. Bush, "State of the Union," U.S. Congress, January 29, 2002.

6. Ilan Pappé, *The Ethnic Cleansing of Palestine* (Oxford, England: One World Publications, 2006), pp. 34-35.

7. Ibid., pp 40, 41.

8. Ibid., p. 82.

9. Ibid., p. 200.

10. Jeffrey Alexander, Ron Eyerman, Bernhard Giesen, Neil J. Smelser, and Piotr Sztompka, *Cultural Trauma and Collective Identity* (Berkeley, CA: University of California Press, 2004), pp. 23-24.

11. Amnon Meranda, "Softened Nakba Law Passes 1st Reading," Ynet, March 16, 2010. http://www.ynetnews.com/articles/0,7340,L-3863825,00.html (accessed March 17, 2010).

12. Barack Obama, speech to the American Israeli Political Action Committee, Washington, D.C., June 4, 2008.

13. A Beirut newspaper, *An Nahar*, estimated that 17,825 civilians were killed along with 10,000 PLO and 675 Israeli soldiers, *Washington Post*, September 3, 1982 as cited in "Secondary Wars and Atrocities of the Twentieth Century," http://users.erols.com/mwhite28/warstat3.htm (accessed March 15, 2010).

14. Scott Lilienfeld and Hal Arkowitz, "What 'Psychopath' Means," *Scientific American Mind*, December 2007/January 2008, pp. 80-81.

15. The Israel Defense Forces Doctrine,"Purity of Arms," The Official Website, 2006. http://web.archive.org/web/20060430031938/http://www1.idf.il/dover/site/mainpage.asp?sl=EN&id=32, (accessed March 24, 2010).

16. Dr. Ruchama Marton, Physicians for Human Rights, YouTube.com, ed. Eran Turbner May 13, 2008.

17. Meira Weiss, *The Chosen Body* (Palo Alto: Stanford University Press, 2002).

18. Joseph Alagha, *The Shifts in Hizbullah's Ideology: Religious Ideology, Political Ideology, and Political Program* (Leiden, Netherlands: Amsterdam, University Press, 2006), see Appendix E, Chronology of Events (1975-2005), pp. 280-291.

19. A. Ezzati, "The Concept of Martyrdom in Islam," *Al-Serat*, Vol XII, 1986, http://www.al-islam.org/al-serat/concept-ezzati.htm (accessed March 21, 2010).

20. Ibid.

21. Ahyia Raved, "Study: Female Suicide Bombers Seek Atonement," *Israel News*, available through Ynet News, January 10, 2006, http://www.ynetnews.com/articles/0,7340,L-3198362,00.html (accessed May 13, 2010). See chapter on female suicide bombers in Mia Bloom, *Dying To Kill: The Allure of Suicide Terror* (New York: Columbia University Press 2005).

22. Ibrahim el-Hussari, "The Gulen Education Movement: An Islamic Response to Terror as a Global Challenge," (paper presented at the Gulen Movement Conference, Georgetown University, November 13-15, 2008), p. 13.

23. El-Hussari cites Quranic verse: *Tirmidhi Diyat*: 22; Abu Dawud, *Sunna*: 32.

24. Lara Deeb, "Hizballah: A Primer," *Middle East Report Online*, July 31, 2006, http://www.merip.org/mero/mero073106.html (accessed March 25, 2010).

25. Deeb, "Hizbullah"; see also Joseph Alagha in "Hizbullah After the Syrian Withdrawal," *Middle East Report*, 237 (Winter 2005): 34-39.

26. Avishai Marglit, "Suicide Bombers," *New York Review of Books*, January 16, 2003, p. 5.

27. Tran Van Tra, *Tet*, in Jayne S. Warner and Luu Doan Huynh, eds., *The Vietnam War: Vietnamese and American Perspectives* (Armonk NY: M.E. Sharpe, 1993), pp. 49, 50.

28. From a radio interview: "Tyler Boudreau, Packing Inferno," *Writers Voice*, Francesca Rheannon, January 10th, 2009, http://www.writersvoice.net/2009/01/tyler-boudreau-packing-inferno/ (accessed March 27, 2010).

29. Nadera Shalhoub-Kevorkian, "Liberating Voices: The Political Implications of Palestinian Mothers Narrating Their Loss," *Women's Studies International Forum*, 25, 5, 2003. p. 394.

30. Ibid., p. 397.

31. Ibid., p. 399.

32. Fatima el Issawi, "Hezbollah: The Mothers of Martyrs," *Asharq Alawsat*, August, 12, 2007.

33. Ibid.

34. Ibid.

35. Over this time period Israel received $10.5 billion in Foreign Military Financing—the Pentagon's biggest military aid program—and $6.3 billion in U.S. arms deliveries, "http://www.worldpolicy.org/projects/arms/reports/israel.lebanon.FINAL2.pdf.

36 Menachem Klein, *The Jerusalem Problem: The Struggle for Permanent Status*, (Gainsville, FL: University Press of Florida, 2003), p.98.

Chapter 10 Colluding in Preparatory War, Lebanon 2006

1. "Deliberate Destruction or 'Collateral Damage'? Israeli Attacks on Civilian Infrastructure," Amnesty International, MDE 18/007/2006, August, 2006, p. 2; according to the report, Israeli attacks on civilian infrastructure included "31 'vi-

tal points' (such as airports, ports, water and sewage treatment plants, electrical facilities) have been completely or partially destroyed, as have around 80 bridges and 94 roads. More than 25 fuel stations and around 900 commercial enterprises were hit. The number of residential properties, offices and shops completely destroyed exceeds 30,000. Two government hospitals—in Bint Jbeil and in Meis al-Jebel—were completely destroyed in Israeli attacks and three others were seriously damaged," p. 3.

2. In Alagha, *The Shifts in Hizbullah's Ideology*, the following are attacks from each side that have been documented up to the 2006 war:

2000, Hizbullah captured 3 Israeli soldiers from the Lebanese Shib'a farms, an area of Lebanon still occupied by Israel.

2002, March: Following an Israeli incursion into the West Bank, Hizbullah waged a 12-day military operation against Israeli forces in the Shi'ba farms.

2004, January 19: An Israeli bulldozer crossed the "Blue Line" and was inside Lebanon when Hizbullah fired an antitank rocket at it, killing one Israeli soldier and wounding another.

2004, May 7: Elite Israeli Egoz commandos moved across the "Blue Line" and were ambushed by Hizbullah fighters, one Israeli soldier killed and 5 wounded.

2005, November 25: An Israeli hang-glider "floated" over the border into Lebanon. Hizbullah rushed to capture it, Israeli troops opened fire on Hizbullah. Around the same time Hizbullah shelled Israeli position in Shi'ba Farms and Israel bombed Hizbullah positions in Lebanon.

3. Tanya Reinhart, "Israel's 'New Middle East'," *Electronic Lebanon*, July 26, 2006, http://electronicintifada.net/v2/article5248.shtml (accessed March 25, 2010).

4. Matthew Kalman, Chronicle Foreign Service, "Israel Set War Plan More Than a Year Ago," SFGATE.com, July 21, 2006.

5. Aluf Benn, "PM: War Planned Months in Advance," Haaretz.com, March 8, 2007.

6. Haartz.com, March 8, 2007; in March 2007 Israel's Prime Minister Olmert appeared before an Israeli commission investigating the 2006 war against Lebanon.

7. Maryam Monalisa Gharavi and Dr. Anat Matar, "Israel Lobby Watch: Israeli Officer Promotes War Crimes at Harvard," *Electronic Intifada*, July 22, 2009, http://electronicintifada.net/v2/article10673.shtml (accessed March26, 2010).

8. Mona Fayard, "To be a Shiite Now..." *Al Nahar*, August 7, 2006.

9. Nir Rosen, "Hizb Allah, Party of God," Truthdig.com, October 3, 2006, http://www.truthdig.com/report/item/200601003_hiz_ballah_party_of_god/ (accessed March 25, 2010).

10. David S. Cloud and Helene Cooper, "U.S. Speeds Up Bomb Delivery for the Israelis," *New York Times*, July 22, 2006, http://www.nytimes.com/2006/07/22/world/middleeast/22military.html (accessed March 25, 2010).

11. Rice used this reference to "Middle East birth pangs" repeatedly; Amr Hamzawy, "Stillborn Illusions," *Al-Ahram Weekly*, Carnegie Endownment for International Peace, August 10-16, 2006, http://www.carnegieendowment.org/publications/index.cfm?fa=view&id=18610 (accessed February 9, 2010).

12. "The Military-Industrial Complex Leaderboard," The Military-Industrial Complex, http://www.militaryindustrialcomplex.com/contracts-leaderboard.asp (accessed April 24, 2007).

13. Story from BBC NEWS, July 29, 2007, http://news.bbc.co.uk/go/pr/fr/-/2/hi/middle_east/6920988.stm (accessed May 15, 2010).

14. See website, Breaking the Silence, "Israeli Soldiers Talk About the Occupied Territories, http://www.shovrimshtika.org/index_e.asp (accessed April 7, 2010).

15. Alagha e-mail correspondence, 2008.

16. "Israel/Lebanon: Israel Responsible for Qana Attack," *Human Rights Watch*, July 30, 2006.

17. Evelyne Accad, "Lebanon, Summer, 2006," *Of War, Siege and Lebanon: Women's Voices from the Middle East and South Asia*, Coalition for Sexual and Bodily Rights in Muslim Societies, http://www.wwhr.org/id_922.

18. Triti Parsi, *Treacherous Alliance: The Secret Dealings of Israel, Iran, and the United States* (New Haven, CT: Yale University Press, 2007), p. 15.

19. Seymour M. Hersh, "Watching Lebanon: Washington's Interests in Israel's War." *New Yorker*, August 21, 2006, http://www.newyorker.com/archive/2006/08/21/060821fa_fact (accessed March 25, 2010).

20. Gharavi and Matar, "Israeli Officer Promotes War Crimes at Harvard."

21. As he indicated in a BBC interview on March 22, 2007, and was reported in "Bolton Admits Lebanon Truce Block," *BBC News*, March 22, 2007, http://news.bbc.co.uk/2/hi/middle_east/6479377.stm (accessed March 29, 2010).

22. Communication with Professor Ibrahim El Hussari, Lebanese American University, August 27, 2009.

23. Sue Pleming, "US Says Israel Cluster Bomb Use Possible Violation," Reuters, *Washington Post*, January 29, 2007, http://www.washingtonpost.com/wpdyn/.../2007/01/29/AR2007012900512.html, (accessed May 14, 2010).

24. Michael F. Brown, "Damaging Congressional Silence on Israeli Violations in Lebanon," *Electronic Lebanon*, April 27, 2007, http://electronicintifada.net/v2/article6844.shtml (accessed March 27, 2010).

25. Rosen, "Hizb Allah."

26. Reinhart, "Israel's 'New Middle East'."

Chapter 11 "No One Understands!"

1. Alexander, *Cultural Trauma*, p. 1.

2. Jonathon Cook, "How Human Rights Watch Lost its Way in Lebanon," September 8, 2006, Antiwar.com, http://www.antiwar.com/cook/?articleid=9667 (accessed March 25, 2010).

3. "Charter," New Profile.org.

4. Jean Améry, *At the Mind's Limits: Contemplations by a Survivor of Auschwitz and Its Realities,* trans. Sidney Rosenfeld, Stella P. Rosenfeld (Bloomington, Indiana: University Press 1980), p. 85.

5. Ibid., pp. 17, 91.

6. Ibid., pp. 99, 100.

7. Ibid., p. 91.

8. Dina Kraft, "Among Israel's Elite, Women Were Perks," *International Herald Tribune,* October 19, 2006.

9. Reported in *International Herald Tribune,* October 19, 2006; see also Steven Meyers, "Putin's Flippant Comments on Israeli Scandal Are Heard," *New York Times,* October 20, 2006.

10. "Transcript of the Hot Line with President of Russia Vladimir Putin," President of Russia, Official Web Portal, October 25, 2006, http://eng.kremlin.ru/text/speeches/2006/10/25/0911_type148987_113064.shtml.

11. Original story was abbreviated in later reporting. "Alleged Rape Victim: 'Katsav Is a Pervert, Serial Sex Offender," *Haartz,* June 30, 2007.

12. *Jerusalem Post,* jpost.com, September 1, 2009.

Chapter 12 Unmaking War

1. United Nations Human Rights Council, "Human Rights In Palestine And Other Occupied Arab Territories, Report of the United Nations Fact Finding Mission on the Gaza Conflict, A/HRC/12/48, September 15, 2009, http://www2.ohchr.org/english/bodies/hrcouncil/specialsession/9/docs/UNFFMGC_Report.pdf (accessed May 15, 2010).

2. Ibid.

3. "Gazans Welcome UN War Crimes Report," *New York Times,* September 16, 2009.

4. Figures from the U.S. Department of the Treasury/Federal Reserve Board, reported on DefeatheDebt.com, May 15, 2010, http://defeatthedebt.com (accessed May 15, 2010).

5. Michael T. Klare, "American Preeminence Is Disappearing Fifteen Years Early, Memo to the CIA" from Tomdispatch, in *Information Clearinghouse,* October 26, 2009.

6. "Remarks of President Barack Obama Speech in Prague, Czech Republic," Re:Obama, April 5, 2009, http://www.reobama.com/SpeechesPrague09.htm, (accessed May 10, 2010).

7. Ibid.

8. Ibid.

9. See "Constitution for the Federation of the Earth," Institute of World Problems, http://www.worldproblems.net/english/fec/constitution_federation_earth_

eng_full_text.htm#article01 (accessed March 27, 2010), which includes the following:

Article 1—Broad Functions of the World Government

1. To prevent war, secure disarmament, and resolve territorial and other disputes which endanger peace and human rights.

2. To protect universal human rights, including life, liberty, security, democracy, and equal opportunities in life.

3. To obtain for all people on earth the conditions required for equitable economic and social development and for diminishing social differences.

4. To regulate world trade, communications, transportation, currency, standards, use of world resources, and other global and international processes.

5. To protect the environment and the ecological fabric of life from all sources of damage, and to control technological innovations whose effects transcend national boundaries, for the purpose of keeping Earth a safe, healthy and happy home for humanity .

6. To devise and implement solutions to all problems which are beyond the capacity of national governments, or which are now or may become of global or international concern or consequence.

Article 2—Basic Structure of World Federation and World Government

1. The Federation of Earth shall be organized as a universal federation, to include all nations and all people, and to encompass all oceans, seas and lands of Earth, inclusive of non-self governing territories, together with the surrounding atmosphere.

2. The World Government for the Federation of Earth shall be non-military and shall be democratic in its own structure, with ultimate sovereignty residing in all the people who live on Earth.

3. The authority and powers granted to the World Government shall be limited to those defined in this Constitution for the Federation of Earth, applicable to problems and affairs which transcend national boundaries, leaving to national governments jurisdiction over the internal affairs of the respective nations but consistent with the authority of the World Government to protect universal human rights as defined in this World Constitution.

10. Susan Hawthorne, *Wild Politics* (North Melbourne, Australia: Spinifex Press, 2002).

11. See Jessica Neuwirth, "Globalization: A Secret Weapon for Feminists," *Sisterhood Is Forever: The Women's Anthology for a New Millennium*, ed. Robin Morgan (New York: Washington Square Press, Simon and Schuster, March 2003) and Cynthia Enloe, *Globalization and Militarism* (MD: Rowman and Littlefield, 2007).

12. Edgar Cardona Quirós, "Mi Verdad," *García Hermanos* (San José, Costa Rica: 1992).

13. Inter-American Treaty of Reciprocal Assistance, signed Sept. 2, 1947, Articles 1-6.

14. Emery Reves, *The Anatomy of Peace* (New York: Harper, 1945), p. 147.

15. Ibid., p. 151.

16. Glen T. Martin, "International Law and the U.N. System," *Ascent to Freedom*, section 10.5, Democratic World Law: The Philosophical Foundations, 2008, http://www.radford.edu/gmartin/Ascent.to.Freedom.selections.pdf (accessed March 25, 2010).

17. Albert Einstein, "To the General Assembly of the United Nations," Open Letter, United Nations World, New York, October 1947, pp. 13-14, http://neutrino.aquaphoenix.com/un-esa/ws1997-letter-einstein.html (accessed March 21, 2010).

18. Samantha Karol, "Prof. Shares Research from Costa Rica," April 2, 2008. www.quchronicle.com/home/index.cfm?event-display Artic (accessed March 17, 2010).

19. "Situación y Análisis del Femicidio en la Región Centroamericana," Instituto Interamericano de Derechos Humanos, Secretaría Técnica, Consejo Centroamericano de Procuradores de Derechos Humanos, Agosto, 2006.

20. L. Heise, M. Ellsberg, and M. Gottemoeller, *Ending Violence Against Women* (Population Reports, series L, no. 11, December, 1999).

21. Clair-Marie Robertson, "Women March Seeking Passage of Anti-Violence Law," *A.M. Costa Rica*, 4 no. 235,(November 26, 2004), http://www.amcostarica.com/112604.htm (accessed April 16, 2010).

22. Danilo Valladares, "Mujeres-América Central: Crece la Barbarie," Inter Press Service, March 28, 2010, http://ipsnoticias.net/print.asp?idnews=94825 (accessed March 28, 2010).

23. Rachel L. Swarns, "School Is Out but Education Doesn't Stop for the Obama Daughters This Summer," *New York Times*, August 2, 2009, http://www.nytimes.com/2009/08/02/us/02summer.html (accessed February 2010).

24. Office of the Press Secretary, *Remarks by the President in Address to the Nation on the Way Forward in Afghanistan and Pakistan,* the White House, (speech given at the United States Military Academy at West Point, West Point, New York, December 1, 2009).

25. Malalai Joya, *A Woman Among Warlords: The Extraordinary Story of an Afghan Who Dared to Raise Her Voice* (New York: Scribner, 2009), p. 52.

26. Zoya interview, Grit TV, December 3, 2009.

27. "Karzai's Approval of 'Marital Rape' Law Leads to International Rift," *The Times*, August 17, 2009.

28. Robert Gates, interview, *Meet the Press,* December 6, 2009.

29. Zoya, (speaking at Women's International League for Peace and Freedom, San Francisco, California, November 7, 2009).

30. Zoya interview, Grit TV.

31. "US to Pay Taliban to Switch Sides," BBC, October 28, 2009.

Chapter 13 Remaking Men, Reknowing Ourselves

1. eMedicineHealth, "Post Traumatic Stress Disorder," 2007.

2. Charles W. Hoge, Carl A. Castro, Stephen C. Messer, Dennis McGurk, Dave I. Cotting, and Robert L. Koffman, "Combat Duty in Iraq and Afghanistan, Mental Health Problems, and Barriers to Care," *M.P.H.* 351, July 1, 2004, 13-22.

3. Norma Perez e-mail dated March 20, 2008 as cited in Larry Scott, "Off With Her Head?" http://www.vawatchdog.com/08/nf08/nfMAY08/nf051908-1.htm (accessed March 21, 2010).

4. National Priorities Project, "The Cost of Wars Since 2001," Costofwar.com.

5. Karl Marx Frederick Engels, *German Ideology* (Cambridge: MIT Press, 1968), p 47.

6. Josh Stieber and Connor Curran, Contagious Love Experiment, 2009, www.contagiousloveexperiment.wordpress.com (accessed March 3, 2010).

7. Josh Stieber and Connor Curran speaking at the Peace and Justice Center, Santa Rosa, CA., Fall, 2009.

8. Iraq Vets Stress Project, http://www.stressproject.org/.

9. Thich Nhat Hanh, Questions and Answers, Letting Go of Suffering, http://dharmaweb.org accessed (March 15, 2010).

10. Maxine Hong Kingston, ed. *Veterans of War, Veterans for Peace* (Maui, Hawaii: Koa Books, 2006) explains how to set up a veterans writing group at http://www.vowvop.org.

Index

CPSIA information can be obtained at www.ICGtesting.com
Printed in the USA
LVOW042258120212

268387LV00001B/2/P